TEARS *for* CROCODILIA

TEARS
for
CROCODILIA

Evolution, Ecology,

and the

Disappearance

of

One of the World's Most

Ancient Animals

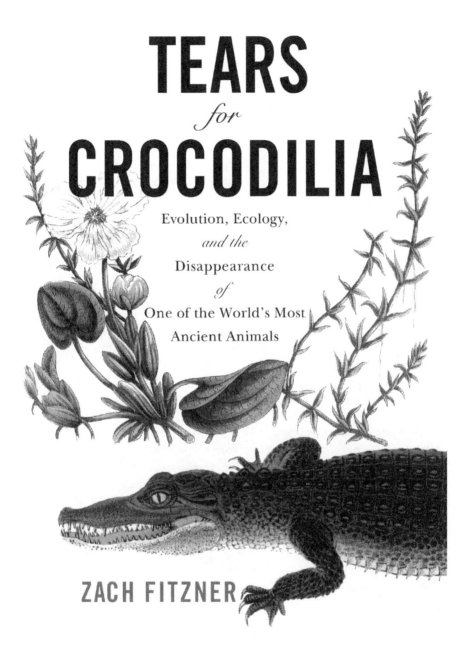

ZACH FITZNER

WESTHOLME
Yardley

Westholme Publishing, LLC
904 Edgewood Road
Yardley, Pennsylvania 19067
Visit our Web site at www.westholmepublishing.com

ISBN: 978-1-59416-380-7
Also available as an eBook.

Printed in the United States of America.

For Erin, who encouraged me to go chasing crocodiles and to all who love unlovely creatures.

CONTENTS

Contents

ILLUSTRATIONS

INTRODUCTION

THE INSPIRATION TO WRITE THIS BOOK came from my firsthand experiences with crocodilian fossils. I worked for years in a business where the skeleton of a giant crocodilian (*Deinosuchus sp.*) lurked in the corner of a side building. Occasionally when I passed by, I would stop and ponder this specter of the distant past. Another experience that haunted me was a childhood stop at the Okefenokee Swamp on a family road trip to Disney World. I remember little of Mickey Mouse, but I can still picture an enormous alligator lying in the water in the rain as the child I was stared with awe.

More recently, I was volunteering at Aransas Wildlife Refuge in Texas on my own time in exchange for a free RV spot and the opportunity to observe wild alligators and their habitat. While I was at Aransas I called up Tom Lindgren of Geo Décor, a paleontology company in Tucson, Arizona, where I had done fossil preparation work in the past. Lindgren told me about a Eocene crocodilian just discovered that summer in Wyoming. That crocodilian ended up being a large fossil preparation project for me, taking up almost as much time and effort as writing this book.

Texas wasn't the last trip I made while researching this book. I traveled to Nepal to find the rare, long-snouted crocodilian gharials and mugger crocodiles in the jungle. In South Carolina I volunteered for alligator behavioral research on golf courses. I canoed Okefenokee in Georgia and I visited the Everglades to see the environment American alligators and American crocodiles share. This is the only place where knowing what is the difference between crocodiles and alligators is useful because you might see both animals. Even in the Everglades, crocodiles, with their more pointed snouts and toothier closed mouths, mostly stay out of alligators' fresh water, opting for salt.

Most of the time I was writing this book, I was also working on the Wyoming crocodilian fossil at Geo Décor in Tucson. Day after day I sat hunched before a vertical slab of stone higher and wider than I am tall, held in a steel support frame. First, with an air-powered chisel I chipped away at the tan-colored stone. Later I blasted the fossil clean with a stylus shooting a stream of white powder—dolomite—to reveal bones ranging from milk chocolate to dark chocolate tones in color. The skull appeared bit by bit, teeth stabbing out at me. The twist of spine, curving and broken appeared like a dark pagan tattoo, thorned with chevrons inked into the pale flesh of rock. Day after day I sat by a garage door, fans blowing over me, forcing the dust outside; although much circled back, settled onto the floor, into my hair, onto my face, and all over my clothes.

The work was like a long road trip—lots of sitting with occasional small movements. There were also many things to discover beneath each layer of rock peeled back. Slowly, over long months stretching to more than half a year, the strange skeletal form of the crocodilian was revealed, a relic of a massive tropical Wyoming lake. Seeing the small details made all the work, the days of monotony, heat, and dust, worth it.

When I realized that my interest in crocodilians was leading to writing a book, I wanted to add to my firsthand experience of the subject. To that end, I traveled to places where crocodilians live today and where fossils have been found. I also dug out my old journals from a college field course in Ecuador where I observed caimans, tropical relatives of alligators, as well as worked with ancient crocodilians preserved in stone. I supplemented my own experiences with interviews I conducted with biologists, anthropologists, paleontologists, and zookeepers. Sources consulted for each chapter—books, scientific papers, and websites—are listed at the back of this volume.

The truth is, crocodilians are beyond human understanding. We humans have a hard time understanding the unique struggles, triumphs, and stories of people with different skin colors, languages, or nationalities; how much harder is it to understand a different species entirely? In this book I've used not only the narrow lens of biology and paleontology but also myth and anthropology. Perhaps imagination can bridge gaps that science alone cannot. I hope what I've written here will inspire deeper reflection on the world we live in and the creatures we share it with—especially those that are scaly and dangerous.

This is *Borealosuchus sp.*, a crocodilian I prepared in Tucson, Arizona, viewed from the ventral side (except for the head which is twisted). At this point this side is only partially prepared as you can see from the tail. *Borealosuchus* is an extinct genus of crocodyliforms, this specimen lived in the Eocene of subtropical Wyoming. (*Geo Décor*)

one

CROCODILIANS *in* STONE

IN WESTERN COLORADO, in a small workshop huddled with other buildings, surrounded by old farm fields and large residential lawns, stands the form of a dead monster. Stripped of muscle and skin, ligaments and tendons, the thing is a skeleton reconstructed in plastic resin. Molded with and cast from high quality rubber, the individual bones are connected by pieces of metal hidden within. The skeleton, painted by hand, is as good a reconstruction as science and art can make.

This is the work carried out at Gaston Design, a commercial paleontology business I worked at on and off for years while going to college and traveling to different field locations as a biology intern. The skeleton is one I've always been impressed with, part of what kept me coming back to Gaston Design.

Mouth agape, back speckled with bone plates (called osteoderms), the skeleton is a bony representation of a nightmare for many. The skeleton is *Deinosuchus*, a crocodilian thirty feet long; almost five feet of which is a peg-toothed killing, crushing, tearing machine of a head. The brown, bony legs bend slightly, flexing for action, the head is raised as if bursting from a great lake upon the unwary; the tail lays behind in a sinuous pattern, like a meandering stream.

A skeleton like the *Deinosuchus* takes a long time to build. I've helped carry the molds of the massive skull from a simple, unlit shed crowded with stacks of other molds to the work room. The outside of the mold is an off-white, hard fiberglass shell, ready to tear at the skin or clothes of the incautious. Around the sharp edges of the mold, holes have been drilled and fitted with bolts. These are circled in marker, lest a bolt be forgotten and the mold spill liquid resin.

After the bolts holding the mold together during storage are removed, the rubber inside is exposed. The soft rubber is similar to one used by jewelry makers. Its intention is to capture the minutia of bone texture and flaws. The rubber is dusted with brown paint powder and the excess removed by the blast of an air compressor hose. To get the skull mold under a fan it was carried into a cramped back room, one side of which is dominated by a hood. Another wall has a door that opens to the large fan pulling air through a screen to the outside. On hot summer days, looking outside through the whirring blades, I have watched horses grazing in the field behind Gaston Design. It's as if I were peering back to a time when equines first evolved in North America.

The end of a day dusting molds like this always left my arms and face darkened with paint colors that I washed off with a preliminary scrub at a large plastic sink near the bathrooms. I dipped hands into white, goopy, industrial cleaners kept in small plastic tubs, smearing them up my arms and across my cheeks and pushed my whole face under the flow of water. I was still filthy when I finished, but cleaned up enough to drive home to a real shower. By the work sink hangs a poster of three-toed, bird-shaped dinosaur footprints in red sandstone, disappearing into the tide of Lake Powell. Outside of the shop at Gaston Design on a spring day, the trees shading the surrounding land are always full of the otherworldly, tinny song of red-winged blackbirds. It's a reminder that dinosaurs are still with us.

After the rubber molds are powdered with color and bolted together with metal supports hidden inside—rods or struts—to give the finished cast long-term stability, the time comes for resin to be poured in.

The casting area of Gaston Design is floored with removable wood panels splattered in plastic; the floor panels appear marked with the remnants of a hundred melted candles. A sandbox raised on wooden table legs stands next to a bank of shelves filled with the smaller miscellaneous molds often used, here stored in untidy stacks. Mammoth teeth and raptor claw molds are near molds of strange armored fishes. Across the room is a shelf full of mostly mammal skull molds—bears, saber-toothed cats, a tiger. On the walls is everything from a Salvador Dali painting (*Burning Giraffes and Telephones*) to a collection of antique padlocks mounted on small rectangles of plywood.

On a bench against the wall closest to the rest of the shop, jugs of resin are kept along with an assortment of plastic containers for measuring and mixing. Some are buckets neatly labeled with graduations, some are old yogurt tubs. There is a stack of clear solo cups next to a dry erase board with magic markers for labeling the cups. Plastic spoons are caked with hardened resin. The only way to clean them is to smash them sharply on the metal leg of a table until the resin breaks off in clumps. This is the room where the reproductions of bones like those making up the *Deinosuchus* skeleton first take form.

With big pieces like the upper and lower skull halves of *Deinosuchus*, Rob Gaston, owner of Gaston Design, and I worked together on pouring them. He'd usually pour in some resin and I'd move the mold vigorously to shake out any air bubbles that might form imperfections in the cast. Rob worked fast to mix up liquid resin in five-gallon buckets, stirring with a long metal attachment on a drill, and pour the resin into the mold before it hardened. Resin solidifies disconcertingly fast on hot summer days, cold winter days being more forgiving. If one is slow or lackadaisical, a pour can be ruined on any day, whatever the weather. The resin itself looks like thick beer. One part perhaps is like an especially light Mexican beer, the other part looks like a darker amber beer. After being stirred together, the two start to get hot and set up into a whitish color. If you mix the two parts of resin together and pour it into an open-top mold, you can see little spirals and spider webs of white start to form in brilliant eruptions as the chemical reaction works. The resin eventually solidifies into a hard plastic representation of whatever mold it was poured into.

The end result of all this work is impressive but somewhat artificial. The languid curve of the spine, threatening mouth posture, and raised head are all within the realm of possibility, but they're also creative decisions made by those building the skeletal mount. Artificial as it is, a mount like this does give the viewer real information and it fuels the imagination. Viewing crocodilians, like viewing any animal (especially extinct), is a flight of imagination. We can never know what it is like to be in another creature's skin. We certainly can never pretend to see the full scope of a lineage's evolutionary history. Slowly, through imagination, we start to view a thread of the tapestry of life—messily woven through and wrapped around all the others, something twisted, not a simple line drawn in textbook diagrams. It was while working at Gaston Design that I started imagining the world of crocodilians.

Over the years I became friends with Rob Gaston. Rob was one of the few people I could tell, "Sometimes the eventual extinction of the human species is my only hope for earth," without being misunderstood or thought deranged.

A tall man with roots in Tennessee, about twenty years my senior, Rob was always quick with fascinating anecdotes about his travels in the Amazon. Rob is also an encyclopedia of natural history knowledge, balanced by an education in art. His shop and his house are incredible museum collections, walls covered in artifacts, tables topped with fossils, animals or skulls. In one room of his home he has an assemblage of small cages where his tarantulas live. The last time I visited him, his three guinea pigs sat in an open-topped enclosure in his living room. A hundred masks from Africa, Asia, and South America stared down from the walls. Near the edge of his property Rob has a greenhouse with everything from a palm tree and cacti to a collection of carnivorous plants. Over the years I worked for Rob on projects ranging from casting to cleaning guinea pig cages to writing exhibit signs.

As I began to write for a museum exhibit Rob was building, I started thinking about how environments shape organisms and how basic physical laws shape those environments. Organisms in some ways are simply manifestations of the land in which they live. Crocodilians are an excellent example. Crocodilians are held to be ancient by many, and indeed in the context of living vertebrate land animals they are, but they're also constantly changing along with their environments.

Deinosuchus is a genus of extinct crocodilian, not a crocodile but more closely related to alligators. Scientists aren't sure how many species of *Deinosuchus* once lived. The fossil record is incomplete, and remains consisting of nothing but teeth can be contested as a new species. Initially, there was only one officially recognized species of *Deinosuchus*—*D. rugosus*, described in 1858 from teeth found in North Carolina. The history of science since *Deinosuchus* was discovered is one of confusion; the genus and various species within it have been renamed more than once, and reconstructions of skulls and skeletons have been found to be faulty. Still, a lot is known about *Deinosuchus*, and a lot guessed at, because it looks so damned familiar.

To most people, including many nonspecialist scientists, *Deinosuchus* is simply a giant alligator—proof of a virtually unchanged lineage. In this way *Deinosuchus* is seen as an ancient relic of a lost world, a giant monster that preyed on other giant monsters living in a place like nothing we know today. *Deinosuchus* is an emissary from a planet without humans. Many *Deinosuchus* fossils have been found in the American Deep South, interestingly the same area where modern alligators live. However, the *Deinosuchus* genus has also been found as far north as New Jersey and as far south as Coahuila, Mexico. Rob Gaston told me he suspects there is much potential left untapped in the deserts of Mexico. I also consulted Hector Rivera, a paleontologist with Museo del Desierto in the Mexican city of Saltillo, Coahuila state, to better understand *Deinosuchus*. Dr. Rivera gave me a wonderful description that I translated from Spanish: "If we can imagine a scenario millions of years ago, we would see herds of hadrosaurs approaching the rivers to drink, and from the turbid waters, a *Deinosuchus* would emerge with such force and speed that the prey would have watched, terrified, as gigantic jaws of more than one meter long and armed with teeth closed violently and quickly on its body. The attack must have been so fast that he could not even feel pain at the time of the attack. . . . For this big crocodile, a dinosaur was nothing more than an appetizer."

Deinosuchus riograndensis fossils, named for the river separating the United States and Mexico, have been found in Texas as well as La Salada in Coahuila, Mexico. Hector Rivera told me that he and other paleontologists searched the area in a 2007 expedition, following up on dinosaur fossils found there the year before. What they found were not only dinosaurs. The area has remains of hadrosaurs that he believes were the favorite prey of *Deinosuchus*, as some of the tail vertebrae had marks on them that appeared to be from the teeth of a giant crocodilian. In the same area *Deinosuchus* bones and osteoderms (bony plates embedded in skin during life) were found.

Deinosuchus in this light was the top predator, a creature capable of killing and eating fully grown dinosaurs as regular meals. In his book *King of the Crocodylians*, paleontologist David R. Schwimmer estimated the total body length for the largest to be 12.0 meters (about 39 feet); from this length Schwimmer estimates the body weight to have been 8.5 tons.* To put this massive weight into context, it's at least 1.5 tons heavier than estimates for the live weight of a *Tyrannosarus rex*. *Deinosuchus* had jaws capable of exerting more force than any living animal and probably more than *T. rex*

---

*In an email, Dr. Schwimmer told me that the sizes between eastern and western *Deinosuchus*, such as the one that Rob Gaston's reconstruction is based on, are such that he suspects the two to possibly be different species of the same genus. Since I first wrote this, classification has changed and there are at least three official species of *Deinosuchus* and possibly more. The eastern species is now *D. rugosus* and the western *D. riograndensis*.

A *Deinosuchus sp.* skull reconstructed from a specimen found in Utah's Grand Staircase-Escalante National Monument with a 22-inch-long modern alligator skull for
comparison. *Deinosuchus* lived 82 to 73 million years ago during the late Cretaceous;
the largest individuals probably measured 35 feet in length. (*Author*)

as well. Schwimmer estimated the bite force of the giant croc to
be about 4,046.6 pounds of force. There is evidence throughout
Deinosuchus' range that the giant crocodilian ate not only
hadrosaurs but also predatory dinosaurs not so different from *T.
rex*. During *Deinosuchus'* time, the waterways of the world were
dominated by crocodilians, the giant ones as well as smaller specimens fighting over scraps, eating each other, maybe even dining
on infant *Deinosuchus*, fishes, turtles, and anything they could catch
at the water's edge.

At Geo Décor, the paleontology company in Tucson one winter
I was set the task of sorting through a collection of dinosaur fossil
pieces that had been wrapped up and put in boxes during the
1990s. Many of the pieces were still embedded in the soft sandstone made of sediments they were deposited in some 68 million
years ago. These were fragments of Edmontosaurus, a type of
hadrosaur like the ones Hector Rivera described in Coahuila. An

Edmontosaurus skull appears to be nothing but a giant duck skull. The so-called duck bill is prominent, and Edmontosaurus has none of the frills or crests other hadrosaurs are known for.

The hadrosaur bones came from roughly the same part of Wyoming where I was born, the flat high plains of the central eastern side of the state, near its border with South Dakota. It's an area that's cold in the winter, unforgiving in the summer, and windblown year round. This place of grass, wind, and ghosts (not all of which are human) is the first place I thought of as home. In geological time, the place is very dynamic, sometimes near an inland sea, sometimes sub-tropical, and other times steppe grassland with harsh winters. The fossils of the Edmontosaurus tell us just one page of the whole story.

Tom, the owner of Geo Décor and one of the men who'd collected the bones, told me they came from a site of a mass mortality. There were different bones from many individuals—younger, older, smaller, larger, female and male. All together these dinosaurs had been caught in a flood, drowned, and left to molder in a retreating river. The fossils range in color from rusty red to a chocolate brown and are textured like bone, similar to rough wood grain. They are embedded in a light yellow sandstone matrix highlighted by roundish globs of clay and occasional chunks of fossil plant and other debris. Mixed with the dinosaur pieces were other chunks of bone with a strangely delicate and familiar pattern. I almost recognized the fragments for what they were but had to be reminded; they were turtle shell. With the turtles and hadrosaurs were pieces of long, sharp, finely serrated teeth. Tyrannosaurs and perhaps other theropod dinosaurs had snacked on the rotting hadrosaur corpses.

Other smaller teeth were mixed in with the remains also; a crocodile or a few crocodiles had lost teeth in the smorgasbord of dinosaur flesh as well. These weren't the teeth of *Deinosuchus* or another animal that could hunt a fully grown hadrosaur; they were the teeth of a smaller crocodile. These smaller crocodiles would have no compunction about eating dead dinosaur when they could. This was a time when reptiles dominated the ranks of larger animals, a world before the "rise of mammals." At roughly 68 million years ago, after the reign of *Deinosuchus*, it was perhaps the twilight of the age of giant reptiles.

To my mind, living crocodilians were a small window into this strange lost world, a glimpse of something beyond the reach of our clumsy ape hands. I asked Dr. Adam Cossette, a paleontologist with a fresh PhD from the University of Iowa, earned working on fossil crocodilians, about this perception; why, I queried, had crocodilians remained so unchanged throughout their long history?

Sure, *Deinosuchus* is enormous, but the fossil contains all the important elements present in its living relatives. The feet look like the clawed paws of a modern crocodile, and the head is the giant version of something Steve Irwin might've once leaped onto while smiling broadly at the camera. The back of *Deinosuchus* is covered in the thick bony armor still found on American alligators and crocodiles. Sure, some things remain similar, but as Adam Cossette told me, the history of crocodilians is much more complex than most people know. "Most, save the long-snouted forms—Gavials and *Tomistoma*—have a generalized snout shape that is moderately long and broad. In the fossil record there is considerable variation in snout shape and much of the variation in the crocodilian skull is concentrated in the snout. The long snouted forms vary from extremely long and tube-like such as *Euthecodon* to long and surf-board shaped such as *Mourasuchus*. Additionally there are giant forms (30+ feet) such as *Purussaurus* and diminutive taxa such as *Procaimanoidea* which have blunt snouts."

In other words, Cossette was saying that although some ancient crocodilians look like modern relatives, many do not. Alligators, crocodiles, and their kin are not living holdovers of some fantastic lost world of the past; like every living thing they are part of the modern world. Cossette went on to tell me that size in crocodilians has changed radically over time: "Most modern species are medium sized with adult sizes being somewhere in the range of 10–15 feet. However adult body sizes were much more variable in deep time. Taxa such as *Procaimanoidea* and species of *Diplocynodon* were only about 3–5 feet long as adults whereas *Purussaurus* and *Deinosuchus* could grow to 30–35 feet as adults."

Cossette then told me about the weirder examples of what croc-odilian evolution had created. Planocraniids, for example, look lit-tle like the modern crocodile form.

Peg teeth in crocodilians are made to hold prey while the pred-ator performs a "death roll," something that sounds exactly like what it is. Animals are held in crocodilian jaws and subjected to something like the washing machine of death. Half-killed by drowning, half-killed by physical trauma, limbs are ripped off in death rolls, making them easier to eat for an animal that can't chew. In planocraniids, the teeth are more like blades, similar to teeth of predatory theropod dinosaurs or modern Komodo drag-ons. Blade-like teeth slash flesh but are useless for a death roll. Death comes simply by bleeding from teeth marks, similar to a knife wound. It makes sense that planocraniids wouldn't have teeth made for a death roll, whose main prerequisite is an aquatic lifestyle. They couldn't death roll anything because they lived out of water.

Planocraniids look a lot like Komodo dragons in general—giant land-walking lizards. Modern crocodilian legs are relatively short and hold the animals just off the ground. Instead of walking, swim-ming is the main way crocodilians move through their world, using powerful tails instead of limbs. Planocraniids had longer legs, though, made for stalking prey on dry land. In one way planocrani-ids do look very crocodilian though: their heads (minus teeth) are very similar to crocodilian heads, at least to the eyes of a casual observer. Adam Cossette pointed out that their snouts are still much more compact.

As strange as it is, planocraniids aren't the first or only dry land walking crocodilians. Before crocodilians took to the swamps and waterways of the world, it seems they were in an evolutionary bat-tle with theropod dinosaurs for the niche of top terrestrial preda-tors. Crocodylomorphs, early ancestors dating to a time before crocodilians broke into the three modern branches of alligators, crocodiles, and gharials, walked on their hind legs. *Carnufex caro-linensis* is an example of this bizarre crocodilian forebear, which must have competed with early dinosaur predators of what is now

This skeletal reconstruction of Planocraniid (*Boverisuchus magnifrons*) was photographed in the Geiseltal Lagerstätte, an important paleontological site in Germany, and used in a 2015 exhibition called, "Gaining Ground: Horse Hunting Crocodiles and Giant Birds." Members of the family Planocraniidae are extinct eusuchian crocodyliforms, sometimes referred to as "hooved crocodiles," because of their adaptations to terrestrial life, including claws resembling hooves. You can see how the legs are more directly beneath the animal compared to modern crocodiles which have a more sprawling stance on land. (*DagdaMor, Creative Commons*)

North Carolina, 231 million years ago in the late Triassic. From a bipedal crocodilian monster, evolution shaped animals more like reptilian jackals, eventually becoming the crocodilians we know today. *Deinosuchus* itself represents one foray into how large a crocodilian could become.

The upshot is that evolution has tinkered a lot with the crocodilian form. The giant *Sarcosuchus*, which the media has dubbed "super croc," is a huge, extinct African crocodilian relative that looks nothing like the American alligator simply because of its size, not to mention its bizarre, thin snout.

Different evolutionary pressures created tiny crocodilians and giant reptilian monsters. Evolution whittled slender snouts and carved broad muzzles. Crocs walking on two legs, on four legs, or almost entirely aquatic all have their place in the history. When you look at the details you can see that *Deinosuchus*, like its modern relatives, is just one animal in a rich tapestry of different forms, some similar, some dissimilar. Modern crocodilians have evolved with the changes in their physical worlds. The differences have been subtle ones, easily missed by a layperson.

TEARS *for* CROCODILIA

Sarcosuchus sp. skull and neck at Gaston Design's workshop. "Super Croc" *Sarcosuchus* lived in the early Cretaceous (133-112 million years ago) in what is now South America and Africa. These animals reached an estimated average length of 30 feet. Although they are not the ancestors of modern crocodilians, they are relatives and probably lived similar lives. (*Author*)

The world has changed radically since crocodilians first appeared. North America, when *Deinosuchus* was alive, would be unrecognizable to the people who live there now. As hard to imagine as it is, the Rocky Mountains, spine of the continent, were built up 300 million years ago and eroded down to very little. The modern Rockies were formed during the Laramide Orogeny, some 80 to 55 million years ago, in a period that must have been punctuated often with earthquakes. *Deinosuchus* lived 80 to 73 million years ago, just at the start of the rise of the Rocky Mountains. Part of Utah was under a vast inland sea that cut North America into eastern and western halves during *Deinosuchus'* time. As can be expected during a period when the world was warmer, it was also wetter. Besides the inland sea, Adam Cossette reminded me that a lot of the southeastern United States was under water as well.

The individual *Deinosuchus* species that so impressed me in Rob Gaston's shop had been found in Grand Staircase-Escalante National Monument. (The original fossil is housed in the Utah Museum of Natural History, Salt Lake City.) Like much of Utah, Grand Staircase-Escalante is a place of desert sandstone; during the life of *Deinosuchus* it was a marshy area at the edge of the sea. Now *Deinosuchus* was the first member of the superfamily Alligatoroidea, which includes modern alligators, discovered in Utah.

The Mexican *Deinosuchus* was found in the Aguja Formation, which lies exposed across the border in Texas in Big Bend National Park as well as Mexico. The formation itself is made of maroon layers of clay overlying a gray-green clay that weathers to a yellowish color. The different colors of clay reveal a habitat that was probably in constant flux. Shifting water conditions deposited clays of different colors as the place changed from an ocean bed to a mix of salt and fresh water and even dry land. North Carolina, which is still populated with alligators, was where some of the first *Deinosuchus* teeth were collected by scientists in 1858, although initially confused with other fossils.* Hector Rivera told me that on the Mexican side, the Aguja Formation isn't quite so pretty and is actually indistinct. When *Deinosuchus* lived in the area, the environment was part of a river delta system. The geology reveals a land of marshes, lakes, and sandbars—an easy habitat in which to imagine a giant crocodilian lurking.

In the Coahuila that *Deinosuchus* lived in, cypress palms grew along with at least five other tropical trees. Abundant plant life

*In 1858, paleontologist Ebenezer Emmons described two teeth found in North Carolina. Initially these teeth were assigned to the genus *Polyptychodon*, then believed to be a giant crocodilian. Eventually it was discovered that *Polyptychodon* was actually a pliosaur, an unrelated marine reptile, and the teeth were reassigned to *P. rugosus*. Today the species *rugosus* is retained but as *Deinosuchus rugosus*. There is a good possibility that Native Americans found *Deinosuchus* remains long before European-American paleontologists. In her book *Fossil Legends of the First Americans*, Adrienne Mayor mentions that in the nineteenth century Europeans noted that the Crow had a word for alligator, despite being far north of the animal's range. Around the year 1880, Chief Medicine Crow made drawings of four reptiles, including an alligator. Ethnologist Ella Clark recorded instances of Crow stories of alligator-like monsters in the Tongue, Rosebud, and Little Bighorn Rivers. Other Crow in the area have reported that finding large alligator teeth was previously a common occurrence.

seemed to entice not just the duck-billed hadrosaurs but also ceratopsians with horned faces and knobby frills. *Yehuecauhceratops* and *Agujaceratops* lived nearby along with heavily armored ankylosaurs, and all could be killed or scavenged by *Deinosuchus* or perhaps other crocodiles. *Deinosuchus* had thicker teeth proportionally and overall harder ones than modern crocodilians, all the better to deal with armor and shells.

The area in which *Deinosuchus riograndensis* lived was humid, frequently flooded by storms. In all that mud, dinosaur footprints were easily formed and fossilized. Tropical woodlands were home to dinosaurs close to the marshes they also frequented. The water held fish, amphibians, and turtles like ponds and rivers of today. Mammals scurried in the underbrush of the forests and drank from the same water where the giant crocodiles swam with their smaller cousins.

From *Deinosuchus riograndensis'* location, scientists ascertain that the animal lived between roughly 72 and 83 million years ago, in the Campian Age. The Aguja Formation reveals a wild world populated with fantastic dinosaurs. The first crocodilians were much older than *Deinosuchus*, though. The oldest known crocodilians (that we'd recognize today as being crocodilians) are about 200 million years old, from the beginning of the Jurassic, compared to the late Cretaceous when *Deinosuchus* lived, only 80 to 73 million years ago.

The story of a crocodilian body plan is even older. Strangely enough, animals with long thin snouts, mouths full of teeth, creatures that lurk in the water waiting to catch their prey suddenly, and short crocodile-like animals have been evolving for a very long time. Just before the rise of the crocodilians, another reptile occupied the same niche as modern crocodiles. Phytosaurs were distantly related reptiles, but at first blush they appear eerily similar to crocodiles. There are the same eyes made for peeking above the water while the massive reptilian body floats just below the surface.

The nostrils, however, are a giveaway that something's not quite right in thinking of the phytosaur as a crocodilian. Crocodilians have nostrils at the end of their long snouts, while the nostrils on phytosaurs are awkwardly bunched together on a protrusion just

Prionosuchus sp., left, is an extinct genus of amphibians that seemed to fill the same ecological niche as modern crocodilians. *Prionosuchus* with the long, thin snout is most similar to extant gharials. Based on comparisons to gharials, some *Prionosuchus* specimens reached lengths of 18 feet. An exceptionally large individual was estimated to have been 30 feet. An approximately 5´ 11˝ snorkeler, right, is shown for comparison. (*Left, sketch by* ДиБгд, *Creative Commons; right, author*)

in front of the eyes. The nostril placement created an animal as strange-looking as it sounds, but the function is the same as the nostrils in modern crocodiles. The location of the nostrils is a telltale sign along with other evidence that the evolution of phytosaurs was separate from the evolution of crocodilians.

The story is even stranger, though, because other animals filled the role of crocodilian-like predator. *Prionosuchus* is perhaps one of the more bizarre examples of a crocodile-like predator. In the Permian, roughly 270 million years ago, *Prionosuchus* prowled the swamps in what seems like a very crocodilian fashion. What makes this especially peculiar is that *Prionosuchus* wasn't even a reptile but a giant amphibian that measured between eight and thirty feet long. Adam Cossette told me that the body plan of these and other crocodile-like animals is "sneaky." The basics of a crocodile body make it a coldly efficient killing machine.

Some of the most interesting fossils in the history of crocodilians come from South America and Africa, which were at the time joined as one landmass, Pangaea. Crocodilians spread across the globe before Pangaea broke up. Alligators are found in the Americas as well as China. Crocodiles live in Asia, Africa, and the Americas. Gharials (also known as gavials) are rarer and found in Asia in quickly dwindling populations. Africa has long been a hotbed of crocodilian diversity despite vastly changing landscapes. *Sarcosuchus*, a cousin to mainline crocodilians, was first found by a French paleontologist on expeditions in what is now the Sahara.

Early British paleontologist Dayrell Botry Pigott's name is associated with many fossil crocodilian species from Rusinga Island near the shores of Lake Victoria in Kenya. Ironically after Pigott's research on fossil crocodilians, he speared a hippopotamus that then overturned his raft. In the chaos that followed, the paleontologist was killed by a Nile crocodile in 1911. Adam Cossette told me being killed by crocodiles remains a possibility today for paleontologists like him working in the area:

> My first encounter with a croc in the wild came . . . while on safari. I was crossing a foot bridge when I noticed two crocs sunning themselves on a sandbar below my position. After hearing the story of Pigott earlier in the summer I could not help but feel uneasy by their presence. I was not the only one who was uneasy, the crocs had a noticeable effect on the other animals in their immediate area as well. Everything seemed to be wary of their presence. Monkeys who were otherwise so quick to vocalize would be absolutely silent while in the presence of a 15 foot Nile Crocodile.

Cossette told me that the landscape of Rusinga Island is a dry one bordering a central volcanic mountain range, a rocky place. The landscape reminded him of central New Mexico near Albuquerque. The idea of comparing an African landscape to the

American Southwest at first surprised me, but not long after receiving Adam Cossette's email I had the pleasure of traveling there. The whole of New Mexico has mountains, prairies, canyons, and plateaus, but it is a hot, dry place. I watched much of the landscape pass me by from the driver's seat of the Ford camper van my then-fiancée Erin and I lived in. Later, we drove south of Tucson, climbing a little higher in elevation to a landscape similar to what we drove through in New Mexico. Stretching towards a horizon broken by dark, rugged mountains was a place of rolling hills. Yellowish grass covered the earth; here and there dispersed in the grass grew gnarled mesquite trees. Looking out over the land, I could easily imagine a herd of zebras grazing or a giraffe cutting in front of a setting sun. I thought then of Adam Cossette's comparison of a landscape like this to the African region where he did field work. The place where he finds his fossil crocs is a place where living crocodiles still lurk. I wondered to myself how far from southern Arizona the nearest wild crocodilian was. Texas is home to American alligators at least, not so very far away. I thought about the fossil *Deinosuchus* found in Utah to the north of Arizona and the one across the border into Mexico to the south. Suddenly the desert seemed filled with the bones of dead crocodilians and bordered by a few live ones.

I considered what would need to change for Utah or Arizona to be home to wild crocodilians again. The answer is, not much really. If Utah was a little bit wetter, maybe a little bit warmer as well, crocodilians could live in what is now desert. Throughout southern Arizona and much of the Southwest, many streams flood and then dry to sandy ditches seasonally. Biology is patient. Will these changes occur before crocodilians are extinct as a whole? We're already melting ice caps, altering so much so fast. Perhaps a few hundred years could bring crocodilians moving along the shores of a new inland sea, crawling and swimming from Texas north to Utah, their ancestral homeland.

I remember a similar place, a grassland in southeastern Colorado where I hiked with my family as a teenager. We made our way past an old Spanish graveyard along a hot, dusty trail to the muddy Purgatoire River. There in the stone near the river's edge were rough shapes punched into mud during the Mesozoic. The place is a dinosaur trackway. Dinosaurs since that time have become pigeons and ducks, penguins and ostriches, hummingbirds and the great wandering albatross. The world has changed, and crocodilians have changed with it. When the world was full of giant reptiles, *Deinosuchus* evolved to giant proportions to prey on them. Before that, they contested dry land on their hind feet. Now, crocodilians have become more secretive, hiding in dense swamps and rainforests, lurking in the shadows of human society. Crocodilians have become successful because they can change while holding onto the things that made them successful.

Crocodiles, alligators, and their relatives the gharials now live in Asia, Africa, North America, South America, and Australia. They're one of the most successful and widespread megafauna. With the rise of clothes-wearing apes, crocodilians changed again, molded to a new world. To our minds, crocodiles, alligators, and their ilk are remnants of a dangerous past. Being ancient predators, however, is only a small part of the crocodilian story. Living crocodilians are more complex, more dynamic than even the fossil record shows. To understand crocodilians, one must see them in context, both in their environment but also in their place in the tree of life.

– two –

OTHER BRANCHES *of the* TREE

THERE'S A POND IN A GRASSY AND SHADED CITY PARK in Tucson where I've often walked our dogs around after dropping my wife Erin off at work in the morning. Just a little after sunrise, when the grass and muddy banks beneath the palm and eucalyptus trees start to warm, you can see red-eared sliders (*Trachemys scripta elegans*) sunning themselves. These little turtles lie inert in small groups or alone, basking in the early sunlight like squat statues. The shells glisten in the early morning light; the tiny heads balance on stretched thin necks. Around the turtles in the grass, gaggles of feral domestic geese honk angrily, and bufflehead ducks and mallards peck the lawn for food. In the water more ducks, American coots, and neotropical cormorants swim past in noisy crowds, searching for edible scraps. In the trees any number of songbirds flit and sing, the bright red vermillion flycatcher being the most conspicuous. One morning I saw a black-crowned night heron standing on spindly legs, slowly swallowing a large fish that spilled out the sides of his beak—a hint of life hidden beneath the pond's surface.

Any of these birds are quick to take noisy flight at the approach of danger, but not the turtles. The only recourse of the turtle is a jerking of limbs and a plop into the cool water, where she can sink and swim away from terrestrial predators into the dark depths. The differences between turtles and birds are too many to mention. This distinction between birds and turtles in almost every way illustrates an evolutionary divide among reptiles. Birds are technically considered reptiles, but they have many novel adaptations most other reptiles lack.

"Normal" scaly reptiles: lizards, snakes, and yes, turtles are ectothermic or, as commonly termed, "cold-blooded"; they depend on outside heat to warm their bodies and lack much in the way of cooling mechanisms. This is perhaps why many reptiles are found only at hotter latitudes.

Lumping all reptiles together (excluding birds) as "ectothermic" is a bit of an oversimplification. In the 1960s keepers at the Bronx Zoo noticed something strange. A nest of Burmese python (*Python molurus bivittatus*) eggs in an enclosure was able to stay warm independently of the exhibit's temperature. Conversely, the temperature of a nearby African python's (*Python sebae*) eggs varied depending on the ambient temperature. Eventually the curious keepers observed the Burmese python wrap her body around her eggs and shiver to keep them warm. The Burmese python evolved for colder conditions than her African relative.

Evolution has found some interesting ways for typically ectothermic animals to warm themselves or their eggs, but there's only so much an animal can do before endothermy is necessary for survival under demanding conditions. There are real physiological reasons that Burmese pythons don't live in Antarctica or high on the Tibetan Plateau (although there is a rare snake, *Thermophis baileyi*, that lives exclusively on the Tibetan Plateau, possibly relying on hot springs for warmth).

Birds, in contrast—penguins, puffins, auklets—all venture into very cold climates. It's not uncommon to see even migratory birds swimming in a small patch of unfrozen water in an icy lake. There isn't much of a geographic analogue for many turtles, lizards, or snakes compared to the very polar species of birds. True enough, sea turtles are great voyagers (leatherback sea turtles, for example, sometimes range from the coast of South America to the coast of Africa), but they're restricted to warmer regions. Crocodilians as well are found exclusively in hot places; North Carolina is about as far north as alligators—the northernmost of crocodilians—venture. Sunlight and warm air temperatures are important for maintaining their health.

Watching American alligators (*Alligator mississippiensis*), one of the first things I noticed is what initially seemed to be a lack. With alligators there is little of the gregarious clucking, flitting, or vigorous swimming seen in the birds. Crocodilians initially appear to be much lazier creatures.

Yet these typically "cold-blooded" aspects of crocodilian lives are only part of the story. As odd as it seems, birds are the closest living relatives to crocodilians; turtles are an offshoot, the next closest living relative to birds and crocodilians together. Crocodilians for their own part are neither bird nor turtle, yet in the same way that we can learn about human biology by studying chimpanzees and other mammals, we can gain insights about the life of crocodilians by looking to birds and even to turtles. For all these groups, life all starts with mating and eggs.

Erin and I once spent a morning inside a tiny blind: a rough plywood shed with fabric covered slits for windows. The hardwood floor and short ceiling made occasional muted shifting of positions—sitting, kneeling, crouching, slouching—imperative for comfort. Sitting quietly in sweaters, we sipped hot coffee from a dented green thermos and listened to the dark hush of a prairie morning. The blind was set up in Buffalo Gap National Grasslands, rolling hills cut into a patchwork of pastures by barbed wire fences and snaking dirt roads. It's the kind of place to drive through slowly, dust billowing behind in dry times, mud sucking at truck tires in the bottom of draws when there was rain. Every so often we stopped to open gates or slowed for the rumbling of crossing a cattle guard. Meandering herds of cattle surrounded the truck, lowing softly before parting as we moved through. We spent the night camping in a small tent on the prairie to be at the blind early the next morning.

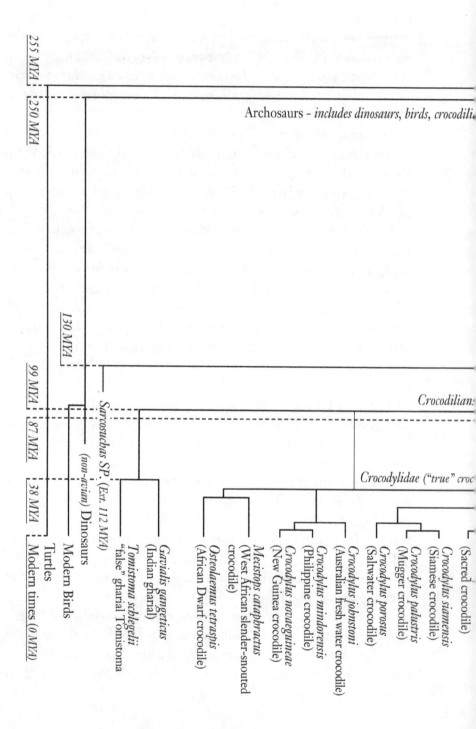

255 MYA

250 MYA

Archosaurs - *includes dinosaurs, birds, crocodili*

130 MYA

99 MYA

Crocodilian

87 MYA

38 MYA

Crocodylidae ("true" croc

Sarcosuchus SP. (Ext. 112 MYA)

(*non-avian*) Dinosaurs

Tomistoma schlegelii "false" gharial Tomistoma

Gavialis gangeticus (Indian gharial)

Osteolaemus tetraspis (African Dwarf crocodile)

Mecistops cataphractus (West African slender-snouted crocodile)

Crocodylus novaeguineae (New Guinea crocodile)

Crocodylus mindorensis (Philippine crocodile)

Crocodylus johnstoni (Australian fresh water crocodile)

Crocodylus porosus (Saltwater crocodile)

Crocodylus palustris (Mugger crocodile)

Crocodylus siamensis (Siamese crocodile)

(Sacred crocodile)

Modern Birds

Turtles

Modern times (0 MYA)

Ancestral Reptiles

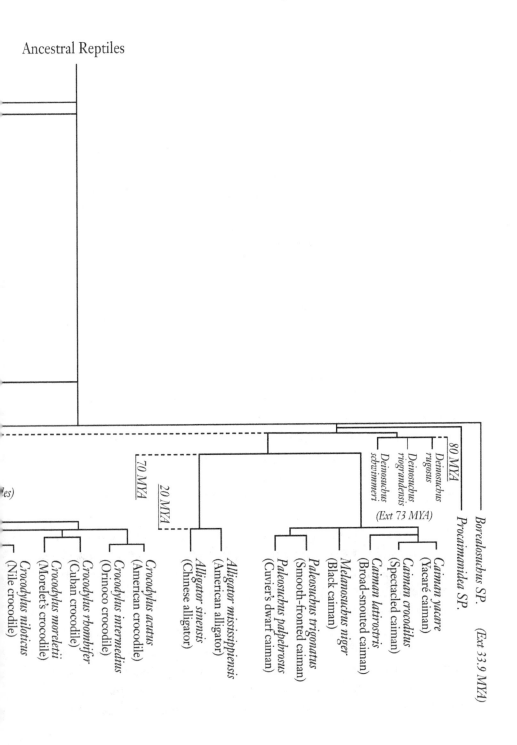

Before the sun rose, the tiny lights from a distant radio tower blinked red at us across the grassland and the moon still outshined the stars in the sky, casting eerie shadows on the fields of knee-high grasses when we crawled from the tent. In the blind, we waited, cramped, with our little Shih Tzu quietly sleeping between us in a mess of extra fleece layers. In the moonlight outside, we could see that the plants nearest us were trampled short and dotted with little fluffs of feathers. It was as if we were in a tiny crop circle misplaced in the prairie. Eventually we heard a soft whispering flap of wings. The birds were gathering. Soon, the area in front of the blind was filled with a small covey of sharp-tailed grouse (*Tympanuchus phasianellus jamesi*). The grouse that we could see were all males. The birds were true to their names with sharp, bladed fans of tail feathers spread as they strutted. Their chests filled with balloon structures as they made eerie drumming noises deep in their bodies. Flapping their wings rigidly, the birds turned in circles in a ritualistic mating display. The wings made sharp sounds as they slapped down in the dirt. The birds whirled like dervishes. The grouse, dancing in their earnestness, brought smiles and quiet giggles as much as fascination. This was a display of males showing off, in hopes of luring in a willing female.

The display is called lekking, and the place is a lek. Sharp-tailed grouse and many other lekking birds return to the same lek location, year after year. There's even a story of a house being built on top of a lek and the birds, undeterred, carried on the next year, lekking on the roof of the house.

If a female is suitably impressed with a lekking male, she'll allow him to join her in disappointingly quick intercourse; blink and you'll miss it. In this way, a top-performing male may mate with several females in a season. Some males will have no luck at all.

Many types of birds lek. Male hummingbirds dance together, showing off their prowess and dazzling colors for the girls, in sunny jungle clearings. Erin and I observed the orange-headed Andean cock of the rock (*Rupicola peruvianus*) doing its own lekking in the dense foliage of a cloud forest in Ecuador, a display filled with hopping on branches and long low whooping calls. Elaborate mating displays, whether in leks or between a male-female pair, are well known in birds. Mating in reptiles is often assumed to be less elaborate and interesting.

In many sea turtles, males merely fight for a position clinging to the back of a prospective female, sometimes forming a Yertle-like stack of swimming, thrashing turtles. It seems the female turtle has little role in choosing a mate and sometimes she's even drowned in the squabbles. Lone males do occasionally approach a female and gently bite her flippers or tail to assess her receptiveness before mounting her without the struggle of competing males. Often, however, competition seems to drive the male turtles into a frenzy.

Competition between crocodilians can be fierce, but there are also mating complexities reminiscent of birds as well. Matt Seney, a friend of mine who worked with alligators in captivity, told me of arriving at work in the early morning while he was a zookeeper and hearing the alligators calling. It was a sound that reminded him of frog choruses, but stranger, a sound he thought he could feel. Alligator calls sometimes have a weird, rattling, croaking quality, but they and other crocodilians also use infrasound, a frequency human ears can't hear but something that can be sensed reverberating through the body.

Infrasound is used by a wide variety of animals. All of the crocodilians studied by science so far use infrasound. Strange birds—the ancient-looking cassowaries of New Guinea—use infrasound to communicate through dense rainforest also. Infrasound frequencies seem to work just as well in the wetlands crocodilians inhabit. Crocodilians are the only reptiles known to produce vocalizations regularly (excluding birds). Turtles only emit noises during sex. Infant crocodilians make small chirping noises to communicate with their parents, and adult males may bellow as part of territorial displays. Probably the most interesting vocalizations and behaviors exhibited by crocodilians deal with mating.

Crocodilians as a group engage in mesmerizing displays at night. Part of the show is the sounds that can't be easily heard by human ears but can be seen or felt. A water dance is the pattern of infrasound vibrations in water across the back of a barely submerged crocodilian. The water can be seen "dancing" along the back of the vocalizing reptile. Only adult male crocodilians do this "water dance" while gathered at meetings designed to find mates.

A whole ritual of roars, head slaps, and water dances is part of a greater mingling of crocodilians, arriving in pairs or alone, swimming amidst each other in swamps and marshes on dark nights. It's something biologist Vladimir Dinets describes in his book *Dragon Songs* as being like a social dance. Vocal displays are clearly a way for a male crocodilian to gain the attention of females. Sometimes after a rather impressive roar, a male alligator will be swarmed with females interested in mating. Mating is just the beginning, however; crocodilians are very different in their parenting than turtles.

I once spent five months over the winter of 2012–2013 at a remote field biology camp in Equatorial Guinea. Off the western coast of Africa, Bioko Island is the seat of the capital of the mostly island nation. Far removed from the capital city, a dirt path through dense, green, wet jungle leads to a camp where primary rainforest is split from the ocean by a band of black sand beach. On a trail that was sometimes completely lost for stretches to the forest, locals left offerings to the forest deities. Soda bottles or bags of chips, things we might consider so much garbage, were left reverentially for nature spirits. After walking through the humid jungle stung by plants and bitten by insects for the better part of the day, arriving at the openness of a beach and the ocean beyond is a revelation. This beach, this ocean, is what brought me and the other research interns to Bioko.

I volunteered to sleep in a hammock under a tarp, to live off canned meat, canned beans, rice, and pasta cooked over a camp fire and eaten in the open air on wooden benches made from native trees. For five months we interns lived this way, bathing in a pool filled with the splash of a waterfall tumbling from high cliffs, drinking this same water filtered for *Giardia sp.* and other contaminants. At nights, the air was filled with the buzz of insects and the strange "bonk, bonk" noises made by hammerhead fruit bats (*Hypsignathus monstrosus*) that sometimes regurgitated seeds while flying over the tarp covering the kitchen. During the day Colobus monkeys played in the trees, chasing each other across branches near our camp, and birdsong flooded the air. We inhabited this wild camp in the jungle by the ocean to monitor the arrival of leatherback sea turtles (*Dermochelys coriacea*) coming to lay their eggs on the beach.

Watching a leatherback, the largest of the extant sea turtles, rise dark and glistening from the waves, to heave herself across the shore on a dark, tropical night feels like a primordial experience. Leatherbacks are huge—they can weigh 500 to 1,500 pounds as adults. The bodies of the large turtles are graceful teardrop shapes, covered in ribbed skin rather than a hard shell, giving them the common name of "leatherback." The skin is black subtly speckled with white—like stars in a sky. The turtles move awkwardly on land, leaving tracks that look like a military tank's tread behind. On scuba trips, I've seen marine turtles in their element, as graceful as ballerinas.

One night I watched a female leatherback encounter a log in her path on the beach; the hapless turtle pushed her head futilely against the log for long minutes, flippers flailing on the loose sand, before eventually returning ponderously to the ocean unsatisfied. On most nights, the turtles dug holes in the beach for their eggs. The flippers moved in rhythmic efficiency while digging. One flipper scoops and dumps, the whole body shifts, and the other flipper scoops its own load of wet sand with the precision of a metronome.

Some holes were dug close to the tide and quickly filled with water. Most turtles abandoned these holes and moved further inland or left altogether to try another night; some turtles did not. The turtles that stayed at flooded holes started laying their eggs in a pool of water at the bottom. The eggs floating in the water were certain to drown quickly. Nest failure rates are high among sea turtles, and youth fatalities are even higher. One study carried out in 2017 found that hatching success rates for leatherback turtles in Sandy Point National Wildlife Refuge in the Virgin Islands has recently fallen. The percent of eggs hatching fell from 74 percent to 55 percent, due, it seems, to changes in climate.

Death and failure happen regularly among young birds and eggs as well, but the approach to parenting between the groups could hardly be more different. Once the turtle lays her eggs, in water or not, with a researcher counting and weighing them or not, near a hungry fishing village or not, she leaves them behind forever. With birds, laying the egg is only the start of parental labor.

Coastal Alaska is a haven for sea birds, especially the lonely islands off the main coast. Even tiny spits of grassy land or jagged rock are given over to messy, squawking, bustling colonies of birds. In the nearly ceaseless Alaskan summer sun, birds can be seen circling around nesting sites in the eerie twilight of 11 p.m. as well as noon. I arrived for my first time in Alaska to be a biology field intern for the United States Geological Survey (USGS). After trips to Costco (where I saw a moose galloping across the parking lot) to buy three months' supply of food for a camp of at least ten people, and some quick planning, we were flown in a cramped bush plane to Middleton Island. The island is a small, relatively flat piece of land with bushes and ferns but not much to count as trees. An exception is the stunted, twisted forest of bushes under which the rhinoceros auklets (aptly named for horned beaks) dig their burrows—bushes still short enough to see over. Middleton is small and contains the decaying remains of old military installations including a Cold War-era radar tower that dominated the insular skyline.

The summer I spent on Middleton was given over to studying a variety of different sea birds, including the black-legged kittiwakes (*Rissa tridactyla*). The kittiwakes I collected data on in Alaska had no obvious differences in physical appearance between males and females. Instead, researchers carefully watch the birds' behavior for clues to gender. Females often engage in "begging" in which she bends forward with her whole body tilted down, her neck arching back up in a graceful curve. Positioned in this way, the bird would jerk her head with mouth open, making little bursts of plaintive cries. The consenting male would regurgitate eaten fish into her mouth. Of course, males also climbed onto the backs of females to mate, which was a much clearer clue to the gender of the birds. There aren't a lot of variable sexual positions in sea birds. This sort of mating behavior is relatively uninteresting compared to the full spectrum of feathered flirting that takes place in other species; love birds have been seen mating for long minutes, apparently relishing the experience. Still, for learning about sea birds, there was hardly a better place than Middleton Island.

The radar tower has been converted into a black-legged kittiwake nesting area and biology laboratory for bird observation. From a distance, the old tower looks like something from Tolkien; a rather tall, ominous building continuously surrounded by the hundreds of birds, hanging nearly motionless in the wind, circling, flapping, squawking on the wing. Black-legged kittiwakes are a smallish gull, mostly white with gray wings (in adult plumage) and black legs ending in small, webbed feet. When kittiwakes come to the tower, they move in an almost orchestrated way, like inhabitants of a busy city, each going their own way yet not colliding in mid-air.

Up close, the tower is a worn remnant from a past, more militarized, Alaskan coast. A flight of rusty metal stairs lead to the single room at the top of the tower. Inside the room, hundreds of small windows are arranged in columns and rows on the nearly circular walls of the room. The sun shining through the windows into a shadowy room with no electric light can be dazzling, like standing inside a dark crystal. The windows are made from mirrored glass; researchers can see out but the sea birds cannot see in. The place is cold enough to warrant a fleece sweater, and the birds sometimes vomited on researchers, warranting full vinyl rain gear. The tower smelled of dead fish, slowly defrosting in the unplugged chest freezers standing in the center of the room, accentuated by the tang of fishy sea bird excrement. It smelled much the way that penguin habitats at zoos stink. Over time, the scent was easy to ignore. Outside each window, mimicking high cliff ledges, was a small wooden platform, divided by little walls into a bird apartment for each window. On these platforms the kittiwakes nested. It's looking out at the birds from these windows that much data is collected on kittiwake behavior. Sometimes, for research, eggs and chicks need to be removed from their nests to be measured and weighed—kidnapped for short periods from their homes.

Most parent kittiwakes sit dutifully on their nests, watching over their young or yet unhatched charges. Mothers and fathers take turns hunting the sea for fish or squid and sitting on the nest as incubators.

When I slid a window open to collect a warm, speckled egg or a fluffy chick, most of the parent kittiwakes would immediately fly away from the perceived danger of a human hand. Only later would the bird return to her nest to find her offspring restored. A few of the parents were another matter entirely.

Some of the birds would violently attack a hand, biting as viciously as a small sea bird can. The aggressive bird's wings sliced the air in violent motion, the beaks slashing desperately at the human interloper. Sometimes blood was drawn, always it was painful. Some parents even found their way inside the tower, flapping, screaming, tearing at the intern holding their chicks— winged fury. This sort of aggressive parenting probably gives a survival advantage to a bird's offspring. Kittiwakes get away with laying only two or three eggs each year by investing more energy into successfully rearing their young, including sometimes protecting their babies with violence. Turtles may put a lot of energy into laying dozens of eggs but none at all in ensuring their success. There's a bit of a trade-off between caring for young intensively and creating a lot of young to fend for themselves.

Parenting and mating seem to be traits that set birds apart from many other reptiles, like the sea turtle. The level of parenting in birds isn't universal, though. Aggression to protect young and other behaviors fluctuate from individual to individual. There are the birds that quickly fly away at the approach of humans and those that vigorously attack. Crocodilians are similar.

Crocodilians are held to be aggressively protective mothers. In his book *American Alligator: Ancient Predator in the Modern World*, Kelby Ouchley said that's often not true, at least in alligators: "Contrary to common belief, the mother alligators do not always

A young alligator photographed at Aransas National Wildlife Refuge. This alligator was seemingly unsupervised and probably a little over a year old. (*Aransas National Wildlife Refuge*)

aggressively protect their nests . . . researchers report that antagonistic behavior towards data collectors is infrequent. It has been my experience that females at nests often hiss and sometimes make threatening advances but always retreat when pressed."

I have no reason to doubt this account of alligator behavior as a generalization. Out on a walk at San Bernard National Wildlife Refuge in Texas, near the beginning of the alligator egg-laying season, my path was a muddy track through grass on a rainy day. I hiked beside the squarish shape of artificial pools created by the refuge to enhance wetland habitats. In the gray windy air over head, I watched a small group of frigate birds bob up and down without seeming to move forward or back. An angry crayfish confronted my boots, raising his claws high in a defiant shake at my intrusion. I carefully stepped over the crustacean and kept walking. My pants were quickly soaked through to the knees from tall wet grass, but the temperature was warm enough. I was glad for my wide-brimmed hat and raincoat.

As I walked near the water, I accidentally startled a few alligators from their spots on the bank of a pond. Rather than fight or even threaten me, the alligators retreated quickly in a flurry of splashing. After looking closer I saw that some of the alligators had left behind large mounds of leaves and plants—nests. The female alligators merely watched from the safety of the water, their eyes and the tips of their noses floating above the muddy surface.

Later I encountered another alligator that I believe was a different kind of mother. A few weeks after watching the alligators splash away from their nests in San Bernard, I was walking along a trail I'd hiked many times at Aransas National Wildlife Refuge. The trail was mildly muddy and ran along a soft division between the relatively fresh water sloughs to my left where alligators were sometimes found and the saltier marshes and beyond the sea to my right where herons and cormorants could be seen. I noticed an alligator in a small pool of water near the trail. A thin veil of plants separated her from me and I paused for a moment, watching her. Suddenly there was a loud splashing noise. My first reaction was to assume I had scared a timid alligator away, but as I watched, the alligator in front of me moved quickly toward me in a veritable charge. I quickly took several steps back and the alligator made her way onto the trail as I continued to backpedal. With her yellow mouth wide open, the alligator faced me with what appeared to be very real malice. I waited and the alligator didn't back down. I returned the way I'd come.

Other hikers reported probably the same alligator chasing them for short distances. The behavior seemed to develop for a short period near the middle of nesting time, and it's an easy assumption that this alligator was a nesting mother. Clearly, some mother alligators protect their young more aggressively than others, and the alligator was much more intimidating than a mother kittiwake.

Crocodilians put a lot of work into parenting. Depending on the species, the mother either digs a hole to deposit her eggs or creates a mound of vegetation and mud for a raised nest. These different nesting structures are important. The heat caused by rotting plants can warm the eggs, working as incubation.

Most species either exclusively dig a hole or create a mound for their eggs; the interesting exception is the American crocodile

Top: Gharial nest on the banks of the Babai River at Dhanuse in Bardia National Park. Bottom: A gharial nest being excavated to remove and transport the eggs to the Gharial Conservation and Breeding Center situated in Chitwan National Park. (*Copyright Ashish Bashyal/Biodiversity Conservancy Nepal, used with permission*)

(*Crocodylus acutus*) when found in southern Florida. Florida's American crocodiles both dig holes and create mounds. This aberration is possibly because these crocodiles are hybridized to one degree or another with Cuban crocodiles (*Crocodylus rhombifer*), since both species live side by side in Cuba and Cuban crocodiles make mound nests. The American crocodile is widespread throughout the new world tropics, and everywhere outside of Florida it only digs holes for eggs. Nesting strategy is a large difference between reproduction in crocodilians and birds. Everyone knows a typical bird nest—a simple cup woven from grass or sticks; birds' nests are usually dry and tidy. Mound nests of some crocodilians use the rot of wet vegetation to warm the eggs; birds incubate with their body heat.

Walking on the top of sea cliffs in places like an Alaskan island, a misplaced foot can sometimes plunge through soft grassy soil into the burrow of a puffin or auklet. Some sea birds painstakingly excavate tunnel systems with forks leading to different "rooms." When I was on Middleton Island I had the job of digging holes into burrows and snaking my hand into the cool moisture of the tunnels to find smooth, warm eggs. If the nest had been abandoned, the cool of a dead egg was obvious. When I was done monitoring the nest, the hole I made was always patched over to not disturb the birds. Sometimes I paused from the work to sit under dripping bushes overlooking the sea and listen for the soft cooing of auklets in their tunnels. These bird burrows are really just tunnels for grassy, feathered nests, places for the birds to hide and sit on their eggs. Holes for birds are usually receptacles for more typical nests.

The holes some crocodilians dig have eggs laid in them then are backfilled with sand, in the same way turtles lay their eggs in holes. Unlike turtles, mother crocodiles stay close to their nest, even if it's simply a hole filled with buried eggs.

Bird chicks make a lot of squalling ruckus to attract parental attention. A nest can be silent as a tomb until a parent arrives with a beak full of tasty worms or small fish. Suddenly the chicks erupt into squawks; what previously looked like innocent balls of fluffy down can appear to be made entirely of yellow gaping mouths and throats. Bird vocalizations are well known to the observant and background music to the lives of everyone else. What would a forest, meadow, or even desert be without the songs, cries, and trills of birds? Babies are sometimes the most raucous of birds when they want attention.

In crocodilians, similar chirping start right after the babies break out of their eggs or even before. The early chirping alerts a watchful mother it's time to carefully tear open her nest to let the babies out. Crocodilians carefully use their noses as shovels to open a nest.

Crocodilians have an "egg tooth" like some birds, which helps them crack their way out of the egg; this tooth is soon lost after hatching. Crocodilian eggs have a soft membrane on the inside but a hard, calcified shell outside, more like bird eggs than the soft, leathery eggs of other reptiles. An Australia's saltwater crocodile (*Crocodylus porosus*) mother will even gently break open the eggs of her young reluctant to hatch on their own by taking an egg in her jaws. Different factors play into the outcome of a hatching reptile nest, including both crocodilians and turtles.

In 2018, *National Geographic* reported on an odd case. Biologists in northern Australia rounded up a large number of Pacific green turtles (*Chelonia mydas*). The scientists launched themselves from motor boats landing onto the backs of the turtles, wrestling them as if they were cowboys in a rodeo or perhaps reincarnations of the late Steve Irwin. The turtles were then steered to shore where blood samples were taken and small cuts made to examine the turtle's reproductive anatomy. The point of all this Chelonian meddling was to determine the genders of the sea turtles swimming around northern Australia. The researchers discovered something shocking.

The turtles turned out to be 99 percent female. This startling ratio comes from the fact that these turtles' gender is determined by the temperature at which the eggs are incubated. A general rule of thumb says that green turtle eggs incubated above 87.8°F will hatch females. Eggs incubated below 81.86°F will hatch males. Eggs incubated somewhere between these temperatures will hatch some males and some females.

Ingram Island, where the research took place, is a small uninhabited atoll located in the Great Barrier Reef Marine Park and an important nesting site for turtles. Overall warm temperatures around the island mean more female turtles have hatched recently. More females born on Ingram Island means a much larger ratio of female Pacific green turtles to males overall. There is no chromosomal difference between male and female green turtles, as gender depends entirely on the warmth of egg incubation. Not all turtles work this way.

Black marsh turtles (*Siebenrockiella crassicollis*) are rather pretty little turtles. As their name suggests, the turtles are mostly dark but with whitish markings along the borders of their shells and a white pattern on their faces that gives them the appearance of having dark goatees and/or white eyebrows depending on the individual. The black marsh turtle is native to Southeast Asia where it lives in slow-moving water with abundant plants—eating snails, tadpoles, almost any small animal.

This turtle is also the first to be discovered with X and Y chromosomes. Gender in these marsh turtles is determined the same way it is in humans, not by temperature. Female marsh turtles have two X chromosomes, one from each parent. Males have one X chromosome from mom and one Y chromosome from dad. In some other turtle species, the chromosomal system is different, and these other turtles have Z and W chromosomes. Males have two Z chromosomes, one from each parent. Females are the odd ones in this case with a Z chromosome from dad and a W chromosome from mom. The differences in how chromosomes determine gender and the fact that some turtles are dependent on temperature to determine gender is informative.

The evolution of chromosomal sex determination is a late development in black marsh turtles; the first turtles were temperature dependent for their sex determination. Different turtles later took different evolutionary paths as far as gender determination is concerned. Strangely, when it comes to gender determination, crocodilians stayed the same as the first turtles, while birds went their own route.

All known birds follow the chromosomal sex determination, with the males having ZZ chromosomes and females having ZW chromosomes. All crocodilians that have been studied to date have temperature-dependent sex determination like green sea turtles. The arrangement and difference of sex determination between crocodilians and birds shows something important.

Crocodilians and birds are the only living animals considered archosaurs, a group that also includes dinosaurs and related animals. The first archosaurs must have been dependent on temperature to determine gender. But since all birds use the same chromosomal sex determination (unlike turtles), gender chromosomes must have evolved in some of the most ancestral of birds. It's a matter of simple reasoning to figure this out. Comparing birds and crocodiles can give us a lot of good ideas about what their common ancestors were probably like—animals not quite crocodile and not quite bird.

The most obvious similarities between birds and crocodilians lie in the beginning of life—early development—inside an egg enclosed in a shell outside the mother's body. Of course, the heritage shared and differences enjoyed among archosaurs are carried in genes throughout their entire lives.

Birds have the unexpressed genes for teeth. When these genes have been "turned on" in laboratory settings and expressed in embryos, the teeth that developed were pointed and set in sockets—like ancestral dinosaurs had—teeth like the crocodilians'. Feathers are simply scales modified by evolution. Perhaps most substantively, birds and crocodilians breathe alike.

Standing on a wooden platform overlooking a slow-moving slough in Texas, I watched an alligator about five feet long lying almost perfectly still at the edge of a copse of cattails. The alligator's left eye squinted shut often, slowly opening again, perhaps from the residual pain of an old battle wound. The only other movement was the delicate flare of the alligator's crescent nostrils, moving with each breath. Most of her body was obscured in the dark water.

The simple act of breathing tells you a lot about the history of crocodilians. At sea level where I stood at the marsh, watching the alligator, my lungs worked exceptionally well. When I hike mountains in Colorado, topping out on jagged peaks around 14,000 feet, I like to think my lungs still do well. The fact of the matter is though, my lungs and heart work much harder to keep my body functioning on the mountain top than near the Gulf of Mexico.

Flying even higher, birds, of course, need more efficient lungs than people. Geese, unlike humans, do not suffer from elevation sickness. Birds have been seen flying over 29,029-foot-tall Mount Everest, apparently as a normal course of action, without seeming to suffer any ill effects.

Humans and other mammals have incredibly simple, inefficient lungs. Our lungs are basically bags of air that inflate and deflate, absorbing some oxygen through the branching tissue of the "bags." Every breath of fresh air we inhale mixes in the lungs with some old air, leaving less oxygen to be absorbed into the bloodstream. Avian breathing is a much more sophisticated affair, something that apparently evolved on an earth which had a much lower atmospheric oxygen content, in dinosaurs living on the ground.

When a bird breathes, air flows not just into the lungs but also into a series of sacs in the body cavity. The extra air sacs allow air to circulate in one direction like a loop instead of simply going in and out in the same way. In the bird's system of breathing, old air isn't mixed with each breath of new air; instead, stale air flows into the air sacs before leaving the body, allowing new air to fill the lungs entirely with each breath and leaving much more oxygen available for absorption into the blood.

Scientists were surprised to discover that crocodilians breathe in the same way birds do, with unidirectional airflow and air sacs, despite having very different needs from their lungs. Crocodilians occasionally need to stay under water for long periods of time—in experiments alligators have shown the ability to stay submerged for two hours—but in the wild, crocodilians rarely stay under longer than fifteen minutes. These impressive breath-holding feats have little to do with crocodilian breathing anatomy—many dives start with the animal emptying its lungs. Instead, crocodilian hearts and blood chemistry seem to be key. The crocodilian breathing apparatus is an evolutionary remnant tying them to birds and other archosaurs instead of a necessary adaptation to crocodilian lifestyle.

It may seem that crocodilians are a mashup of different traits—an inherited patchwork quilt of genes snipped and stitched together by evolution. Crocodilians have the strange temperature-driven sex determination of turtles but the parenting skills of birds. The truth is, every organism bears the mark of generations before, and these remnants can help us understand their evolution, but it's only a piece of the story. Among crocodilians, each genera and species, even each individual in each species, is unto itself unique but also part of the greater whole. Roots can teach us about budding branches, but only so much. To learn more about an animal, you must eventually look directly at that animal itself.

An American alligator at Bear Island Campground in the Big Cypress National Preserve, Florida. (*Bobyellow/Creative Commons*)

– three –

PHYSICAL ADAPTATIONS

CROCODILIANS CAN SEEM ALMOST SLEEPY. An alligator lying quietly in a marsh, body disappearing into murky brown water below, only eyes and nose protruding above the tepid surface, might fool you. It may look like the alligator is almost insensible to the world around her; the only sign of life is the flaring of nostrils.

A professor of mine worked with alligators during graduate school. One day he was sure he found an alligator that had choked to death on an especially large piece of prey. He approached the alligator, thinking to perhaps retrieve the animal for taxidermy. When he was nearly to the 'gator, the large reptile lunged in his direction, startling my professor but giving him a good lesson: alligators are masters at being still.

As alligators lie in the water, their brains are actually awash with signals from sensory equipment that humans cannot match. It's possible that crocodilians may even sense the small electrical fields created by other animals. A crocodilian's skin is very thick and embedded with the "armor" of osteoderms: round pieces of bone rising to a sharp ridge called a keel, covered in collagen in life. These give crocodilian backs their distinctive pattern. It may seem like a forgone conclusion that such thick and ornamented skin would be completely insensitive to the surrounding world, but in the case of the crocodilians, evolution has found a way.

Bundles of nerves hide in small pits within a crocodilian's skin, creating extremely sensitive areas. These nerve pits are known as integumentary sense organs (ISO). These sensory bundles allow a crocodilian to navigate all but blind in dark, murky waters and catch prey with no visibility. In experiments, alligators with their eyes and nostrils covered will lunge directly at a drop of water in a pool; when their ISOs are masked, they don't respond.

One of the most sensitive body parts is the crocodilian snout, which is more delicate than a pair of human lips due to the large number of ISOs found there. Alligators have the highest concentrations of these ISOs around and even inside their mouths, possibly allowing them to control their bite pressure with precision. Gharials and crocodiles in contrast have ISOs spread throughout their body rather than focused in any one specific location. There are some other interesting physical differences between the different lineages of crocodilians.

One strange difference between alligatorids (alligators and caimans) and crocodiles is that even freshwater crocodiles avoid drinking seawater if they're exposed to it. Alligatorids will drink seawater to the point of death if they're in the salt for too long. It seems that the ISOs found throughout the bodies (below the head) of crocodiles are also used in sensing the saltiness (osmotic pressure) of water. Other animals have organs that sense osmotic pressure but not in their external skin. ISOs are not only sensitive to touch and salt, they are also sensitive to changes in temperature and pH, making this organ unique among vertebrates.

Specialized sensory organs, whatever their exact purpose, undoubtedly help crocodilians moving below the surface of dark waters where eyes help very little. This might explain why gharials, one of the largest crocodilians, can survive by eating mainly fish; not only is the body efficient with the food it gets, gharials are efficient predators. Crocodilians not only have adaptations for close quarters hunting and navigation but can find their way home over incredibly long distances.

When crocodiles are caught in areas where they too often come into conflict with humans, it can be a challenge to keep them from returning. Crocodiles in Florida, Australia, and other places are captured, relocated, and, to the frustration of wildlife managers, can turn up right where they started again. Recently, some scientists have simply started taping a magnet to the crocodile's head while transporting the animal to a new location. This strange but simple technique comes from the idea that crocodilians can sense the earth's magnetic field and use it for navigation. Much like homing pigeons or other birds on long migrations, crocodilians can find their way by sensing electric fields. The magnet is supposed to temporarily disrupt this sense, confusing the reptile and making it harder to get home. I imagine it's similar to covering your eyes and turning in circles until you're dizzy and then immediately trying to find your way in unfamiliar surroundings. However interesting that image may be, we're still left scratching our heads when we try to imagine the sensation itself. Crocodilians seem to behold the world in a profoundly different way than we do.

Even crocodile eyes function unlike ours. If you spend enough time looking at crocodilians, you notice something a little eerie: from almost any direction you approach them, the animal can make eye contact with you. Eyes that appear facing forward when you're nose to nose, easily track you from the side without a twitch of head movement. The only place possibly outside its vision is directly behind the creature. In this way, an alligator can lay quietly on the surface of a pond, taking in all of its surroundings without betraying its presence to anyone by turning. The eyes are also protected by a clear third eyelid (nictitating membrane) that can cover the eye and work as a sort of swimming goggle when underwater. This especially helps animals living in water that is clear enough to see through. The eyes are generally protected by a bony brow below which they can be retracted during fights. Crocodilian eyes see quite differently from ours too, able to focus across an extremely wide field of vision from very close to very far away.

Because of the difference of light through saltwater (which has more blues and greens) than freshwater (which has more reds),

A young crocodile's eye photographed in Australia. Crocodile eyes have a wide field of vision, contributing to their success as ambush predators. The eyes are also situated to be above water when the rest of the animal is submerged. You can also see the Integumentary Sensory Organs (ISO): they are the black dots on the skin. (*Photo by David Clode/Unsplash*)

crocodile eyes are adapted to the water they live in. A study on the eyes of Australia's freshwater crocodiles found they were more sensitive to red light than the eyes of their saltwater cousins. This isn't to say that the eyesight is crisp and clear by our standards; it isn't—crocodile vision is somewhat blurry. Crocodilians have relatively excellent night vision though. If you ever find yourself on a warm night in a swamp or marsh where these animals live, shine a light around and watch for the glowing of eye shine on the water. The eye shine is caused by the reflection of crystals behind the retina of the eye; these tapetum lucidum are used to reflect as much light from the surrounding environment as possible, making the most of dim illumination. This isn't unique to crocodilians; experienced naturalists can often identify creatures at night by the color, size, and location of their eye shine. If you've ever been frustrated by the strange glowing appearance of your dog's or cat's eyes in a flash photo, you've seen evidence of tapetum lucidum. Like vision, crocodilian's other senses have evolved to function both on dry land and submerged in water.

Crocodilians can hear a wide range of sounds above water, nearly as well as many terrestrial animals, but focused on the lower end of the spectrum. Underwater, the hearing is slightly limited but still quite useful for the animals.

Smell is similar. Crocodilians seem to be able to smell airborne particles on land and waterborne particles and chemicals below water. Alligators and possibly other crocodilians release musk from glands at the back of their jaws as well as from their cloacas during courtship displays; apparently smell is part of their social behavior. But how can we know what it's like to smell the world as a crocodilian, much less peer into their inner lives?

We only incompletely understand the world as experienced by other humans, so it's hubris to think we can see the world from a crocodilian's eyes. Still, science can help us gain, however foggily, more of an appreciation of the world as seen from their perspective. Through careful observation we can perhaps understand a crocodile's skin, if not what it's like to live in that skin.

Crocodilian skin isn't just sensitive to the outside world, it's also studded with the osteoderms I mentioned earlier. Holding one of these strange pieces of bone in your hand, the idea of armor is immediately appealing. Osteoderms are porous, full of tiny pits, but they're also strong, and with the keel—almost a little sharp—making the structures seem like lines of dull blades attached to the back of the animal. Interestingly, there is an enormous amount of vascularization in the osteoderms—they're filled with blood vessels—more than the surrounding skin. A large number of blood vessels seems like a strange feature of armor, and the vascularization of the osteoderms points to another function.

Biologist Matthew Shirley told me that osteoderms act like "little solar panels," meaning they're important in regulating temperature from the sun. The osteoderms are always cooler than the surrounding skin; the question is, why? This difference in temperature suggests that blood is pulled from these osteoderms and circulated through the animal's core, warming the internal body. Because the blood is quickly pumped away from the osteoderms

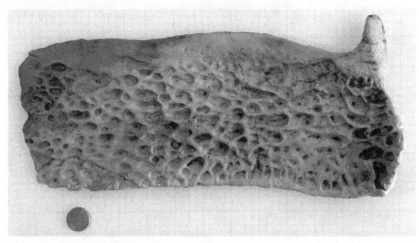

An osteoderm (cast) from a *Sarcosuchus sp.*, top, with a U.S. nickel for scale. This is an osteoderm from the dorsal area of the animal and is rather large and rectangular when compared to many other species (such as the American alligator osteoderm). The rugosity is typical of both extant and extinct crocodilian osteoderms. Bottom, an American alligator osteoderm, much smaller than the *Sarosuchus*. The rugosity shows where blood vessels could be found in the live animal. (*Top, author, bottom, Zach Piotrowski*)

as it warms, they remain cooler than nearby tissue. Osteoderms thus probably help warm the crocodilians internal organs. Osteoderms may also help with a classic physiology problem for egg-laying animals.

For a mother alligator, the cost of reproduction is high. Time, effort, and extra nutrients are required to bring the next generation of alligators into the world. Among nutrients, few are as important as calcium when it comes to making eggs. Researchers estimate that a full batch of as many as forty alligator eggs needs 90 to 200 grams of calcium for eggshells. Female birds store calcium in medullary bones, structures that dissolve when needed to supply calcium for egg production. Frog tadpoles have tiny sacs near the base of their heads that store calcium which is used for the ossification of their skeletons as they develop into adult frogs. Researchers thought perhaps crocodilians use similar sacs for egg production, but the sacs appear the same before and after egg laying in mother alligators. Instead, alligators (and perhaps other crocodilians) dissolve some of their osteoderms to create eggshells for their young. Researchers found that osteoderms in nesting alligators are 10 percent lighter than other alligators, suggesting that some of the mother's armor was sacrificed for her young. If, indeed, osteoderms still function as armor at all.

There's a problem with interpreting osteoderms as armor; the little pieces of bone are the least useful when the animals are the most vulnerable to attack. Large adult crocodilians are nearly invulnerable to predation, except from humans. The young, however, are just another smallish tidbit to eat. Juvenile crocodilians don't have well-developed osteoderms useful for protection. Why would armor only appear on animals that are large enough for it to be superfluous? In caimans, the picture is a bit more complicated by the fact that their bellies are also covered in osteoderms. Osteoderms in the belly would serve little function in heat regulation and could possibly be armor. Perhaps the osteoderms play a role in fights between adults, perhaps not. When it comes to making functional forms such as armor, evolution is sometimes messy. There are physical features that seem to serve no purpose or are quite inefficient, but as long as the body holds together well enough to reproduce, the form isn't selected against. From an evolutionary perspective, what matters is reproduction. If osteoderms don't change an animal's chances of reproduction, there's no evolutionary selective pressure. Sometimes traits "drift" one way or another, for no discernible reason beyond statistical probability. The whole truth of the many functions of osteoderms may always be a mystery.

One thing that's easy to miss in crocodilian physiology when looking at bones and osteoderms is the color of the skin that covers them. Crocodilians are colored darker on their backs and lighter on their bellies, an arrangement common to aquatic animals— think of penguins or many fishes or dolphins. They all have a color pattern called counter shading, a type of camouflage that makes an animal appear flatter when viewed from the side, and thus harder to detect. It works like this: when sunlight is hitting the top of an object, it appears lighter, while the lower parts of the object (or animal) appear darker. Counter shading unbalances this effect of sunlight, making an animal appear flat, less shaded. In the water, this effect also helps when looking down from above or up from below at a crocodile. From the surface, the water typically appears dark below and so the dark upper part of a crocodilian is camouflaged. From the bottom of a lake looking up, the surface appears bright and so the crocodilian's white underbelly is still camouflaged. Rare cases of albinism have appeared in wild crocodilians, but they've never been known to survive long in the wild—partially because they're easy prey when young and partially because their skin is sensitive to the sun.

When I was a child, my parents took me on a visit to an alligator park. A popular gimmick in places like that is to have chickens, the type you'd buy at the grocery store, headless, footless, white and plucked of all feathers, dangled on a rope. Alligators can leap impressive distances with such enticement. Alligators and crocodiles don't leave the water entirely like a frolicking dolphin or humpback whale: these mammals start well below the water's surface to get up to leaping speed before they leave the water. Crocodilians start a leap from a dead stop and use the powerful muscles of their tails to push most of their body above the surface. In shallow water, crocodilians use their short but strong legs to push off the substrate base as well. More than a leap, crocodilians have impressive

A saltwater crocodile (*Crocodylus porosus*) jumps from a river in Australia's Northern Territory. (*Photo by Simon Watkinson/Unsplash*)

lunges. Many species use this ability to startle hapless prey drinking at a waterhole: think of a zebra grabbed in the powerful jaws of a Nile crocodile or a deer fawn overpowered by an American alligator. Smaller prey can be captured by lunging crocodilians as well, in surprising ways. That chicken hanging from a rope disappears quickly.

African dwarf crocodiles (*Osteolaemus tetraspis*) in Gabon have been found eating bats in caves, and saltwater crocodiles of Australia and Asia (*Crocodylus porosus*) have been seen leaping up to grab black flying foxes (*Pteropus alecto*) hanging sleepily from branches. Birds are sometimes eaten from a tree by a patient and watchful crocodilian lunging at just the right moment. Crocodiles, alligators, and caimans all eat fruit on occasion and even pluck it from relatively low-hanging limbs. Adam Britton, a crocodile biologist from Australia, has a photograph of a crocodile lunging from the water toward a hanging fruit bat on his website. Britton explained what was going on in the photograph and how he obtained it.

> Wild crocodiles will occasionally try and leap up to grab birds and bats in overhanging branches; I've seen it myself twice over the space of 25 years, so it's pretty rare to actually witness it, even though crocs hang around under fruit bat colonies all the time. Getting a decent photo of it is nigh on impossible . . . we had an opportunity many years ago when I worked at a facility with crocodiles that lived in a large lagoon. The local Power and Water Corporation regularly removed dead fruit bats that had electrocuted themselves on power lines, and they offered us a handful of dead bats to feed the crocodiles. Rather than just throw the bats in there to be eaten, we decided to offer the crocs some behavioural enrichment by setting up a natural feeding situation, and suspended bats from branches above the water. This encouraged the crocs to search for them and jump up to grab them, and I got a few great photos that have been useful for teaching purposes for many years.

Not only can crocodiles leap high enough to snag an unlikely bat from a tree branch, they sometimes even climb into trees themselves. Near the pre-Columbian ruins of the walled city of Tulum in Mexico's Yucatán Peninsula, locals have noticed juvenile American crocodiles (*Crocodylus acutus*) crawling into mangroves to sun themselves. Likewise, saltwater crocodiles scale the understory sometimes, and a young New Guinea crocodile (*C. novaeguineae*) has been photographed hanging out in a tree. Central African slender-snouted crocodiles (*Mecistops cataphractus*) have been seen regularly basking in the tree limbs of the dense forests of the Congo. Even American alligators (*Alligator mississippiensis*) have been seen in trees. A former zookeeper friend of mine told me that alligators have climbed chain-link fences to escape. Adam Britton reported in a paper published with two other scientists in 2013 that he's watched Australian freshwater crocodiles attempt climbing chain-link fences as well. The interesting thing is that the more arboreal aspects of crocodilian lives have been generally ignored by scientists, with the first formal descriptions appearing in that 2013 paper. Mostly crocodilians have been thought of as swimming creatures, and their abilities in trees and on land have been largely overlooked.

There's a silly myth that if you run away from a crocodile in a zigzag pattern, it won't be able to catch you. The truth is, in short spurts crocodiles can run very fast indeed. If a sudden burst from the water doesn't catch prey immediately, crocodilians can also gallop after their victim, a form of locomotion unique to them among reptilia. A galloping croc seems to move more like a wolf or lion than most reptiles: the rear legs move in tandem, reaching forward and framing the front legs, allowing them to next spring forward in turn. Five species of crocodile have been observed galloping. Research suggests that differences in musculature deprives alligators of this ability—crocodiles have longer muscle fibers in their legs and chests than do alligators. Despite minor differences among crocodilians, their overall body plans are remarkably similar and remarkably successful. Even alligators despite their handicap have been seen hunting on land, waiting patiently by trails at night. The flexibility but solidness of the crocodilian body form has allowed it incredible resilience.

Evolution almost seems to have its favorites, body plans that are consistently successful. The crocodilian body layout is certainly one of them. Well before the first crocodilian burst from a river in a spray of water to lock crushing jaws on struggling prey, there were animals that looked and acted in a very similar manner. I already discussed some of the animals with similar body plans in Chapter 1.

Crocodilians are large, low, and long reptiles that live in aquatic environments. Ambushing prey seems to be a regular part of crocodilian life: long periods of lying unmoving just at the surface of the water followed by acts of violence at very fast speeds. The body of the crocodilian is built for a life waiting in the slow-moving waters of the tropics and subtropics. Most of their lives are spent in warm water dappled with sunlight filtering through trees or tall marsh plants. The waters rich with tannin and heavy of sediment are often dark, hard to see through. Crocodilians often go long periods without eating, a feast or famine creature. The bodies of crocodilians are finely tuned to match their lives and their habitats, carefully shaped through the happenstance of biological evolution.

While I was doing beginning preparation work on an Eocene crocodilian (*Borealosuchus sp.*) fossil cut from rock in a Wyoming quarry, I took a break from chiseling into the stone slab with an air-powered scribe to ponder an alligator skull sitting on a bench nearby. The skull was a bleached white thing from an American alligator that died in captivity of natural causes. The crocodile, meanwhile, looked to be little more than a rounded impression of raised stone lying over a contorted but remarkably complete skeletal remains. The whole skeleton was in a flat slab of rock leaning against a table in front of a stool I sat on as I worked. Slowly, the strange sponge-like texture seen in the skulls of living and extinct crocodiles emerged from the rock, as sharp black teeth, like chips of obsidian, were uncovered.

Considering the skull of a crocodilian, one thing that strikes you is the size of the brain case; buried in thick bone as it is, the brain is necessarily small. It's not that crocodilians are especially dim-witted: when you learn about the complex behaviors they exhibit, it's impressive how much they can do with such little "gray matter." Birds have similar body-to-brain ratios as crocodiles and none of the bias against them (more about this in later chapters). Brains are just not the first thing to come to mind when considering the crocodile skull.

More obvious parts of a crocodilian skull are the teeth. Alligator teeth are thick pegs, rather dull and rounded but very sturdy. These teeth are more for gripping the prey tightly in the viselike bite—saltwater crocodile bites have been measured up to 3,700 pounds per square inch, while the bite of an American alligator has been measured at 2,125 pounds per square inch.

Of course lunging and grabbing an animal is only the beginning of a nightmare for prey and the making of a meal for a crocodilian. The classic way of killing prey for a crocodilian is the "death roll," which I already described as being akin to a "washing machine of death." This innovative move not only kills an animal but also can tear the poor creature limb from limb, allowing smaller body chunks to be swallowed by the crocodilian (crocodilians can't chew, instead swallowing large pieces of their prey whole). A few novel adaptations make the death roll possible. Paleontologist Adam Cossette had an interesting answer to my question of what the most important crocodilian adaptations are.

> The secondary palate is the most important morphological adaptation found in crocodilians. It allows them to simultaneously eat and breathe without having to leave the water. This allows them to be exceptional semi-aquatic ambush predators. The secondary palate is shared with mammals but was derived independently and for different purposes.
>
> The most significant behavioral adaptation is the extremely destructive feeding behavior called the "death roll" where the animal will latch onto a limb, for example, and perform a powerful roll in the water. This behavior allows for the dismemberment and consumption of large prey— think of a Nile Crocodile feeding upon a Wildebeest.

The secondary palate divides the nasal cavity from the mouth, which is why you can open your mouth underwater without drowning. This palate allows a floating alligator to breath calmly through the nostrils just above the waterline, while water fills her toothy muzzle. Obviously crocodilians have a huge need to open their mouths under water—to bite something without choking.

I've seen the inside of an angry American alligator's mouth, and what was immediately obvious the first time (besides the threat of teeth) is that I couldn't see down the animal's throat. A flap at the

A Nile crocodile photographed in Kruger National Park, probably sunning itself. You get a good view of the inside of the mouth which seems to "dead-end" because the palatal valve is engaged, closing the mouth off. (*Photo by Ansie Potgieter/Unsplash*)

back of the mouth closed off the throat from the mouth; this is known as the palatal valve. Sometimes this valve opens, for instance, when the crocodilian in question is eating or mouth breathing when basking. The conundrum of the palatal valve is that if a croc opens her palatal valve under water, an enormous amount of water would flood into the trachea. Some have suggested pushing open the palatal valve with an injured fist or leg lodged in a crocodile mouth as a way to survive being pulled under water. If your arm (or leg) is already in the mouth, you *might* be able to accomplish this, which *may* cause the suddenly choking crocodile to let you go. But it seems like a very desperate measure to me. The ability to grab an animal in the water and quickly kill while breaking it into bite-sized chunks is what makes the typical crocodilian lifestyle possible. The durability and broad applicability of the niche facilitated by this is attested to by the vast scales of time and space that crocodilians inhabit, circling the globe for much longer than the entire history of primates.

Of course if you're going to kill and swallow large prey, you still need to digest them as they're swallowed—bones, hair, hooves, and all. Digestion in crocodilians is connected to their hearts, which are like no others. A valve in the heart can be opened or closed, allowing crocodilians to shunt blood past their lungs, a strange ability to say the least. The idea that this redirection of blood was important for diving was popular among scientists, but a vicious and bloody experimentation proved differently. Scientist C. G. Farmer cut open some crocodiles and altered them so they could no longer shunt blood past their lungs. Interestingly in crocodilians that are intact, the blood shunt past the lungs then flows through a special aorta straight to the stomach. Farmer and her colleagues showed that this ability allows crocodilians to produce gastric acid at rates ten times greater than any other animal measured. This unique set up in their hearts allows crocodilians to eat, and digest, 23 percent of their body weight in one sitting. Most four-chambered hearts, like yours or mine, have only one aorta. The extra aorta crocodilians have shunts the oxygen-poor blood away from the heart and to the stomach, bypassing the lungs where blood is usually scrubbed of carbon dioxide and replenished with oxygen.

When I talked to crocodile biologist Matthew Shirley, he told me there's something else that impresses him about crocodilians related to blood: their toughness allows them to survive. Crocodiles can live for years after horrific injuries that would certainly kill the average human, especially without intensive medical intervention. "Crocodiles as organisms are amazing," Shirley observed. "They have the kind of immune system that's built to withstand their social aggressions. When it comes to living in habitats that are prone to infection, this is massively helpful. Most people lose a limb, they'd bleed out and die within minutes. While crocodiles take that to a whole new extreme, not only can they shut off blood flow to certain parts of their body, if they get their tail bit off they can literally stop blood flow to the tail so it's not going to bleed out. Then they don't get infections and they can heal."

Jay Young, who owns Colorado Gators, a reptile park, told me he's seen alligators lose an entire limb in a fight only to sit in the sun and heal from the wound completely and in short order with no treatment. He's watched injuries that would quickly kill a human go unnoticed in a crocodilian for as long as a year. Crocodilians are not just great predators, they're tough.

Crocodilians' blood in itself is effective at fighting infections. The antibiotic properties of the blood have potential as a treatment for different sicknesses in humans as well. Some crocodile farms in Thailand actually give out capsules of dried crocodile blood as an unsubstantiated treatment for cancer. Although it's unlikely that capsules of dried crocodile blood can help with cancer, the antibiotic quality of that same blood is very real. Blood from the critically endangered Siamese crocodile of Southeast Asia has been tested against human pathogens. Blood plasma from the crocs reduced growth of some human bacteria and viruses by 40 percent and others by 80 percent. Leukocytes extracted from American alligator blood have also shown themselves to have broad antimicrobial impact, they're especially good at stopping fungal growth. Some hope that these properties of crocodilian blood could lead to major medical breakthroughs, even the cure for HIV. I personally worry that blood might soon be harvested for unscientific "medicine," threatening crocodilian survival for little or no real value. Even when it comes as a benefit to humans, who are we to sacrifice the life of another for our own? Either way, part of crocodilians' survival secret is locked in their blood; part of their survival is due to evolutionary tactics.

In some ways crocodilians don't follow the normal rules for survival. In general terms there are two strategies for reproduction. In the first strategy you have a lot of young and hope that some of them live. Sea turtles are this type of parent, laying thirty or more eggs at a time, burying them and then crawling off into the surf, leaving the next generation on its own.

The next typical plan for fostering young is perhaps more familiar to humans. In the second strategy, you only have a few young and spend a lot of time caring for them, to give them the greatest chance at life possible. The sea birds I worked with on Middleton Island are an example of this type of parenting, laying one to at the most three eggs and feeding their young diligently until they fledge. This strategy isn't always as benign as it sounds; the second hatched chick is often underfed and pecked bald by the older, stronger sibling stealing all the fish left in the nest. It's heart-rending to watch the cowering, malnourished form of the younger bird slowly wasting away or disappearing overnight from the sudden push of a sibling.

Crocodilians don't follow either of these strategies. Instead, they follow both, laying many eggs and then attending to the young by guarding them from predators (although the young must find their own food). This connects them to their nearest relatives, the birds, as well as to other reptiles, and is also the basis of crocodilian social lives and a sign of high intelligence, which we'll look at next.

four

INTELLIGENCE

A COSTA RICAN FISHERMAN found a crocodile (*C. acutus*) marred by a bullet hole to the head and speculated that the reptile had been shot by a farmer while trying to eat a cow. Feeling sympathy for the large animal, the man brought the crocodile home and revived him, feeding him chicken or sometimes chewing fish to encourage the skinny beast to eat. It was during this time a bond started to develop.

The man's wife and daughter were a bit nervous about a large American crocodile living in their house, but the man persisted, slowly acclimating the wild creature to his presence. He started by petting the beast's scaly tail and slowly, over many days, moving toward his head. Eventually he was able to show his wife that he could safely place his hand inside the crocodile's mouth. After a while it was clear that the crocodile was healthy and strong again, so Chito, the man, put his crocodile friend Pocho into his truck and drove him out to the forest where he'd found him. The next morning, Chito was surprised to see that Pocho had returned to sleep beside his house. Several times Chito tried releasing the crocodile into the wild, with the same results. (Another version of this story I read has Chito unloading Pocho from his truck, after waiting a long time for the croc to leave, he ends up bringing him back home.) Whichever story you believe, it seems possible that the two were truly friends in the real sense of the word.

Eventually Pocho and Chito (whose full name is Gilberto Shedden) made a show of their relationship. There are YouTube videos of the two swimming and playing together. In a NatGeo Wild episode, Chito described the peace he got from his reptile friend and said that swimming with Pocho at night was like being with God. The two splashed and frolicked together in the water for over twenty years until eventually Pocho died of natural causes and was afforded a somewhat public funeral. Transformed by taxidermy, his body now lies in a museum in Costa Rica.

It's possible that the gun wound to the head changed Pocho's behavior, but the amount of friendliness, or at least intelligence, exhibited by Pocho isn't completely unique among crocodilians. Once you start asking people, there are many stories of cleverness in crocodilians.

I met Jay Young, who owns a reptile park in Colorado, while I was working with fossils in Arizona. Jay is a relatively short man in his forties, with a wide-brimmed leather hat decorated by a band holding crocodilian teeth. He was particularly interested in the Eocene crocodilian fossil found in a Wyoming quarry by Geo Décor that I happened to be preparing at the time. We discussed crocodilians, living and fossilized in Geo Décor's showroom and lab.

I asked Young a bit about crocodile intelligence and he told me about a problem alligator he caught and transported to his facility in Colorado. The animal was aggressive, lunging as if to attack Young every time he entered the reptile's enclosure. Once he entered to catch the alligator, carrying a rope into the pen for the first time since the creature's capture two years earlier. The animal immediately fled from Young on this encounter, swimming to the bottom of his pond instead of the usual aggressive posturing. The thought is that the alligator recognized the rope, understood what it meant, and reacted accordingly. Anecdotal accounts like this are common among people who've worked with captive crocodilians.

A friend of mine who worked at a reptile zoo told me his own story of alligator smarts. In his zoo, the alligators were fenced in with basic chain link. On a single day, not one but three alligators escaped by climbing the fence. The story is remarkable not because an alligator could climb a fence; what's remarkable is that after one alligator realized it could climb the fence and escape, the other two watched, learned, and acted on this knowledge as well. Being able to watch another do something and realize your own ability requires a certain amount of self-realization and empathy, abilities not often accorded to any (non-avian) reptile. For a long time crocodilians and other reptiles have been written off as primitive-brained half-wits, but more and more evidence—both scientific and anecdotal—is showing that crocs are a lot cleverer than we assumed.

Science in particular can be slow to recognize new information that flies in the face of old dogma, but there are scientific papers now showing signs that crocodilians have richer inner lives than we imagined. In 2015 Vladimir Dinets published a paper in *Animal Behavior and Cognition* reporting on several instances of crocodilian play.

Dinets told of captive American alligators sliding down slopes into water only to scramble back up, and a broad-snouted caiman hatchling repeatedly riding a jet of water across a pool in a zoo in Bolivia. A estuarine crocodile was seen surfing waves off the coast of Australia. Alligators have been observed snapping at water dripping or streaming from pipes, apparently enjoying a mock fight with a watery foe. A Cuban crocodile in a zoo played with a ball, attacking it and blowing bubbles at it, not so very different from what we see dogs doing to toys. Other crocodilians have been seen attacking and pushing sticks, floating flowers, and other objects. Nile crocodiles and black caimans have been noticed playing with each other in mock fights or swimming around each other in small circles.

In a most memorable observation, Dinets tells of seeing for himself an alligator playing with otters. The otters would approach the alligator until the reptile lunged at them and then swim quickly away, just out of reach of its jaws. Eventually one otter was caught in the alligator's mouth. What was extraordinary is that the alligator didn't harm the otter but instead took the mammal under water for a short bit before releasing him to swim safely away. The end result of this encounter suggests that the alligator might have actually been playing with the otters as a mutual participant. Observations like these contend with what we once thought we knew about neuroanatomy and reptilian intelligence. The question is no longer *are crocodilians intelligent?* but *how do crocodilian brains support such obvious intelligence?*

It was once thought by brain scientists and even popular science luminaries such as Carl Sagan that crocodilian, or "reptile," brains were primitive. Scientists and laypeople alike began referring to the part of the human brain responsible for things like anger or violence as the "reptilian brain." The "reptilian brain" was, as some scientists explained, the central part of the brain, with new mammalian structures built around it, layered like an onion, with the reptile brain at the center; making the two quite distinctly different. Of course, this view is at odds with the complex social and learning behavior seen in crocodilians, to say nothing of birds, whose brains closely resemble in structure those of other reptiles but are similar in proportion to those of mammals. Modern neuroscience has likewise shown that this view is just plain wrong. Older vertebrates—sharks, reptiles, etc.—have many analogous brain components to those of mammals, although arranged slightly differently. New technology now allows scientists to test how different reptile and mammal brains are from each other like never before.

It's helpful to look at the beginning of crocodilian brain development. Many anatomy studies, including those of the brain, begin with embryos. In a 2015 paper, "Crocodilian Forebrain: Evolution and Development," scientist Michael Pritz wrote, "very early development of the brain in *Alligator* is similar to that of other amniotes." Amniotes for our purposes are other mammals, reptiles, and birds. From a similar beginning, differences do start to arise between crocodilian (or reptilian) and other brains, but not as many as some might expect.

According to a 2019 paper in *Brain Behavior & Evolution*, brains in birds are typically assumed to be ten times bigger than in other reptiles of similar mass. There are some problems with this number and this comparison, though. A reptile of the same body mass (weight) as a bird will inevitably have a smaller body size than the bird, which is generally much lighter—built for flight. Crocodilians have scutes, long tails, and other relatively weighty body elements; feathered birds with lightweight bones do not. In the end, when these obvious differences in the evolution of body plans in reptiles and birds are taken into account, there seems to be a smaller but lingering gap in the brain-to-body ratio between the two groups.

Birds unquestionably have larger brains in comparison to non-avian reptiles (including crocodilians). However, this brain size difference is not as important as many have previously thought. Reptiles actually show a complex range of behaviors but are continuously stereotyped as slow and dim-witted. This bias only reinforces itself, because reptile cognition is rarely tested by scientists. The reality is that science hasn't come to any conclusions about what the size of brains means within species or across taxa; we're left trying to explain why animals with smaller brains actually show what seems to be so much intelligent and complex behavior.

Since we humans are the only ones writing scientific papers, the literature of science (and other disciplines) tends to judge us, *Homo sapiens*, as the most intelligent life form on earth. We may be biased; the human brain is the one we all know the most intimately, the spring from which pours the entirety of our experience. So it makes sense that when looking at the brains of other creatures, we compare them to the only brain we know what it's like to be inside—ours. Intelligence, as we often understand it, is the ability to solve problems with novel solutions—solutions that are created by an active mind not by repetition or "instinct." Such a definition necessarily oversimplifies a complex and controversial idea.

We all probably think we know what intelligence is, but when it comes to measuring it, things get fuzzier. Many think of the intelligence quotient (IQ) test as a real measure of inherent intelligence, something perhaps we're born with. Research shows, however, that overall IQ scores have grown throughout the developed world in recent years and indeed, a person's IQ can grow in a lifetime. In this light, does an IQ test reflect intelligence or education or perhaps a mixture of both? Intelligence is a notoriously tricky subject to examine.

Think of a dog. Which is more intelligent—the dog who has learned to sit and wait patiently while a human prepares her bowl of food, or, the unruly dog who leaps onto a table and grabs the food bowl, consuming the kibble before being offered? There's no way to tell, the details are in context. Both good and unruly behavior can achieve similar ends. The same basic concept can be used when comparing the intelligence of one species to another. Keeping in mind the inherent flaws involved in comparing different intelligences, it can still be interesting to try to peer into the workings of another mind.

One suggested way to measure intelligence is to look at the "information processing capacity." Information processing capacity (IPC) can be examined in different animal and human brains as well as computers. In fact, the invention of the computer became influential in psychology and the understanding of the brain and was used in developing IPC specifically. The computer itself is a powerful metaphor for the brain and thinking, and the development of computers through time shows that there are different ways to reach the same goal.

Computational machines of days gone by used to fill entire rooms and were less capable than smartphones carried easily in the pocket today. In a similar way, the size of a brain isn't the important aspect of intelligence but rather, its overall form. As with many things, more than one design works. For instance, the IPC for parrots is comparable to that of intelligent mammals, like monkeys, yet the brains are very different. Parrots have small brains packed with neurons rather than larger brains with fewer neurons, as is the case with whales and dolphins (still intelligent animals but with lower IPC than parrots and corvids, the family including crows and ravens). Basically, parrot brains are able to rival those of some primates not because of the size of the brain but because of the density of neurons within their (relatively) tiny brains.

Besides the obvious difference between avian reptile brains and mammals, when it comes to strategies of neuron packing, there is good evidence that many of the differences between brains are superficial. Until recently, it was impossible to analyze the gene expression of a brain on the cellular level. Now with the advancement of technology scientists are able to compare how genes in individual cells are expressed in mammal and reptile "gray matter." This allows us to compare brain regions between these two lineages, to see if brains are as different as they appear at first blush.

Looking at the gross anatomy of the brain, the six-layered neocortex, which seems to be found only in mammals, is huge in humans, making up 76 percent of your total brain volume. You use the neocortex when hearing music, interpreting lyrics, or noticing the bright flash of a red flower thrown towards a stage. The neocortex is responsible for what we think of as "higher" functions: perception, language, motor skills, and conscious thought. The neocortex is the upper part of our brains; in humans and other primates it is full of the classic ridges we think of when we think "brain," allowing for more neurons. In smaller mammals like mice, the neocortex is smooth. The neocortex is divided into different lobes with different functions like auditory and visual functions, and a lobe important for sleep.

Lacking an obvious mammalian neocortex, reptiles have their own unique brain structure. The dorsal ventricular ridge (DVR) is a bulging structure found in reptiles but not mammals. Although non-avian reptiles generally have proportionally smaller brains than birds or mammals the DVR significantly contributes to the overall size of the reptile brain. Research suggests that the DVR has a parallel function to the missing neocortex in crocodilian (and other reptilian) brains. The DVR and neocortex evolved separately. Just as insect, bird, and bat wings prove that evolution finds different ways to fly, the DVR and neocortex suggest there are also different ways to think. It's a case of convergent evolution. This means when a crocodile hears the peep of a baby or sees the flash of a fish in the sun, she's using her DVR, as we'd use our neocortex. Despite the difference in anatomy between mammal and reptile brains, new scientific techniques are showing the function between the two is not so very different.

In 2018 scientists published research using single-cell transcriptomics to look at the differences and similarities between human, mouse, turtle, and lizard brains. This technique looks at the RNA in individual cells to compare gene expression between the different brains on a cellular level. Similarities between functions of brain regions can be assessed, even when those regions at first glance, look very different. The study found that cells in the pallium (the area containing the DVR) in bearded dragons and turtles were very similar in function to cells in the neocortex of humans and mice. Considering the history of bearded dragons, turtles, mice, and even humans, it's all but a sure thing that brain functions essentially shared between all groups will also be found in crocodilians. It's also important to remember that birds are more closely related to crocodilians than other reptiles.

It might seem obvious, but the brain acts differently asleep than awake. Attaching an EEG to the head of a person before and after they fall asleep demonstrates this nicely. As we fall asleep, our heartbeat slows, sometimes our fingers, toes, faces twitch. Our muscles relax and, critically, our brain waves fall into a slower sleeping pattern and our temperature drops. As we fall deeper to sleep, our brain waves continue to slow but show small bursts of activity. Later, during REM (rapid eye movement) sleep, our eyes move quickly behind closed lids and our brain function comes closer to that of our waking selves.

Birds show similar patterns in their sleeping (anesthetized) brains. Their brain waves slow as they fall asleep and change again during REM sleep, much like in mammals. The same seems to be true of Nile crocodiles. Unfortunately, it's not clear whether the different types of brain waves found in crocodiles directly correlate to those found in birds or mammals, but a similar pattern seems to exist. Either way, the similarities between bird brains and those of mammals, who last shared an amniotic ancestor some 300 million years ago, suggests that much of the brain is very old and likely shared with crocodiles as well as birds and mammals. However, as I've already said, there are some real differences between crocodile brains and those of birds and mammals.

One strange and unique feature of crocodilians is that they continue to grow (although later quite slowly) throughout their lives. This is obvious of the massive bodies of very old crocodilians but it's also true of crocodilian brains. Interestingly, as the body grows, the parts of the brain which control the body directly—the brain stem and diencephalon (which relays sensory signals, controls hormones, sleep patterns, and appetite, among other things)—show smaller but continual changes, not adding any neurons. Other parts of the brain increase in size but add neurons at much slower rates as well. Studies like the one showing this change raise many questions about what it means to have an indeterminately growing brain and what it means for intelligence. All too often, when looking for intelligence in animals, we start by looking for intelligence as we define it, a type of human or mammalian cleverness that may or may not be useful for reptiles or other animals. We sometimes look to confirm a bias for or against intelligence. Less research has been carried out on reptile intelligence than on mammals', a disproportionate scientific focus emphasizing our bias.

Recently crocodilian intelligence received some attention as a research subject possibly pointing toward systematic change. It's been noticed that alligators and other crocodilians enjoy spending time below trees where birds nest. It's likely that this allows the crocodilians a ready snack any time an unprepared fledgling plops into the water below, flapping ineffectively. Or possibly the birds choose areas with crocodilians in order to protect their nests from tree-climbing predators. Even in alligator farms with trees, egret nests eventually take up occupancy and alligators sometimes snack on fallen chicks. This simple observation has led to a more complex hypothesis. Vladimir Dinets thought he observed crocodilians doing something quite remarkable.

These egrets were photographed sitting on tree branches just barely above the water in a pond with multiple alligators in South Carolina. Although all of the alligators I noticed were quite small, they were still large enough to eat an egret. (*Author*)

In 2013 Dinets and other scientists published a paper in *Ethology, Ecology & Evolution* titled, "Crocodilians Use Tools for Hunting." The provocative title says it all: the scientists observed what they described as crocodilian tool use. The researchers observed captive crocodiles and alligators floating in the water with sticks resting on their snouts. Sometimes a bird would fly down to retrieve a stick for nest building and sometimes the crocodilian would snap up the bird for a meal. Not only did alligators observed in the wild also float with sticks "displayed" on their snouts, they were observed with sticks more often during the birds' mating and nest-building season. A truism of science says correlation doesn't mean causation. Unfortunately the presence of sticks on alligator snouts during mating season is correlation not necessarily causation, a fact acknowledged in the paper but not dealt with directly.

Other researchers took up the challenge of pushing crocodilian tool use from correlative evidence to scientifically tested hypothesis. Adam Rosenblatt and Alyssa Johnson actually took sticks and added them to ponds with wild alligator populations. The idea was to then see if alligators near nesting sites would be observed balancing the sticks on their snouts more often than the alligators away from nesting sites.

Unfortunately, there was no evidence that the alligators used the sticks offered them more often when birds were nearby collecting sticks. The jury is still out as to whether crocodilians have the ability to use tools, but the research highlights the complexity of gauging intelligence and interpreting behavior in other animals. Even if a crocodilian is never found using a tool for any purpose, it doesn't show the animal to be unintelligent. It simply shows our bias towards looking for intelligence that mirrors our own.

From what I and others have seen, it seems clear that crocodilians have rich inner lives that accommodate their own bodies well. We will never be able to inhabit the mind or body of a crocodilian, so some aspects of their existence will always be mysterious. One thing we can do is look more closely at the interactions between crocodilians, which also reveal a certain intelligence.

– five –

The SOCIAL LIVES *of* CROCODILIANS

RESEARCH ON CROCODILIAN SOCIAL BEHAVIOR has proceeded slowly since the animals were first looked at by science. Partially the lack of research was due to a bias which assumed there was no crocodilian social behavior to look for. Partially it's due to the fact that crocodilians spend much of their lives in watery environments that are alien to us humans and hard to access. Recent efforts to breed crocodilians in captivity for entertainment, conservation, or the skin trade have made close observations of behavior easier than in the wild. It was thus by coincidence that in the 1980s, while science was starting to truly revolutionize our view of dinosaurs, that biologists could look closely at the behavior of another group of archosaurs—crocodilians. In captivity it's a simpler task to watch many animals accustomed to the presence of humans in a relatively controlled environment. It's easier to install cameras and recording devices where the animals are known to be. It's easier to visit a captive animal than a wild animal in a wetland, and it's easier to manipulate behavior to answer scientific questions. Unfortunately, this might mean that some behaviors observed for the first time in captivity are not necessarily normal in the wild.

One thing we know for sure is something I've already mentioned—crocodilians are often devoted parents compared to many reptiles; sea turtles for instance. Mother crocodilians go through some effort to create good nests for their eggs. Expecting alligators create mounds of rotting vegetation and mud to deposit their eggs in. Spectacled caimans and some other crocodilians make similar nests. American crocodiles dig holes in sand, similar to turtles. Gharials and many other crocodilians do the same, laying their eggs to incubate underground. Sometimes crocodilian mothers nest in close proximity to each other. Crocodilians that nest with holes have been observed more often nesting near each other than mound-nesting animals. This could be because there are fewer good banks for digging nests into, it could be a data collection bias, or it could mean some crocodilians are actually more social. Either way, all crocodilians either time their nesting or the hatching of their nest for their particular location's rainy season.

After the eggs are laid, the mother crocodilian remains nearby. In the case of gharials, it seems that the father remains close by as well. Some evidence suggests other male crocodilians may also remain in the immediate area, but research is lacking. How much actual aggression the mothers display toward intruders depends on the species and individuals involved, but it is thought that her mere presence might convey some protection to her unhatched young. Mother alligators are known to sometimes urinate on their nests when they become either too dry or too hot.

From the very beginning of the young crocodilians' lives, vocalizations are important. Vocalizations are a normal part of everyday life for crocodilians, which are the most vocal of non-avian reptiles, voicing communication in ways lizards, turtles, and snakes do not.

Experiments where calls from young animals were played back to mothers showed that most crocodilian calls seem to be mutually understandable among different lineages of the group. For instance, a mother American alligator can understand the calls of a

A mother alligator floats near her babies (two, at lower left), in South Carolina. (*Author*)

young American crocodile and vice versa. This makes sense, suggesting that dinosaurs and ancestral crocodilians were vocal as well. In the case of living crocodilians, communication starts inside the egg with the tiny voice of a hatching youngster.

Experiments with eggs of alligators and crocodiles in laboratory incubators have shown that the little animals vocalize during the last two weeks before hatching and will even respond to each other's cries. Tapping on the egg container resulted in the embryos responding with pecking noises.

When it comes time for a nest to hatch, the mother's presence becomes even more important. In 2008, researchers using playback recordings proved something long suspected—that these inner egg vocalizations serve an important purpose. In the experiment, the eggs of Nile crocodiles in zoos are removed from their nests early on. Speakers were hidden near the empty nests, still guarded by faithful—if duped—mothers. Near the expected hatching date, vocalizations of pre-hatching embryos were played, and many of the mothers responded by digging, in an apparent attempt to find their missing young and help them enter the world.

The cries of Nile crocodile young seem to coordinate hatching, saying to the others, "it's time to hatch"; yet they also are directed to the mother, calling on her to dig up her nest and help her young crack their shells. In this way, the young and mother act together to make sure they all come out of the nest under the supervision of a protective adult. It seems likely this is the case for all other species of crocodilian and has often been observed anecdotally. The mother digs open her nest, helping her young escape, then crocodilian mother takes her young in her jaws and carries the babies to the water. The exception is the gharial, whose mouth is too narrow to carry young, and must be content to simply be near the young, allowing them to find their own way to water. After this point, it seems that the mother's main job is to simply watch over her progeny. When a youngster is seized, they make an alarm call that attracts the full attention of an angry mother. Beyond protection from predation, there is some evidence that at least occasionally mothers do a bit more.

A zookeeper made a video of a mother Philippines crocodile carrying a piece of meat to her young, then holding the morsel in her mouth while the babies tore pieces off. African dwarf crocodiles have also been seen sharing meat with their young. Orinoco crocodiles seem to sometimes feed their babies as well. It's possible that this behavior is more common than we know, considering how much we've learned about crocodilian parenting in recent years. The first time a mother crocodile was observed carrying her young in her jaws, it was misinterpreted by scientists as cannibalistic behavior, highlighting the bias of the times. Who knows what we'll discover about crocodilian parenting in the future?

It's not all cries and mothering for baby crocodilians, though. Saltwater crocodiles (*Crocodylus porosus*) have been observed fighting with each other shortly after leaving their eggs. "Salties" have a reputation of being among the most aggressive crocodilians in the world, so it's not surprising that violence starts early.

The first signs of this behavior, when the animals are only a week old, usually involves physical contact between two or more of the young crocodiles and seems undirected. By thirteen and

Gharial hatchlings in nursery at the Gharial Conservation and Breeding Center, Chitwan National Park, Nepal. (*Copyright Ashish Bashyal/Biodiversity Conservancy Nepal, used with permission*)

forty weeks, though, a sort of hierarchy has evolved and often a dominant animal will merely threaten a subordinate and the other animal meekly runs away.

It seems that the point of this antagonistic behavior is to determine social standing. This is possibly why a certain percentage of captive crocodile young die—perhaps unable to compete effectively from the role they're relegated to on the bottom of the hierarchy, they simply die. Antagonism may also limit the growth of unlucky crocodiles in captivity.

Some antagonism between young is normal in most, if not all, crocodilians, although it varies depending on the species. Gharials and other slender-snouted species tend to raise their heads when fighting, to keep their delicate jaws out of the fray. Johnstone's crocodiles in turn push each other down with their heads. New Guinea crocodiles sweep their tails back and forth violently, and salties strike with the sides of their heads while also swinging their tails.

Interestingly, almost no fighting happens on land; instead, crocodilians seem to prefer conflicts in the open water. Clashes may arise when two animals accidentally swim into each other, but at other times it's intentional and seemingly calculated. During approach and aggressive signaling, the reptiles facing off might gape their mouths, snap their jaws, or wag their tails. Usually an animal walks away from a fight but sometimes a violent confrontation is inevitable. When a fight gets physical, crocodilians push each other with their heads or bite or strike each other. It's hard to test for sure, but there may be more conflicts between young animals in captivity—where they cannot escape each other—than in the wild.

In the wild, eventually the stress from struggling with other saltwater crocodiles is too much and the young disperse at the relatively early age of thirteen weeks old. Being spread farther apart relieves some pressure of social competition. In the freshwater Johnstone's crocodile (*Crocodylus johnstoni*), young males disperse farther from their nests than their sisters, probably to avoid male-male conflict. It may also play a role in preventing inbreeding.

The situation is a little different with American alligators. For as long as two years, the young alligators stay close to their mothers. This means that you can sometimes see a mother alligator with young from two different seasons floating in the water near her. During this time, the babies tussle with each other in playful fights and catch insects, small fishes, amphibians and snails for their meals. A mother alligator mostly passively protects her babies by the threat of her hulking presence.

While helping on research in South Carolina, I approached a female alligator in a pond only to hear the telltale chirping of babies from a bush near the edge of the water. The mother swam close to the bush, quietly watching the humans as her babies chirped and yellow butterflies danced near the bush's purple flowers. This motherly attention to potential threats is normal for alligators, but all good things must come to an end. Eventually, for alligators as with other crocodiles, families disband as young leave their mothers behind and find their own territories and mates.

Violence is a part of the social lives of crocodilians. In Bardia National Park, Nepal, I photographed this larger mugger crocodile (*Crocodylus palustris*) lunging and biting the smaller crocodile at the base of the tail. The smaller crocodile reacted with obvious pain or surprise and then twisted around in an attempt to defend. Eventually the larger crocodile released the smaller one, and it fled. (*Author*)

In an experiment in the Okavango Delta of Botswana, recordings of hatchlings and juvenile Nile crocodiles were played near adult females. It was shown that the females react by moving toward the calls of hatchlings more often than older juveniles. The pitch of vocalizations may play a role in changing mothering behavior over time. Eventually mother Nile crocodiles stop responding to their young altogether, even chasing them away, perhaps when they become more of a competition for food resources and it's time for them to find their own space.

Crocodilians as a whole are known to be territorial rather than overly friendly. If some captive male salties are not carefully supervised, it's relatively common for them to kill females meant as mates. In the wild, territories are fluid, females move into males territories during mating season, and several subordinate males may also share a territory with the dominant male. More space outside of captivity allows for a more peaceable existence, where everyone can maintain a comfortable distance. The wild simply allows subordinates and females the opportunity to escape with only minor injuries, when they might be killed if contained in a pen with no other recourse.

The mugger crocodiles (*Crocodylus palustris*) I watched in Nepal would sometimes skirmish with each other, usually ending with a larger, more powerful animal chasing away a smaller one. I even captured a series of pictures of one crocodile biting another's tail. Still, most of the time I saw the muggers lying relatively close to each other basking on sand and gravel bars with no conflict. There could have been more conflict in deeper water that I was simply unable to observe. Gharials would share basking space on many of the bars as well, apparently unafraid of threats from the smaller but more dangerously equipped muggers. The open spaces of the wild also allow a surprising amount of mingling for some crocodilians.

As I discussed in the last chapter, American alligators socialize in what some observers have described as a sort of "ball" or "dance" where animals mingle and sometimes pair off together and swim away to flirt at the fringes of the group. In these gatherings, late at night, the alligators bellow and swim together.

Caimans seem to also display with bellowing and slapping their heads on the water in groups. The purpose of these gatherings isn't entirely known. Whatever the reason for these mixers, it must be quite important because even mothers with babies have been seen leaving their young unguarded for a few hours of socializing.

Researchers have observed Nile crocodiles, in Zimbabwe, court and mate from late June into August during the dry season when the Runde River dries up and the animals congregate in remnant pools of water. The females nested later—from September through the beginning of October—at the beginning of the rainy season when the river begins to flow again. For notoriously aggressive animals, the mating was a rather social affair. Crocodiles basked on a sandy shore overlooking the watery arena while fighting, courtship, and mating took place in pools below. The female crocodile often initiated sexual behavior; floating high in the water, the entire top of her head exposed (as opposed to only the eyes

Breeding group of gharials consisting of one male (middle) identified by the presence of ghara at tip of snout flanked by two adult females at Soth Khola by the Babai River, Bardia National Park, Nepal. (*Copyright Ashish Bashyal/Biodiversity Conservancy Nepal, used with permission*)

and nostrils as usual). She and an interested male swam toward one another, the female angling away and passing him by as they came close. The aroused female would sometimes rub the "gular" or throat region of the male with her head or rub her own gular region on the snout of a male. Nile crocodiles aren't the only crocodilians to display these sophisticated behaviors.

Mating behavior in crocodilians is fascinating. Males will tickle their intended by blowing. (This may be part of the reason male gharials have such strange protuberances on their noses.) It isn't just gharials that blow bubbles but alligators and other crocodilians as well although it may be important to them in particular. Preludes to sex also include "singing" crocodilians bellowing and responding to each other, almost like a chorus of frogs, as I mentioned before. Some crocodilians splash with their tails, expand their throats, and open their mouths. Slapping their heads on the water and clapping jaws together are all part of the performance. Many crocodilians playfully chase each other during courtship as well, something other young animals also do.

"Playful" isn't a word that many would use to describe crocodilians, but sometimes it's accurate. Young black caimans (*Melanosuchus niger*) have been seen swimming in circles, pursuing each other at night in Brazil. There are videos of Nile crocodiles roughhousing with siblings. Scientist Vladimir Dinets watched a female Cuban crocodile climb onto the back of a courting male as he swam around giving her a sort of crocodile "piggy back" ride. This behavior had never been observed before, and Dinets speculates that it was simply improvised play between the two courting reptiles. Crocodilians are sometimes playful, but as one might expect, not all of the interactions with each other are quite so cordial.

Violence, as I've already mentioned, is common among captive animals, and it's also a less common but not abnormal feature of life in the wild. Violence between individual crocodilians, especially males of the same species, has a long history. Wounds were found on the jaws of an Eocene semi-aquatic crocodilian fossil from Mali. The wounds match up to teeth marks of the same species, so paleontologists have interpreted them as evidence of old infraspecific fighting. Fighting now, and probably then, often has to do with territory and mating.

As with saltwater crocodiles, it's thought that in most species dominant males establish territories during mating season, patrolling the area, mating with any females within its boundaries, and chasing off other males. This doesn't always work out for the dominant male as well as he'd hope. Inevitably, some of the less dominant males are able to mate as well, as territories are sometimes very large and a dominant male can't be everywhere at once. In some crocodile species, females also form separate hierarchies with large dominant females.

Studies of black caiman in Brazil's Anavilhanas National Park found multiple paternity; nests laid by individual females were the product of breeding with different males. In contrast, a genetic study of American crocodile young in Costa Rica suggested mate fidelity. It could be that American crocodiles are more faithful, or possibly it's hard enough to find one American crocodile to mate with in Costa Rica, let alone two. Alligators in Rockefeller National Wildlife Refuge on Louisiana's Gulf Coast were found to have partial mate fidelity. The majority of females mated with the same male year after year but not exclusively, the norm being a clutch of eggs with multiple fathers. Not all mating hierarchies revolve around a male (unsuccessfully) defending a territory where females are welcome but other males are not.

Spectacled caimans seem to have a social hierarchy built around male size rather than territory. The larger males have greater access to females and chase away smaller males, without reference to a particular geographic region. One study showed that of twenty spectacled caiman nests surveyed, nineteen had more than one dad. Yacare caiman and Orinoco crocodile nests also show multiple paternity. Despite questionable genetic paternity, some crocodilians are good fathers.

Young gharials associate with their nest mates as well as the young in nearby nests, to form groups of sometimes hundreds of individuals called "crèches." The infant gharials communicate with each other and attendant adults and vice versa. Young swim with and climb on nearby parents, who seem willing to protect them from the potential dangers of predators. Unfortunately many young still die, from opportunistic predators and from uncontrollable elements like flooding. Fathers guard their young as well as mothers. Sometimes dads are left to watch out for the babies while mothers forage for food and sometimes moms take their turn babysitting.

Siamese crocodiles (*Crocodylus siamensis*) also share parental duties. A male Siamese crocodile in captivity has been seen carrying a piece of meat to his young, allowing one baby to even climb in his mouth to eat. After the food was consumed, the male was seen bringing another piece of meat back to his babies again. A male mugger crocodile was once observed carrying his offspring to the water, raising the possibility that it happens more often than we've seen.

Interestingly, it seems that in the "false" gharial (*Tomistoma schlegelii*), parenting isn't quite so equitable. Although very little documentation on parenting in the species exists, one study found that females were much more likely to respond to recordings of

A "crèche" of gharial hatchlings swimming in the Babai River at Dhanuse in Bardia National Park, Nepal. (*Copyright Ashish Bashyal/Biodiversity Conservancy Nepal, used with permission*)

distress signals of young crocodilians played back to them than males. In the wild it seems that sometimes human presence scares the shy *Tomistoma* enough for her to abandon her nest, while in captivity, animals accustomed to human presence continue to guard their nests when observed. Parental behaviors like these have been known to change depending on circumstances. In general, animals in areas with large amounts of human disturbance sometimes show less nest-guarding behavior, possibly in acknowledgment of the futility of intimidating the humans. Some scientists believe that crocodilian parents are able to assess which parental behaviors best suit given circumstances and adapt their behavior.

Good parenting in the form of nest guarding is only one of many traits shared between crocodilians, birds, and other archosaurs.

Harris' hawks are a species of modest-sized raptors found in the southwestern United States, including the cactus-studded Sonoran Desert, south to Argentina. The hawk is a pretty enough animal of rich brown plumage, but not too striking in appearance. What makes the Harris' hawk interesting is its behavior, for they've been known to hunt in packs. Chasing prey away from one animal and into the waiting talons of another, the hawks sometimes even pursue prey on the ground as if re-enacting *Jurassic Park* scenes. Recent studies have found that the Aplomado falcon (*Falco femoralis*) also works in pairs when chasing down prey. Many scientists think that some dinosaur predators likewise hunted cooperatively. It's interesting that some of the closest relatives of crocodilians hunt together, something scientists have only recently noticed in crocs themselves.

In his book *Dragon Songs*, Vladimir Dinets tells of seeing crocodiles hunting together. One example involved a pig trotting along a path in New Guinea. A crocodile erupted from the water in front of the unlucky mammal. In terror, the pig stumbled backward, practically falling into the jaws of two smaller crocodiles. His interest piqued by this one observation, Dinets was able to find accounts of similar hunting behavior in crocodilians in Georgia, Australia, Venezuela, and Botswana. Although evidence is anecdotal, it's quite likely that crocodilians, like their closest relatives, help each other hunt more efficiently.

A reptile zookeeper in Australia watched Johnstone's crocodiles herd fishes toward their compatriots in shallow water, allowing them to catch the fish more easily. Alligators have been seen hunting piscine prey in a similar way in Okefenokee National Wildlife Refuge, where some of the animals apparently waited their turn to join in the hunt, others resting after eating their catch. Spectacled caiman in Venezuela have been seen flushing frogs from the shore to other caimans waiting in the water.

The advantages of a higher success rate in cooperative hunting are just some of the overall benefits of social living. The protection afforded by a parent to their offspring is another plus to social life, as are the sharing of information and resources. These are advantages shared by almost all social animals and may help in the spread of their genes. Taking this into consideration, it becomes not so surprising at all that crocodilians are social beasts. Instead, what becomes surprising is how long it took for scientists to see the social behavior in front of their own eyes. Further, it begs the question, how much social behavior is really lacking in reptiles in general and how much of it is overlooked by researchers? Recent scientific papers suggest that more social behavior in reptiles will be found if only more detailed and focused research looks for it.

What seems to emerge with the better science available today is a view of not just crocodilians but all non-avian reptiles as more sentient and more gregarious than previously thought possible. Research on Australia's sleepy lizard now shows an animal that comes together to mate with the same individual for decades. In fact, a survey of all lizards shows that many of them display complex social behaviors. The slow change of attitude from crocodiles as dull, slow-witted monsters to intelligent, caring parents may presage a change in attitudes about all reptiles. The closer we look at any group of organisms, the more dynamic, interesting, and worthy of our respect they appear. The crocodilians that have been extensively studied seem to show more interesting behaviors, but this is because in general we know more about the animals we study more.

Alligators in particular are relatively well studied and much of their social behavior well documented, simply because for American researchers at least, they're easily accessible. While I wrote this book, I was also able to observe more alligators than any other extant species of crocodilian. Alligators are also not very dangerous compared to some crocodilians. The next four chapters will each focus on, in turn, alligators, caimans, crocodiles, and gharials.

six

ALLIGATORS

THE AMERICAN ALLIGATOR (*Alligator mississippiensis*) is undoubtedly the most famous member of the genus *Alligator* alive today. The only other extant alligator is the shyer, smaller and more mysterious Chinese alligator (*Alligator sinensis*). The distribution of two alligators found in distinct parts of the world is truly strange and requires an explanation.

In the past, North America and China were much closer geographically than today. Magnolias, pines, sycamores—all genera common in the southeastern United States—are also found growing in the Anhui Province of China, near where alligators live. Closely related arachnids, fungi, and even surprisingly large salamanders* are found in both China and the southeastern U.S. as well. As odd as it may seem today, it appears that alligators first evolved in North America and traveled over the Bering land

---

*The hellbender (*Cryptobranchus alleganiensis*) is the only American member of the Cryptobranchidae family of salamanders. This family also includes "giant" salamander species in Japan and China. Together, these are the largest amphibians alive today. *Andrias sligoi*, the South China giant salamander (newly described as a distinct species), is probably the largest, measuring as much as two meters long.

bridge to China. A string of alligators between the two places must've lived in the balmier world that once was. Eventually the two populations of alligators diverged into two new species in isolation.

Driving from the saguaro-filled Sonoran desert of southern Arizona where I live, the nearest American alligator habitat is in central and eastern Texas, where alligators can be found in rivers, marshes, and swamps. The trip is mostly a long ride through dry cactus country of southern New Mexico and western Texas. As you get closer to the Gulf of Mexico, larger trees appear and the heat becomes sticky; water is more abundant and with it, aquatic animals. Alligators are to be found in canals and swimming pools, golf course water hazards—in any sort of water. I once saw an alligator swimming in San Antonio Bay (in the Gulf of Mexico) with what appeared to be an egret in its jaws. Alligators have even been spotted at Padre Island National Seashore, a peaceful island of sand and grass more known for sea turtle nests and moonlit crab-covered beaches. One thing that separates alligators from crocodiles is the first's inability to expel salt; alligators can only spend short periods in the ocean but they seem to travel through it with few problems. Yet alligators still venture into ocean and brackish waters for short spells when it suits them (more on this below).

I spent most of my time in Texas watching the American alligator at Aransas National Wildlife Refuge, originally established by Franklin Roosevelt on December 31, 1937, for migratory bird protection. Alligators use a lot of the same habitats as birds visiting the Gulf of Mexico and so preserving habitat for the birds inadvertently helped the alligator as well.

Aransas is a tangle of short but widely sprawling blackjack oak trees (*Quercus marilandica*) twisted with vines, marshy lakes the tannin-color of tea, and thick vegetation of all kinds along the edge of the Gulf in central Texas. Wild grapes with unimpressive flavor hang from trees. Patches of coastal prairie, muddy sloughs, and coastal salt marshes form the refuge's other habitats.

Walking along paths in June, I at first felt as if I could hardly breathe for the thick gauze of humid heat in the air. When I

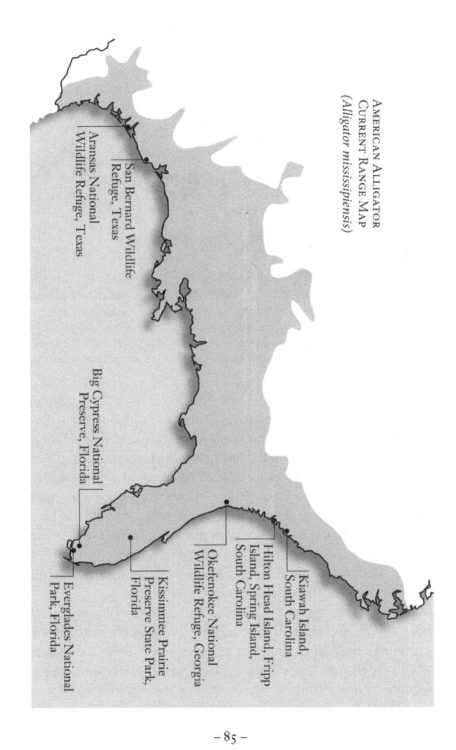

AMERICAN ALLIGATOR
CURRENT RANGE MAP
(*Alligator mississipiensis*)

San Bernard Wildlife
Refuge, Texas

Aransas National
Wildlife Refuge, Texas

Big Cypress National
Preserve, Florida

Everglades National
Park, Florida

Kissimmee Prairie
Preserve State Park,
Florida

Okefenokee National
Wildlife Refuge, Georgia

Hilton Head Island, Fripp
Island, Spring Island,
South Carolina

Kiawah Island,
South Carolina

A juvenile American alligator at Aransas National Wildlife Refuge, Texas. Young alligators have protective coloring probably to camouflage them from potential predators. Very young alligators are also usually close to their mothers. This juvenile crawled over and through the algae and other plant life as much as swam when I saw it. (*Author*)

stopped in the shade, mosquitoes covered me with buzzing malevolence. Only a few trails wander off from the paved wildlife-viewing road and into the swelter and swarming insects.

A ramp climbs through a copse of oak trees near the road to a tower platform overlooking the tidal flats, the open sea, and brackish Mustang Lake. In the other direction forest stretches as far as I can see. From the forty-foot high platform, there is deliverance from oppressive heat and insect clouds in a near constant salty breeze. Because the time I spent there was unusually dry, virtually all of the insects were gone by August.

All of the refuge's trails are less than two miles long, perhaps because building trails in such terrain is a constant struggle with plants and mud in the hot shade. A more generous assessment would say that the trails and even road are relatively short to give wildlife its peace from human bumbling and aggression. Most of the refuge is a trail-less "wild" place of sun, riotous life, salt water, fresh water, ancient oak trees, and shrubby saw palmettos.

People often seemed confused about what sort of place Aransas is. Menacing signs stand at the entrances of many of the refuge's wetland areas. The signs are simple metal rectangles featuring a black and white illustration of an alligator, mouth open in a fierce pose. The signs say, "Caution. Alligators are WILD DO NOT FEED." The signs seem to be often ignored as evidenced by marshmallows floating in the water and the purported friendliness of some of the alligators to an approaching human. I'm not sure many people take the alligators very seriously.

One late afternoon, I was walking a trail back toward the road when two tourists with German accents asked politely if I'd seen an alligator. I told them I had and walked back to show them, this being much easier than attempting to explain how to find the animal. Just as I was about to leave, one of the tourists said to me how surprising it was that people were allowed to walk around here like this. Then he said he supposed the alligators never eat people, "even the big ones." I told the man that, in fact, I'd heard of two people who'd been consumed at Aransas, only it was supposed that both had died first and the alligators merely ate their lifeless bodies. The two tourists grew quiet for a moment after that. I then said good-bye and the men thanked me before I walked down the trail towards the road and my campsite beyond.

Although much of the refuge is set aside for wildlife with no regular human access, alligators have a way of being pulled into conflict with people. Another time, a family told me that an aggressive alligator had chased them down the path. I advised them to give the alligator, which was sitting quietly in a slough nearby, plenty of space. After this warning, the man edged closer and closer to the alligator to get a photo. As the alligator wriggled in agitation, I told the man that now it was time to move along and leave the alligator alone. The man wore a holstered gun and police badge on his hip. Too often alligators are antagonized by humans and end up being punished for defending themselves. This particular alligator was most likely a new mother guarding her nest.

A paved road runs as the main artery through all of Aransas that can be accessed by the public. Unlike many national parks, there is no backcountry. Kayaking is the only way to really distance one-self from the sharp edges of asphalt. Even from a kayak, views of offshore oil platforms clearly sign the assumed mastery of man over the place. If you paddle out too far, you may get in the way of oil tankers that often pass by Aransas. All of this together leaves a human footprint that makes the place feel slightly like an artificial wildlife park. Texas is after all a place where the wealthy can hunt African game roaming about on large private ranches that also collect oil royalties.

Across from the visitor contact station at Aransas is a wooden deck surrounded by a hand rail, overlooking a small body of water, with a sign designating it as an alligator viewing platform. It feels almost as if you should check when the feeding time is or expect to see a trainer asking the alligators to perform tricks.

There is another side to Aransas though. On a bike ride in the least popular section of road in the refuge, I was startled to see a bristled mother javelina (collared peccary) sprinting across the road with her baby "red" trying its best to keep up. Armadillos sniff and dig in the grass around the visitor contact station near twilight. I've heard the sharp exhalation of a breaching dolphin nearby while kayaking many times at Aransas. Deer and wild turkeys are everywhere; the whole place with its rich range of habitats is known for bird diversity. Cottonmouths and coral snakes sun themselves on hot roads, and tree frogs swarm the observation towers in the early morning hours. Alligators lie quietly in almost all bodies of water at the refuge, often hidden or statuesque but always present and alert.

Aransas is in the western part of the American alligator's range, although alligators are found a bit farther inland in Texas as well. Alligators are the northern-most crocodilian, being found as far north as some of Oklahoma, a large portion of Arkansas, and the eastern quarter of North Carolina. The Chinese alligator, like its American cousin, lives in relatively colder northern subtropical rather than tropical climates as well.

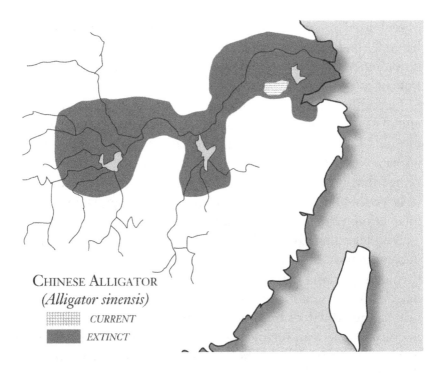

CHINESE ALLIGATOR
(Alligator sinensis)
CURRENT
EXTINCT

To deal with colder climates, Chinese alligators spend nearly half of the year underground. Similar to their American relatives, at the northern end of their range, the smaller alligator digs elaborate tunnels and underground burrows or dens to stay warm through chilly winter days. Chinese alligators lie dormant in their dens from the end of October until mid-April. The dens vary in size, and sometimes several individuals can be found together. The tunnels are often connected below water to rivers; when the Yangtze River floods, it sometimes drowns Chinese alligators in their dens. Some think that these burrows inspired notions of dragons hidden in underground lairs in China. In especially warm places like southern Florida, American alligators don't dig burrows, remaining active year round in the subtropical sun.

I arrived at Aransas on the last day of May to begin a two-month stint as a volunteer for the Fish and Wildlife Service. In exchange for three work days per week, I got four days off and an RV pad on which to park my camper van. Not only did I have most of each week to explore the refuge and take in alligators and their habitat, I had such fancy amenities as electricity, and even air conditioning. My arrival at Aransas coincided not just with the hottest time of the year—it was also an important time for alligators.

Officially, mating season for alligators at Aransas runs until the end of May, but of course alligators don't adhere to human schedules, and I didn't observe mating behavior at Aransas. Then again, it's hard to see mating behavior that occurs after dark at a wildlife refuge that is closed at night. After mating, there is the building of large mounds of plants used for nests, then egg laying and an incubation period of sixty-eight to seventy days.

A bit later than their American counterparts, Chinese alligators become active in the spring weather of May, spending less time in their dens, basking in the sun and maintaining daytime diurnal behaviors. As the year moves into summer and the weather becomes hotter, the alligators become more nocturnal, like their mostly nocturnal American relatives. By mid-June the Chinese alligator mating season peaks and the animals go about courtship in the dark of night. In late June and July Chinese alligators make nests and lay their eggs, which hatch sometime in September.

Aransas was full of babies of all kinds when I arrived. Two deer fawns ran away as I first drove through the entrance gate. Under the sprawling canopy of an oak tree next to my camp spot, a turkey pecked at the ground, tailed by her scurrying chicks, still in coats of down. After my trip from Tucson, my tired mind wondered if there were small alligators out there in the water somewhere. Dinner my first night was salsa mixed with a can of black beans spooned up with tortilla chips. I ate, then, I slept. It had been a long two days of driving from Arizona.

My first full day at Aransas came bright and hot. My official volunteer duties didn't start for a week, so I ventured out to see a bit of the place that morning. I had agreed to meet the volunteer coordinator, Zach Piotrowski, at the visitor contact station that day, but I had a bit of time to kill. I unloaded my old, blue, somewhat rusty mountain bike from the rack on the rear of the van and pedaled out onto the road. Almost directly across from the staff and volunteer housing was a sign proclaiming "Rail Trail." I pushed my bike down the grassy trail lined with dense plant life. Soon I noticed little breaks in the bushes and cattails leading into the water. These were places where alligators had pushed their hulking bodies through the plants and over the banks of lazily moving sloughs, smashing pathways through the brush. These routes wind through the water as well, creating open areas in sloughs that otherwise are often choked with flora. These pathways, Piotrowski told me, are important because they allow water to flow and circulate more freely. Alligator trails serve another purpose as well—other animals sometimes travel them, although perhaps at some risk. Alligators make movement of water, nutrients, and animals possible in otherwise plant-bound marshes. It was just off the trail, peering through one of the breaks in the vegetation, that I saw my first alligators at Aransas. Three small reptiles, dark with the yellow stripes of the young, lay in the water; one made a quiet squeaking noise. I was enthralled and excited to see alligators so quickly, so easily. Almost every day I spent at Aransas was punctuated by at least one alligator sighting.

On a Sunday afternoon after my volunteer duties were finished for the week, I took a walk. The day had been hot, clear, and muggy, but the afternoon was cooling off. I stopped at a platform overlooking a coastal marsh and the calm ocean beyond it. From the raised position, I enjoyed a steady, cool breeze. A raccoon picked its way across the mud, but distracted, I lost track of his whereabouts. Tourists arrived at the platform to watch wildlife and I continued my walk down the trail. I passed two coffee-dark sloughs where alligators were sometimes found; I saw nothing and turned back, my mind filled with visions of a hearty pasta dinner to come. Slowly, I became aware of strange, low, long growling noises coming from a marshy pool hidden behind dense foliage.

Alligator? My mind asked and my body moved to answer the question. I pushed through the grasses on the edge of the trail and out into a muddy high point between two sloughs where an inch or two of water sloshed over the top of my sandals. I couldn't see the animals making the growling noises—the vegetation was too thick—but I saw something moving in the slough beside me. An alligator I estimated to be between seven and ten feet long swam toward the far bank; its sharp tail like a scaled knife blade moved effortlessly through the water. The alligator stopped with head and tail both held high, a position that looks a bit awkward. The alligator growled low and long, a rumbling, primordial sound. The quieter growls now behind me were clearly other alligators. The large alligator growled again and the other animals slowly quieted themselves. The big alligator seemed satisfied and slowly sank back into the water until only the top of his head, mainly his eyes, were above the water. I waited a few minutes, but the creature was still. Perhaps the most striking aspect of alligators is their quiet patience, their stillness. Crocodilians aren't actively searching as predators; they're hair-trigger traps waiting for the unwary to stumble by.

In *Alligators: Prehistoric Presence in the American Landscape*, LeRoy Overstreet wrote about a peculiarity in alligator hunting behavior. Alligators lying perfectly still near a bank can easily be mistaken for a log by an unobservant animal searching for a place to drink. Sometimes the unlucky critter, say a rabbit, will carefully ease onto the back of the alligator, nose twitching, slowly hopping down the back to taste a sip of marsh water. The alligator lies perfectly still until the animal returns and hops toward the shore. As soon as the prey steps off the alligator, the reptile erupts into motion and catches the animal in powerful jaws. Sometimes, even a human may unwittingly step onto the back of an alligator. Overstreet told of a man wading in a swamp who accidentally stepped onto the back of an alligator and called for help. Boats were positioned on either side and the man was lifted quickly off of the alligator, but the animal still managed to grab one of his legs which was badly mangled once freed.

The classic example of crocodilian hunting, the climax of a hundred nature documentaries, is that of a thirsty prey animal nervously edging up to a pool of water only to be caught in the leaping jaws of the crocodile. Ethologist (a biologist focusing on animal behavior) Vladimir Dinets has also observed alligators in Florida waiting out of water along paths at night. A jogger was even attacked and killed by an alligator hunting relatively far from water. An old woman was killed while watering her garden in Florida. Hunting away from water is unusual but seems to be within the range of normal behavior for alligators.

The typical quick lunge followed by the horrific "death roll" that actually kills and dismembers the prey is what crocodilians are known for. Teeth are one of the essential components of the alligator's hunting apparatus.

When a group of young boys visited Aransas for a service project of planting native trees, bushes, and grasses, Zach Piotrowski also treated them to a short lecture on alligators. I fetched a cast of an alligator skull from the office, carrying three alligator teeth used for props in my hand.

American alligator skulls contain 74 to 80 teeth; Chinese alligators, 78 to 82. The teeth are somewhat unique to archosaurs—relatively stubby but powerful and sharp cones, designed to stab and hold onto flesh and sometimes crack open shellfish. Outside of the mouth with their roots revealed, alligator teeth are much longer and hollow. As the tooth grows outward, another tooth grows inside its root, waiting for the outer tooth to be pulled loose in a struggle with a potential meal. The next tooth pushes upward, replacing the lost tooth, so that an alligator is never unarmed. Only very old alligators lose the ability to regrow teeth. Kelby Ouchley, in his book *American Alligator*, writes that an alligator may use as many as 2,000 to 3,000 teeth in a lifetime. Alligator teeth are very similar in this way to the teeth of carnivorous dinosaurs. Teeth in the mouth of alligators wait for just a few sharp moments of grabbing and can be lost in an instant. These brief moments of violent action punctuate a rather placid day-to-day reality.

Even yearling alligators, still quite small, give the impression of serenity, without the hyperactive leaping or running of young cows or deer, bighorn sheep, or rabbits. To the casual observer, these young, diminutive alligators are only slightly more mobile than the hulking adults. Movements are graceful but not frequent. When an alligator swims, the whole body aligns with the movement and the reptile that looks like an overgrown lizard becomes serpentine or piscine (like a fish) while swimming. The very small alligators stop the graceful swimming motion when they come to thick clumps of algae or floating rafts of broken cattails, instead crawling their way through the debris with their front claws splayed. It takes more substantial obstacles to slow larger alligators. In water, alligators can move incredibly fast but even their slower movements seem effortless, as if simply propelled by the power of lazy thoughts. I've stood at a dock on the edge of a lake looking for alligators only to be startled when I turned to find one floating in the brownish water only about fifteen feet away. The alligator just lay suspended for a long time with no obvious intent, and then slowly the body sunk beneath the water and disappeared eerily as if by forces beyond the animal's own will.

One morning I found a young alligator, probably a bit shy of two feet long, on a bridge at the end of a hiking trail. I'd seen this alligator or its siblings before in the marsh beneath this bridge, their dark bodies striped with gold, making them camouflaged like tigers. I'd observed them in the water many times, lazing about, occasionally munching on whatever prey happened past. The alligators were probably about a year old; it was near the end of mating time but not yet egg-hatching time, and these babies were clearly no longer watched over by their mother much. On the bridge, out of her element, the little alligator gaped her mouth, hissing slightly at my presence, but didn't run and scramble for the safety of water. I snapped a few photos and quickly skirted past the small creature. Thinking it best to leave her in peace, I walked away.

Alligators show their curiosity about the world quietly. Vanishing, then appearing. Walking onto bridges or into buildings, exploring. Humans, despite our superior views of ourselves, may react by thoughtlessly killing these animals. Early European explorers in the Americas often shot alligators as a matter of course, and most "nuisance alligators" in the United States are killed rather than relocated. When the alligators were unprotected by law, Chinese farmers often set snares near the entrances of dens,

Juvenile American alligator on a bridge, Aransas National Wildlife Refuge, Texas. This alligator hissed at me and fled the bridge as I came a bit closer. (*Author*)

killing the animals on principle, using them as food as something of an afterthought.

In the early years of alligator hunting, an almost casual desire to kill the alligators took hold, along the same thoughtless lines that advanced Manifest Destiny. For many it seemed that the only good alligator was a dead alligator. The first record of using alligator skin comes from the early 1800s. In the beginning, tanning techniques couldn't make alligator skins into very practical boots (they leaked), so after the first initial foray into large-scale commercial hunting, the alligator skin trade declined. Fat from alligators was used to lubricate machinery such as the cotton gin, but hunting alligators was far from a booming business.

The Civil War created a new market for alligator skins. Naval blockades stopped cowhide from arriving in Southern ports, and the Confederates had little choice but to use alligator skins for boots and saddles. After the war, the skins became more fashionable, leading to an increase in alligator hunting. The trend of alligator and other crocodilian clothes and accessories spread to Europe. Alligator meat became "Cajun sausage" and over time a tourist novelty food. The scale of alligator hunting and the connected skin trade was enormous, and between 1880 and 1933, 3.5 million alligators were skinned in Louisiana alone, according to Louisiana Wildlife and Fisheries. Much of this changed within the scope of a human lifetime.

When my father was born, in 1953, it wasn't yet widely understood how much of a negative impact hunting was having on alligators. American alligators were killed, mainly for their skin, without management until the 1960s, when states started to regulate their alligator populations. Louisiana made hunting alligators over five feet long illegal in 1960 and established a hunting season, outside of which hunting was illegal. Two years later, all alligator hunting was outlawed in Louisiana. Hunting alligators was made illegal in Florida in 1961. State laws like these were the first alligator conservation legislation put into place, but state regulations weren't enough to stop the decline of alligators. Simply put, poaching alligators was still easy because the skins could be moved across state lines and sold where such sales were legal.

Federal laws were needed to protect American alligators. In 1967 alligators were protected federally under a law predating the 1973 Endangered Species Act. Alligators were on the first list of endangered species in America. Intense federal efforts aided by state governments and organizations led to the growth of American alligator populations that were pronounced recovered in 1987, the year I turned two. This was also the year that the American alligator was declared the official state reptile of Florida. Today the American crocodile is listed on the endangered species list as "threatened due to similarity of appearance," meaning an endangered crocodilian could be mistaken for an American alligator. In such a relatively short period of time, marked against a typical human timescale, alligators in the United States reached their

Adult American alligator resting near the official "alligator viewing area," Aransas National Wildlife Refuge, Texas. She was very quiet and still. This photo clearly shows the alligator's rounded snout, in contrast to the crocodile's more angular and pointed one. (*Author*)

darkest period and rebounded impressively. In less than thirty years conservation efforts are said to have led to the recovery of alligator populations.

In recent years the American alligator has continued its comeback from a historic low created mainly by overhunting and habitat destruction. There are an estimated 5 million American alligators alive in the wild today, 1.25 million of them in Florida. As many as 30,000 alligators were legally killed by hunting in one recent year in Louisiana alone. There is still much conflict between humans and alligators, partially because both populations keep increasing.

People throughout the Southeast have moved into areas historically given over to wetlands. Golf courses, swimming pools, and shopping malls have been built where once swamps, marshes, and lakes were ruled over by alligators. Human populations throughout the region have grown. As the alligator population rises closer and closer to historic levels, the animals leave places like the Everglades or Okefenokee Swamp looking for new territory. They find places that were once their wetland habitats but are now the domain of *Homo sapiens*.

Louisiana has the largest population of alligators of any U.S. state (more than 2 million in the wild), but Florida has the highest rates of conflicts with humans, mainly because of the larger number of people living in and visiting the Sunshine State. Alligator access to much of their previous habitat is now contested by human development and intolerance to large reptiles.

The Chinese alligator faces a similar problem on a much larger scale. Most of the Chinese alligator's habitat has been destroyed by agriculture and urban development. Some of the last shreds of habitat for the Chinese alligators, such as Dongtan Wetland Park, are on the edges of Shanghai, China's largest city. It's estimated that there are fewer than 150 Chinese alligators living in the wild today. Thousands of Chinese alligators have been bred in captivity with the hope that some small area of wild habitat might be found to reintroduce them to.

Chinese alligator populations were brought low by a trade in skin as well as development and human conflict. Unlike their American cousins, the Chinese gator is small enough to pose no direct threat to humans at all. Instead, Chinese alligator meat has been promoted as a cure for everything from the common cold to cancer. Alligator parts are even used as an ingredient in skin creams, as a source of collagen. While the American alligators were finishing their official recovery in the wild, their Chinese counterparts were in severe decline. Surveys in 1985 and 1987 of the number of wild alligators in the National Chinese Alligator Reserve, estimated the population at roughly 735. This is the only protected area where Chinese alligators live in the wild and the only place where a viable breeding population had any possibility of being established. The population has been estimated to have declined by 90 percent from 1,000 individuals in 1979 to a mere 100 in 2003.

Although it's easy to blame hunting of alligators for medicine, skin, meat, or retaliation for their decline, development is more

Chinese Alligator (*Alligator sinensis*). (*U.S. Fish and Wildlife Service*)

to blame for the decrease in Chinese alligators. The growth of the Chinese population has created a sprawling web of rice paddies where once alligators lived in the wild. Along with the paddies, rivers were diverted and water flow changed to suit human desire. Demand for electricity and water has dammed rivers that once ran unencumbered. These obstacles not only decimated the Chinese alligator population but continue to make its recovery in the wild nearly impossible. Habitat destruction, not hunting, is the real threat to the Chinese alligator.

In America, decades of wanton killing of alligators led to a huge decline in populations. With fewer alligators, swamps were drained, houses built, crops irrigated. With conservation efforts in place, alligator populations grew, quickly filling in the protected lands and spilling into human spaces. Thus collisions between alligators and people are inevitable, usually ending in death for the reptiles.

Chinese alligators have little habitat to which to return. Because of years of official payments for Chinese alligator eggs to be raised in captivity, there are more alligators in captive breeding facilities

than in nature. This has created an impossible situation for reintroducing alligators in China and little political will to create large
areas of protected land for them in their native habitat.

With growing human populations, even the best conservation
efforts, like those to preserve the American alligator, will be tested.
If we want to live with alligators, we need to not be complacent
but instead actively embrace a wilder world.

seven

CAIMANS

CAIMANS ARE A SUBFAMILY (Camaininae) within the alligator family. Unlike their more northerly relatives, caimans are native only to the tropics of Mexico and Central and South America. My own first encounter with wild caimans was in Ecuador in college, but my interest started earlier.

In elementary school, I encountered a book (the title of which I don't remember) on tropical rainforests that sparked a fascination still burning in me today. I read about not only caimans but piranhas, jaguars, sloths, and monkeys. I stared in awe at photographs of a human infant floating suspended on the pad of a giant water lily and of the bright colors of a toucan's beak. I also learned that tropical rainforests were endangered—threatened by logging, mining, and poaching. Inspired by my reading, I set up an impromptu fundraising effort. With a card table at the edge of my family's yard in Gillette, Wyoming, I sat with a homemade sign saying something like, "Save the Rainforest." I collected money (although I doubt it was much), simply by asking passersby, and then sent the earnings to Rainforest Action Network (RAN), an activist group I still find inspiring. I continued to read more books about the tropics, some about tropical frogs, some about bats, and some about the ecology, but in many ways that first book was special as a catalyst.

Given my childhood interests, when I saw a flyer advertising a tropical field biology class in the hall of Mesa State College, where I was studying, I immediately emailed the professor. Shortly afterward I received a phone call.

The professor organizing the field biology course asked me over the phone where I lived. This seemed an odd question, but I told him the intersection where my basement apartment was located. Great, he told me, he wasn't too far away. Could I meet him at the crossroads so he could pick me up in his van and talk to me about the field course? I was determined to find myself studying a tropical rainforest in person and quickly agreed. So, I waited on the corner and the time for our meeting passed. The professor called me back twenty minutes later to apologize. He'd fallen asleep, but he told me but he could pick me up right now. I was game.

The man who pulled up in a Volkswagen camper van was in his late thirties with blonde hair falling below his shoulders and a happy, easygoing manner that made me trust him immediately. I climbed into the van and Dr. Walla introduced me to his children sitting on the bench seat in the back as we pulled away from the curb. He told me about the cost, time frame, and wonders of the trip. I knew I had to do whatever was necessary to participate. That fall, I took out student loans to pay my way to Ecuador and never looked back.

Ecuador is a field biologist's dream, a country the size of Colorado but with ecological diversity ranging from the stunning Galápagos Islands, where tortoises graze and iguanas dive for algae, to the snow-topped volcano of Chimborazo, 20,548 feet in elevation. Due to the bulge of the earth, Chimborazo is the point farthest from the earth's center, despite being shorter than several other peaks. Ecuador is like that, there's less Amazon in it than Peru but a greater diversity of landscapes. It's one of the world's biodiversity hotspots with less than 1 percent of earth's surface but about 5 percent of the reptile species, 8 percent of mammals, and

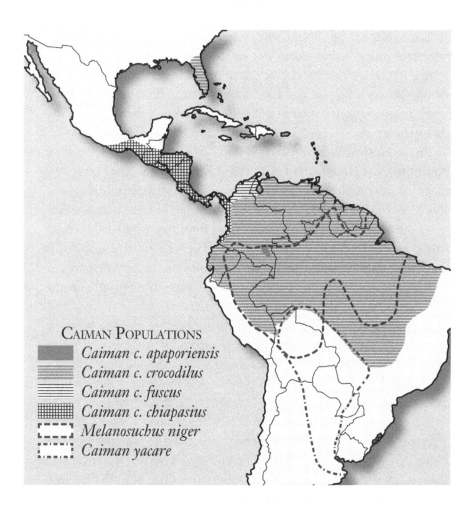

CAIMAN POPULATIONS
- *Caiman c. apaporiensis*
- *Caiman c. crocodilus*
- *Caiman c. fuscus*
- *Caiman c. chiapasius*
- *Melanosuchus niger*
- *Caiman yacare*

16 percent of birds, including 140 species of hummingbird. I landed in Quito with the rest of the class and checked into a hotel. I still remember standing on the balcony listening to a chorus of tropical frogs in the December night.

The next morning brought an unfortunate accident. I slipped in the hotel bathtub and struck my forehead hard on the edge. For a moment I felt woozy and thought I might black out. Instead I cleaned the blood from the split goose egg rising above my right eyebrow and tied a bandana over it. My professor looked at the wound, told me he should probably take me to the doctor, but it was my choice. I wanted to get to the lowland forest and wasn't going to miss the experience for the world, certainly not for a bruise on my head. By late morning I was boarding a small plane.

From the colonial capital of Quito, a bumpy, roller coaster ride by air (at least one student looked pretty green) landed our class in the modest oilfield town known as "El Coca." Until recently a community service provided by the oil companies that built "El Coca" was spraying dirt roads with crude oil to keep dust down. I've heard stories of happy children running after the trucks splattering the earth and their bodies with a fluid that eventually would bring cancer to many in the region. When I visited the town, it was still a slightly rough place on the knife's edge between an advancing tourism economy and a vast self-governing jungle crumbling into ruin in the face of human development.

We were now in a region of eastern Ecuador and the western Amazon, a place locals simply call *el oriente*. It was from here, at the confluence of the Rio Coca and the Rio Napo, that Spanish conquistador Francisco De Orellana is said to have set out by boat to eventually be one of the first Europeans to float down the entire Amazon River. At the end of the trip, Orellana and his men rebuilt a ship and sailed to Spain. Orellana's accounts first shaped western views of the rainforest, creating the image of female warriors and forever giving it the name "Amazon" from Greek myth and history. Orellana's often discounted stories of vast numbers of humans living in the region are gaining more and more traction as archaeologists find more corroborating evidence. It appears that an epidemic ravaged those living there not long after Orellana. By the time large numbers of Europeans visited the Amazon, indigenous populations had already been decimated. This new, dehumanized Amazon is the legacy of Western disease and promotes a myth of separate "wilderness" and human centers.

After landing in El Coca, a stop at the garden of the El Auca hotel allowed us to watch capuchin monkeys clamoring for the bananas growing from small trees. The more shy agoutis quietly sniffed, moving in their peculiar hopping manner in the grass below.

Leaving in an open-sided bus, we rode past trees with woven oropendola nests hanging like grass pendulums from branches. The air was fresh and full of the thrum of insects when we stopped at the banks of a muddy river thickly walled with vegetation. Huaoroni men with ear lobes drooping from gauge piercings held long fishing spears as they stood waiting for another bus while we boarded a motorized canoe.

As the boat took us downriver on the Rio Shiripuno, Dr. Walla talked excitedly about the forest, about how we were entering a region more remote than any in the lower forty-eight states of the U.S. The boat sped past miles of green jungle, broken only once by a traditionally Huaoroni village—a cluster of simple huts—which quickly disappeared again amidst vine-tangled trees. It felt like traveling through a massive museum diorama. As darkness fell, the stars glittered overhead and we smiled up at the southern cross—bright in an unpolluted sky. The canoe snagged once on tree limbs in the coffee-brown water and there was a tense moment before we pushed clear and rumbled downstream.

At the research station, I found my way upstairs and across an opening in the forest to a simple cabin lit by candles and a bed protected by an insect net. Once during my stay, I found a tarantula on the top of the net as I went to climb into bed. If I'd flipped the net down without first looking with my flashlight, the tarantula would've been flipped into bed with me. To me, seeing a tarantula, along with other wild animals, was a joy rather than a horror. The calming throb of life was everywhere in the night, I fell into reverie and then sleep hypnotized by the screams, screeches, and buzzes of insects, bats, frogs, night monkeys, and maybe caimans singing of sex and death and life.

Another night on the Shiripuno meant floating in a canoe with the motor off and a bright flashlight cutting across the water. All around us on the river's surface reflected eyes glowed like fiery balls. These were caimans, small crocodilians hunting the water at night. Seeing how their eyes shone with an orange glow in the beam, it would be easy to believe the Papua New Guineans, who think crocodile eyes glow with the light of ancestral ghosts.

Caimans are not quite "true" crocodiles, though, and are more closely related to alligators.

There are three extant genera of caiman and five species (many more species and genera are extinct). Black caimans (*Melanosuchus niger*) are the largest and most dangerous to humans, measuring at least sixteen feet and up to twenty. In *Land of Ghosts*, author David Campbell describes black caimans, locally known as *jacaré preta* on a river in the western Brazilian Amazon where he worked for years as a botanist: "An adult can grow to eight meters long and a meter wide—bigger than our canoes. It is one of the most formidable crocodilians on Earth, but individuals that size are rare now. The jacaré loves the snarled, closed vegetation of the váreza [flooded forest], especially fallen tree trunks, from which it can ambush its prey. Fiercely territorial on the nest, a mother black caiman can swim as fast as a torpedo and swamp a dugout canoe, swiping it with her tail, butting it with her head, or even crushing it in her jaws."

Another species, the Yacare caiman (*Caiman yacare*), is found mainly in the Pantanal, a seasonally flooded plains area located in southwestern Brazil and portions of Bolivia and Paraguay. There, as many as ten million caiman live crowded together in the largest population of a single crocodilian species anywhere in the world. *National Geographic* called the Yacare the "comeback croc" because of the incredible rebound from low populations caused by the slaughter of the skin trade. Caimans are truly tropical animals, sharing water with heavily armored catfish, strange frogs that make an alarm call disconcertingly similar to a baby's cry, bright stingrays colored like butterflies, and river dolphins. Caimans are caught in the tangle of biological interactions—eating and being eaten—of the tropical rainforest.

Brazilian researchers found that as many as 70 percent of caiman deaths in the dry season were due to jaguars hunting them for food. Another study found that jaguars only preyed on caimans in seasonally flooded habitats, where perhaps rising water levels brought the reptiles right to the cats' proverbial doorstep. In different places caimans of different species played varying roles in

Top: A Black caiman (*Melanosuchus niger*). (*David Stanley/Creative Commons*) Bottom: A Yacare caiman (*Caiman yacare*). (*Lea Maimone/Creative Commons*)

jaguar diet. The big cats are one of the few predators adult caimans have in the wild, besides anacondas and, of course, humans.

Eggs are another matter. Along with jaguars, beautifully striped black and yellow tegu lizards consume caiman eggs, and monkeys dig up the nests for a protein rich snack. A photo of a capuchin monkey *Cebus* (*spp.*) digging with a stick was even captured by a camera monitoring a caiman nest. Humans have long indulged in occasionally raiding caiman nests of eggs as well, although crocodilian eggs are said to taste unappetizingly fishy.

Being both predator and prey makes caimans important players in the middle of the intricate and diverse ecosystems they live in. Even in Puerto Rico, where they're not native, some suggest that caimans play a valuable role as an early indicator of water pollutants.

Very young caimans, like juvenile American alligators, have black and golden striped skin, patterned not unlike that of a tiger. With tigers, although such skins appear vibrant in the starkness of the zoo, they blend with the verdant jungle when the cats seek prey among the trees. Caimans' pattern allows the reptiles to lay unnoticed by hunters in the dripping pools of swamp and marsh.

Some hungry beasts can still see through camouflage. Swarms of native fire ants (*Solenopsis spp.*) colonize nests of Yacare caiman and Morelet's crocodiles (*Crocodylus moreletii*) in Central and South America. As the crocodilian nests hatch, the ants attack, killing and consuming the weakest of the young caimans, like a scene from some pulp adventure novel. Sometimes almost the entire clutch of crocodilian babies is killed and eaten by the hungry ants. As these ants have moved into North America following warming climates, the same attacks have been observed on American alligators and American crocodiles in Florida.

In some cases, ants may not be all bad. A painful ant sting on the paw may keep a hungry capuchin monkey away, allowing caimans at least the chance of scrambling to the water in a mad dash to escape burning insect bites. Some biologists have interpreted fire ants this way—as risky and sometimes costly but overall beneficial to crocodilian nests—but the jury is still out on the dynamic details between the two animals.

There are myriad other weird, interesting affinities between caiman and different species. Carlos de la Rosa, an aquatic ecologist from Venezuela now working in Costa Rica, told me how butterflies sometimes land on the faces of caimans and turtles sunning themselves, to taste their tears. De la Rosa told me in an email,

Lachryphagous insects have found yet another source of salts and nutrients in the eyes of reptiles such as caimans and river turtles, and also mammals and birds, and even in humans! Tears are produced by animals as lubrication for the eyes . . . the butterflies that visit caiman's and turtle eyes to imbibe their tears use the minerals in the production of their spermatophores (structures that carry the sperm of males).

A spectacled caiman (*Caiman crocodilus*) basking as a butterfly and bee take advantage by drinking the animal's tears (lachryphagia) in Costa Rica. (© *Carlos L. de la Rosa, used with permission*)

What fascinates me the most is how these serendipitous events, such as a butterfly finding a new source of minerals, evolve and become innate behaviors for species. . . . I was on a small boat with my research assistant and colleague, Socorro Avila, collecting chironomids [flies similar in appearance to mosquitos] in the Puerto Viejo River . . . I noticed that a caiman sunning on a log had several . . . butterflies and bees . . . hovering around its head . . . I was able to get very close. I was surprised to see the solitary bee also approaching the caiman and drinking its tears. . . . Butterflies drink from turtles but while the caimans are usually very passive about the whole affair, turtles do get bothered by it and often shoo the butterflies away as they land on their heads. . . . Some of these butterflies irritate the eyes so they produce more tears. It must not hurt the caimans, since they let them do it, as opposed to turtles that are reluctant to allow them. Nevertheless, both turtles and caimans need to sun in order to warm up . . . so they have to put up with the butterflies in order to carry on with their physiological needs. . . . Butter-flies drinking tears from the eyes of caimans is one of those fantastic, curious, extraordinary, and even weird things we find in nature, tidbits that fascinate us and make us curious about what else is there.

Caimans are fascinating in their own right but impossible to truly see when separated from their tropical homes. Like many other crocodilians, the largest threat to many caimans is habitat destruction, things like deforestation and hydroelectric dam construction.

Being a group of different species and even different genera makes generalizations about caimans somewhat problematic, but caimans do have some similarities when compared to other groups.

As my nighttime encounter testifies, caimans, like alligators, are mostly nocturnal, I was only in Ecuador's lowlands for a short time and never saw a caiman during the day. The glowing eyes seen on a river at night show that caimans have good night vision, just like the glowing eyes of a dog or cat caught in a headlamp—both animals with better night vision than humans.

Caimans have another unique adaptation—the ability to live in large populations. Most crocodilians are not so tolerant of being so close to each other and spread out in the wild. Perhaps living in larger densities has allowed caimans a survival advantage; it also makes them easier to keep in captivity than many crocodilians. The tropics of South and Central America have an abundance of caimans—six extant species, none of which is listed as endangered. The story of caimans doesn't end in their native land though.

I remember seeing young caimans for sale in a pet store in Wyoming and desperately wanting one as a child—a desire that was never fulfilled but has since abated. Regardless of my parents' doubt and disapproval, I thought I could keep one, perhaps in a kiddie pool in the garage, before realizing later in life that this would be unfair to the caiman and possibly dangerous to me. Caimans are incredibly fast and have strong bites. Despite this, people continue to buy them as pets.

A Spectacled caiman (*Caiman crocodilus*) caught in a lasso, similar to how some Puerto Rican's capture (non-native) caimans. (*Carlos ZGZ/Creative Commons*)

After it was made illegal to have pet crocodiles in the United States in the early 1950s, caimans began to be imported for hobbyists from their homes in the tropics from Mexico to Argentina. In the 1960s and 1970s a pet caiman could be purchased cheaply at stores like Woolworth's at a life stage when the animal was still lizard-sized and deceptively harmless.

The smallest caiman species, Cuvier's dwarf caiman (*Paleosuchus palpebrosus*), reaches only approximately four to five feet in length as adults, with a maximum weight of about fifteen pounds. The spectacled caiman (*Caiman crocodilus*), also sometimes kept as a pet, usually only reaches a length of six feet. It's clear why someone would choose a pet caiman over an eight-foot-long alligator. However, caimans are still not exactly small pets, and dangerous enough to be challenging companions to say the least.

Caimans quickly associate a person arriving at the edge of their enclosure with food and are quick to jump for a bite at meal time. Sometimes a feeding hand gets caught in the reptile's sharp teeth.

Many people bitten by their cold-blooded pet or scared of their increasing size decide to turn the animal loose in whatever body of water happens to be nearby, leading to caimans living outside their native range.

Spectacled caimans were first introduced to Puerto Rico over fifty years ago, making Tortuguero Lagoon Natural Reserve the center of a new caiman population. Today the crocodilians have established a healthy breeding population and are top predators in the area—juveniles eating insects and other small prey, adults feeding mainly on fishes.

According to the *Seattle Times*, caimans have become part of normal daily life in parts of Puerto Rico. Some neighborhoods are filled with amateur caiman hunters, who routinely use horses as transportation and lasso caimans just as easily as they catch crabs for food. A local school assigns chaperones to walk children to the bathroom after heavy rains, as they try to raise the money to build a concrete wall around the grounds to keep crocodilians at bay. There is even a bizarre story of Puerto Rican drug gangs purportedly feeding the bodies of murder victims to pet caimans apparently kept for the task.

Outside Puerto Rico, caimans have shown up in rivers flowing through the Arizona desert, school ponds in chilly Michigan, and—much more to their liking—Everglades National Park, where the young are easy to mistake for alligators.

Spectacled caimans are thought to have the largest range of any new world crocodilian, being widely distributed across South and Central America. Now they've become distributed outside of that range in and out of captivity. The spread is caused by an irresponsible pet industry and ignorant caiman buyers. In the end, the caimans must go somewhere when the owner can no longer care for them. For the lucky ones, this means a sanctuary.

Phoenix Herpetological Sanctuary is a large complex of outdoor pens and buildings stocked full of cages and aquariums on the edge of the desert near Phoenix, Arizona. Turning from asphalt, a short dirt road leads to the complex. Driving in feels more like an approach to a house in a nice rural neighborhood than to a reptile rescue facility. My wife Erin and I arrived at the sanctuary and, after signing waivers on an iPad, a large young man led us through a maze of walkways past caged animals basking next to pools of water.

We entered a trailer full of the hot humidity of simulated tropics and the smell of snakes. Inside, was an open room, a large table and a scattering of cages around the periphery. Erin needed to use the bathroom, so I wandered down a hallway lined on both sides with glass fronted cages stacked three high. The young volunteer who led us to the building told me of a man who wore a pet rattlesnake around his neck at a party. The snake ended up biting him. The man thought he'd sleep off the snake bite by the next morning and be ok; instead, his throat swelled shut and he died. His snake found a new home at the sanctuary. Three spectacled cobras joined the sanctuary's numbers when the police raided a house producing methamphetamines; apparently some drug dealers like the idea of dangerous pets. As Erin came out of the bathroom, I walked out of the hall and noticed a baby alligator, still with prominent yellow stripes, sitting on a gravel bar in an aquarium next to a pool made into a stream by a pump.

Later, we were led back to the entrance for only a short wait in a group of ten to twelve people before our tour of the facility began. A couple stood by their daughter in a stroller, and one man wore a black t-shirt with an image of a kitten pawing at an assault rifle with the legend "arm the animals."

The man who guided the tour was in his fifties or sixties, short graying hair, wearing a long-sleeved shirt pushed up to reveal a tattoo of a scorpion on one forearm and one on the other reading, "We the people . . . " in calligraphic font. He picked up some small tortoises, flipping them over to show the bottoms of the shells, roughly tapping on the carapace. I flinched, remembering the gentle, sensitive nature of a box turtle I once had. The tour guide told us the small Russian tortoises are actually native to southern reaches of the former Soviet Union, roughly the same latitude as southern Arizona, not Russia itself. The guide explained to us the nutritional needs of many tortoises that arrive at the sanctuary, comparing the problem to a child kept in a closet for a year and fed little but junk food. Without vitamin D from the sun or proper nutrition, the tortoises sometimes develop abnormal shells; one such tortoise has cables glued to the shell, hopefully to build a flattened shell into a normal, healthy one.

Next we watched Aldabra tortoises and Galapagos tortoises munch in slow contemplation and watch us with big, dark eyes. "Look, she's so beautiful!" Erin whispered to me and I looked over the low wall and found a tortoise very close with soulful chelonian eyes locked on me; she *was* beautiful. The guide's message about the Galapagos tortoise was more stark than beautiful. Of the quarter million individual tortoises alive when Darwin arrived; decimation by whaling ships has dropped the number to 17,000 today, still higher now than the lowest point decades earlier. Many of the Phoenix sanctuary's turtles were acquired, via veritable mountains of paperwork, from a sanctuary that closed in Florida.

The guide explained how there are now more Aldabra tortoises in captivity, many kept as pets, than in the wild. As we started to move away from the enclosure, a woman asked the guide whether it was a good thing for the tortoises to be kept as pets. He sighed, and after a second told her that it's a tricky situation. Being kept as pets would indeed help the species survive, but it's also sad to think of them separated from the wild.

Erin interjected, "It's complicated."

"Yes, it's complicated." He nodded and led us along to the next tortoise enclosure.

We watched sulcata tortoises mounting each other amidst a quiet but persistent chorus of grunts from the surrounding tortoise crowd. We reentered the building full of venomous snakes and I looked harder at the animals behind the glass, thinking of Darwin peering at a venomous snake in a zoo. Erin excitedly pointed to a delicate sidewinder in the bottom cage. I noticed green and black mambas, snakes I feared encountering during my time in Equatorial Guinea. The guide explained that the black mambas are so named not from the color of their bodies but from the color of their inner mouths. The guide took a veiled chameleon from a mesh-sided cage near the door to climb his arm and explained how they're extremely hard to take care of—not good pets, a refrain I heard repeatedly during our tour.

Stepping outside again, we walked down a concrete path, threaded at ninety degree angles between a maze of chain link enclosures. This was where the crocodilians are kept. The sanctuary, I was told, has all species of crocodilians except for the Indian gharial and the mugger crocodile. Alligators are illegal to keep as pets in Arizona and our guide told us that one animal will land you a fine; two will mean a short stint in prison.

A pair of small American alligators basked next to a pool in an enclosure with eleven spectacled caimans. Our guide pointed out the caiman's distinctive eye crests, which also give them the name "spectacled." Some of the animals were missing tips of their tails, or digits, old battle wounds. Our guide told us that they received these caimans from a facility in Canada. Before arriving in Arizona, none of the caimans had ever been outside. A depressing thought.

Near the caimans and alligators, we stopped by an enclosure where two Cuban crocodiles basked, facing in opposite directions with their mouths agape. We're told that the two are male and female, but it's thought that the male is too young to produce viable sperm. In any case, the sanctuary is in contact with the government of Cuba, which is interested in reintroducing any viable young that may eventually come from the pair. We passed an enclosure of broad-snouted caiman and stood in front of a pen with two alligators.

Inside a bald man cleaned the pool where the two gators soaked, heads raised and mouths open. They hissed at the pool net as it passed over them. The man was Russ, founder of the sanctuary, who smiled at us while cleaning, occasionally interjecting a comment on the guide's monologue. Behind us an enclosure held a false gharial laying in a pool quietly, calmly, watching with a strange needle-snouted face. Next to the false gharial was an American crocodile.

We were shown the Orinoco crocodile of the famed Venezuelan jungles, sitting in a largely barren pen. Yeti, an enormous American crocodile, was basking against the fence, and Russ cautioned the tour guide to be careful what he said, because Yeti's "sensitive about his weight." He continued his rounds, cleaning out the pool in Yeti's enclosure. Behind us female black caimans basked in their own enclosure.

We made our way to "murderer's row," which we were told is only a half-joke; indeed, these are some of the most dangerous reptiles at the sanctuary. The guide explained to us how he tells his wife, if he's bitten by a snake, there's treatment, but if he's eaten by a saltwater crocodile, he's done. He told us that there's a video of a mother Nile crocodile attacking a bull elephant to chase the pachyderm away from her nest. The enclosures here are the largest to accommodate the bigger crocodilians, and we're shaded by a walkway overhead. The guide joked that he tells people if the fall from the walkway doesn't kill you, the crocodiles will finish the job.

We passed by an enclosure of Yacare caiman, and Erin giggled and pointed at one looking goofy with only one eye open. We walked past a pen with a pair of West African slender-snouted crocodiles and then we entered another building, leaving the crocodilians behind.

We watched as the guide opened a large glass enclosure with Asian water monitors. One of the massive lizards climbed the guide's arm and lay a scaled head on his shoulder, reminding me forcefully of the three-year-old mixed breed dog we have at home.

I'm excited to see a Dumeril's boa in a cage, reminding me of holding a wild boa at the research station in Madagascar where Erin and I met. We saw coiled anacondas and we are told it's virtually impossible for a snake to swallow an adult human. Soon we stepped back outside.

Chickens pecked around the building as they do everywhere at the sanctuary, and now at the end of the tour, this avian reptile is finally addressed. Chickens, we were told, eat scorpions, which actually pose a threat to crocodilians that may try to eat them. They're also an educational tool, something to show to people wanting to see a "real" dinosaur.

At the end of the tour I smiled at the chickens clucking around, crowing, chasing scorpions and undoubtedly many other creatures for food. It occurred to me later that the chickens are actually the most free-ranging animals at the sanctuary.

After our tour was over I picked out a baseball cap with an alligator on it from the gift shop. Erin found a piece of jewelry she liked. We wandered around the small shop as a woman carried in two boxes with ball pythons inside. These were animals she was giving to the sanctuary. A few polite questions about feeding habits and temperament were asked. The woman paid a fee and the snakes became part of the sanctuary. Ball pythons are easy to take care of compared to many of the reptiles found at the sanctuary. Measuring only four to five feet and living for about thirty years, the serpents don't compare to the tortoises weighing hundreds of pounds and living over a hundred years. The snakes were carried away, the counter cleared. We paid for our purchases and left.

Erin and I ate a lunch of fry bread topped with tomato, onion, and beans at a nearby restaurant, sitting outside in the warm January sun of southern Arizona. We talked about what we saw at the sanctuary, how exciting it was to see this or that creature. One thing we said little about is one thing I know we both agree on—the sanctuary was doing good, even necessary work, but it'd be better if it didn't exist.

If many people can't take care of even small pythons eating a diet of frozen mice, what chance do caimans have? No person can possibly make up for the wild forest rivers and lakes that these creatures call home. I thought of how the whole diversity of the Amazon jungle can be reduced to a large reptile in a concrete pen through the avarice and ignorance of humans.

eight

CROCODILES

THERE'S ONLY ONE PLACE IN THE WORLD where crocodiles and alligators both live—southern Florida. This biogeographic anomaly has given rise to the age-old question of tourists in the Sunshine State, *how to tell an alligator from a American crocodile?* It's easier than many think.

The most obvious difference between the anatomy of the two is their heads. American alligators have rounded snouts, where crocodiles' are more angular and pointed. The closed mouth of a crocodile is toothier than that of the alligator as well. When an alligator's mouth is closed, only some of the teeth from the upper jaw are exposed, pointing downward. The lower teeth fit into the larger upper jaw, hidden from view when the mouth is closed. When a crocodile's mouth is closed, however, teeth pointing both up and down from both jaws are exposed. Further, American alligators typically have darker skin than American crocodiles and the crocodile's feet are more webbed. These are little differences. The biggest dissimilarity between the two animals is in their habitat.

American crocodiles have a functional salt excretion gland in the mouth that alligators lack. It's true that I saw an alligator swimming in the ocean, but this is a temporary and somewhat rare event. American crocodiles (and some other species) spend long periods in the ocean, which is why in the Everglades, I looked for them in Florida Bay. I had only a little luck, but crocodiles have made the most of the ocean.

With their adaptation to salt water, crocodiles have spread by sea across enormous areas. American crocodiles inhabit the Caribbean, as well as the Florida Keys, small islands like Cozumel off Mexico's Yucatán Peninsula, Central America, and into northern South America.

In Asia and the Pacific, other crocodiles have been able to move from the mainland to populate Papua New Guinea and Australia. Crocodiles live throughout much of Africa as well as Madagascar. In spreading through the warmer parts of the globe, crocodiles have diversified into thirteen (some say fourteen) species worldwide.

Crocodiles make up the family Crocodylidae, which also includes the subfamily Tomistominae, holding only one species, the lonely "false" gharial (*Tomistoma schlegelii*). There is now some evidence, however, suggesting that the "false" gharial should be included in the family Gavialidae along with "true" gharials.

"True" crocodiles, animals of the subfamily Crocodylinae, are probably the first crocodilians humans encountered, before we even left Africa. They're some of the most widely represented, celebrated, and villainized in human culture. Movies like *Crocodile Dundee* and the late Steve Irwin's show, *Crocodile Hunter*, have ensconced the saltwater crocodile (*Crocodylus porosus*) of Australia, Southeast Asia, and Oceania, specifically, in our collective pop culture. Many popular portrayals of crocodiles make the animals into little more than props illustrating a human's rugged strength. Indeed, saltwater crocodiles are impressive, and impressively dangerous animals, but their threat to humans is also grossly exaggerated. International Union for Conservation of Nature (IUCN) data shows that from 2000 to 2007, there was an average rate of 3.6 attacks on humans per year in Australia. (The IUCN, the United Nations's main biological conservation arm, maintains a catalogue of the conservation status of species.)

Australia's less well-known crocodile, the Johnstone's crocodile (*Crocodylus johnstoni*), is even less dangerous to people, eating mainly fishes, frogs, crustaceans, small mammals, and birds. It's also a more freshwater species than its larger "saltie" cousin, with rarer estuarine populations.

My own encounters with wild crocodiles in Nepal were also quite peaceful—at first. In Bardia National Park, while out looking for gharials, I sometimes settled for watching their more bountiful reptilian relative, the mugger crocodile (*Crocodylus palustris*). I have an image in my mind of a mugger, probably about five feet long, lying on a gravel bank, as still as an exquisitely carved statue, the dark body reflected into the quiet stream nearby. I saw what seemed to be the same crocodile lying in the same spot more than once on different days. The passive beauty of the creature I observed belies their potential for violence. Watching from a bridge at another time, I saw a large mugger quickly lunge at a smaller crocodile, grabbing the tail in his mouth. In spasms of pain, the smaller crocodile bent back toward the attacker with mouth agape, trying in vain to defend. Soon enough the larger animal released, leaving the smaller to splash quickly away. In a minute or two, the scene was as peaceful and still as it had been before. Mugger crocodiles, like their Australian cousins, do sometimes attack people. Neither is as deadly as the Nile crocodile (*Crocodylus niloticus*).

A Nile crocodile ended the life of South African outdoorsman and author Johannes Hendrik Coetzee while he was kayaking in 2010. Coetzee, a former South African army medic, was experienced on the water and had many previous encounters with crocodiles. In 2004 he led a kayaking expedition from the source of the Nile River at Lake Victoria to the Mediterranean Sea. Coetzee also completed daring first solo trips through Uganda's Murchison Falls National Park. Murchison Falls has some of the world's highest concentrations of hippopotamus and crocodiles. Alone on one trip, he even threw his helmet as a decoy to distract a quickly approaching crocodile.

Leading two Americans on a kayak expedition on the Lukuga River in the Democratic Republic of the Congo (DRC), Coetzee

Mugger crocodile (*Crocodylus palustris*) basking on stream bank, Bardia National Park, Nepal. (*Author*)

didn't initially consider wildlife in the area a primary concern. Crocodiles are often thought of as most dangerous in protected areas, where they have little to fear from people with weapons. The Lukuga wasn't protected, but violence in the area led to bodies dumped into the river, presenting the crocodiles with an abundant source of human flesh for food. Possibly because of this, a large crocodile approached Coetzee while he was slightly behind the other two kayakers, rising quickly from deep water. After the crocodile grabbed his shoulder, Coetzee's last words were "Oh my God," before being pulled under, leaving his kayak bobbing empty on the surface. The two American men paddled hard, scared for their lives. At the next village, the two men asked through sign language and broken French to use a motor boat to go upstream to search for their friend's body. They were told the villagers had given up on boat travel after too many of them were killed by crocodiles. Many Africans going about their daily lives come into conflict with Nile crocodiles every year.

An adult Nile crocodile can take prey as large as the famed wildebeest (*Connochaetes sp.*) and even the massive Cape buffalo (*Syncerus caffer*), so a human would pose little problem. Indeed, conflicts with most crocodiles all over the world have increased as the human population swells and protected habitat shrinks.

Even with a long history of clashes with humans and our live-stock, crocodiles still manage to cohabitate with us in relatively large numbers. Nile crocodiles are widely distributed throughout sub-Saharan Africa; the IUCN estimates their populations at a stable 50,000 to 70,000. Some countries within the Nile croco-dile's range have started to classify the conservation status of their populations separately. Many threats to Nile crocodiles are pres-ent on local levels, such as villagers hunting the animals, rather than on national or continental scales. Most people first consider the threat of Nile crocodiles to them rather than the other way around. Despite the optics of an enormous reptile eating a human, we are by far a greater threat to not only Nile crocodiles but all crocodiles.

Africa is home to several other species of crocodile: the sacred crocodile, the slender-snouted crocodile, the West African slen-der-snouted crocodile, and the African dwarf crocodile. For a long time science recognized only three species. but genetic analysis identified the sacred crocodile as a distinct species from the Nile crocodile, and the west slender-snouted crocodile as distinct from the slender-snouted crocodile.

Once thought to be part of the genus *Crocodylus*, the slender-snouted crocodile (*M. leptorhynchus*) and West African slender-snouted crocodile (*M. cataphractus*) now make up the genus *Mecistops*, which is possibly basal to the family Crocodylidae, meaning it could represent the ancestral form of crocodiles.

Recently a new species, Hall's New Guinea crocodile (*Crocodylus halli*), was split from the New Guinea crocodile (*Crocodylus no-vaeguineae*) as well. In the 1980s, Philip Hall, a scientist with the University of Florida, noticed behavioral differences in mating and nesting between crocodiles on the northern and southern parts of New Guinea. It wasn't until after his death that other scientists

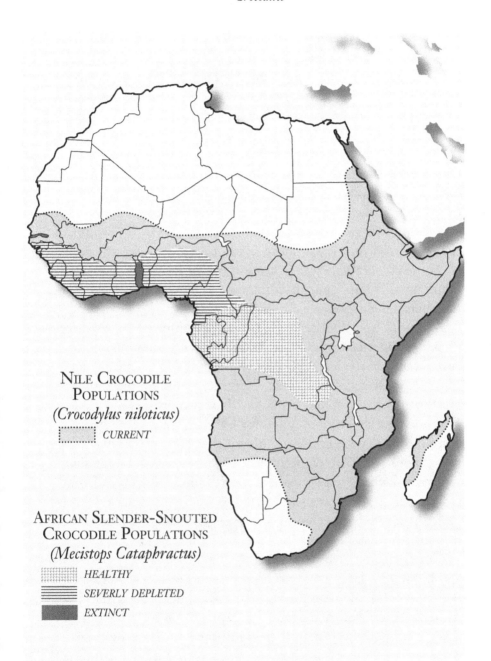

NILE CROCODILE
POPULATIONS
(*Crocodylus niloticus*)
   CURRENT

AFRICAN SLENDER-SNOUTED
CROCODILE POPULATIONS
(*Mecistops Cataphractus*)
   HEALTHY
   SEVERLY DEPLETED
   EXTINCT

completed his work, looking at skulls of museum specimens to realize what Hall suspected, that there were two crocodile species endemic to New Guinea. Such quickly changing taxonomy makes greater demands on conservation. Two distinct species with a smaller population means each is more vulnerable than one species with a larger population. The New Guinea crocodile was listed on the IUCN Red List as a species of "least concern," showing little threat to its survival. Now it seems a closer look will need to be taken at both kinds of crocodile to determine the conservation status of each, if the new species classification isn't contested. Either way, it shows how vulnerable crocodiles can be to the whims of changing science or even public opinion.

These vulnerabilities are a product of the modern world. Crocodiles now live in a human-dominated planet, where more often than being their food, we are their aggressors.

At Punta Sur Eco Beach Park on Cozumel Island, Mexico, there are American crocodiles. As a teenager, I found myself on a family vacation to Cozumel, a name which in Mayan means something like "Island of swallows." Cozumel is a small piece of land off the Yucatán replete with small Mayan ruins, an ancient Catholic church, and not much for beaches but an abundance of surrounding marine life. We came for the renowned scuba diving to be found in the Mesoamerican Reef, but we also did some sightseeing on land. There's a lighthouse at Punta Sur you can climb to look out over the ocean and wetlands where the American crocodiles live. I remember seeing the large reptiles shrunk to the size of lizards by distance.

Not far from Cozumel is Banco Chinchorro, a protected atoll and home to a large concentration of American crocodiles. The only people who inhabit the atoll are park rangers and fishermen, who lived there before the atoll was protected as a marine reserve. The fishermen dwell mainly in traditional stilt houses over the water, where they clean their catch, throwing guts into the sea below, attracting crocodiles. This agreeable arrangement for crocodiles and fishermen evolved into something else over time—a tourism enterprise. Today a tourist can pay to go snorkeling with

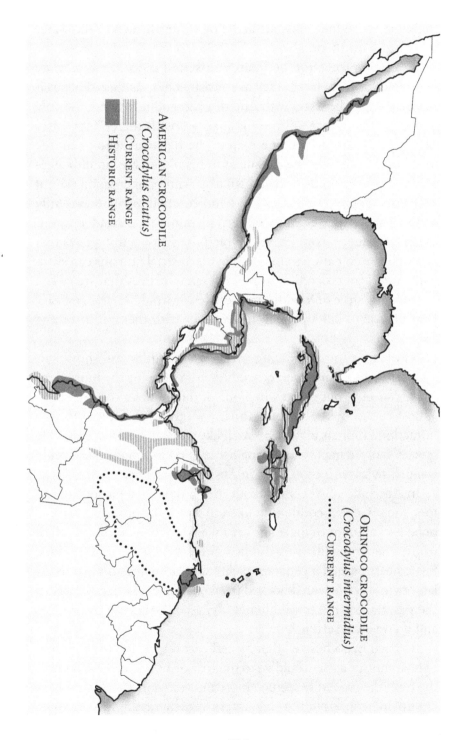

AMERICAN CROCODILE
(*Crocodylus acutus*)
CURRENT RANGE
HISTORIC RANGE

ORINOCO CROCODILE
(*Crocodylus intermidius*)
CURRENT RANGE

the same crocodiles, now attracted by chum thrown in the water specifically for them.

The only protection between tourist and crocodile is a safety diver in the ocean and guides in a nearby boat. As incredible as it seems to enter the water with American crocodiles, it's not the only example of someone swimming unarmed with them. Years after my visit to Cozumel I met a man in the Bahamas who once free dived with crocodiles near Cuba. On his phone was an unbelievable video—the fluidly moving tail of a swimming crocodile swept past the camera, and the man's hand reached out and carefully gripped it, letting the crocodile pull him deeper under water. Without video, I would have doubted the story, but it shows that crocodiles aren't always violent. That terrestrial humans can swim with American crocodiles in relative safety proves that we're not much of a source of food for the reptiles. It would seem to be easy for the croc to kill a person in the water with them, if it wanted to.

Snorkeling and free diving with any crocodiles also shows our own arrogance. American crocodiles aren't one of the more dangerous species, but if and when one of them bites a tourist, it will almost certainly be the animal that pays the higher price for the infraction. Tourists in Mexico are lucky in dealing with a crocodile species evolved mainly for eating fishes. No knowing person would want to swim with crocodiles in Australia or Africa.

In Australia's Sweets Lookout, there once lived a seventeen-foot-long male crocodile who liked to attack the outboard motors of boats. In honor of his home's name and perhaps with a touch of irony, the crocodile was dubbed Sweetheart. Over the years, Sweetheart earned a reputation that belied his friendly name. At least twice people were knocked from boats as Sweetheart attacked their crafts, but the crocodile never chased the people themselves and no one was seriously hurt.

It's been hypothesized that Sweetheart responded to the sound of boat motors as he would've to the roar of a rival male. Whatever the case, the crocodile seemed more interested in attacking watercraft than people, but the encounters were increasingly worrisome to authorities. On July 19, 1979, the Australian Parks and Wildlife Commission and Northern Territory trapped Sweetheart. The crocodile was anesthetized with the idea of relocating him to a more remote location where encounters with motorboats were less common. As Sweetheart was being hauled to shore, he became tangled with a submerged log and drowned, thus ending the life of one of Australia's most infamous crocodiles. Today Sweetheart's remains, preserved through taxidermy, can be found in collections at the Museum and Art Gallery of the Northern Territory. In his stomach were the remains of a pig, two turtles and a fish. No human remains.

The Orinoco crocodile (*Crocodylus intermedius*) is critically endangered, indeed, it's one of the most endangered crocodilian species in the world. Found only in freshwater environments of Venezuela and Colombia, primarily the Orinoco River system, the crocodile has a relatively small range. In this limited area, crocodiles inhabited a wide variety of habitats from tropical evergreen forests to foothill streams and lakes. The crocodiles share the river with caimans, anacondas, river dolphins, giant otters, and more than a thousand species of fish. Mainly the crocodiles could be found in lowland Llanos savannas. During the dry season of January and February, the female crocodiles bury clutches of thirty- or forty-some eggs in holes dug in sandy river banks. When the waters rise at the beginning of the rainy season, the baby crocodiles emerge from their eggs.

The Orinoco River, despite occupying a small piece of the world, is not a small river. By water volume discharge, the Orinoco is the fourth largest river in the world. Flowing 1,700 miles from the Guiana Highlands to the Atlantic, it's the northernmost of South America's major river systems and extensively used for transportation. Unlike many large rivers, the Orinoco system is mainly intact. As roads bring hunters into many parts of the world, large rivers bring hunters into the interior of South America's rainforests. During the dry season, the crocodiles become concentrated in remaining pools as the rivers dry up. Condensed into large numbers in small bodies of water, crocodile populations become vulnerable to devastation by hunters hungry for profit. Starting at the end of the 1920s, commercial hunting decimated Orinoco crocodile populations by the 1960s. In 1974 and 1976 surveys of Colombian habitat found evidence of only 280 adults in the areas that once held the highest population densities. Surveys in 1994 through 1995 showed a worsening situation. Surveys from 1999 through 2001 suggested that populations of adults had fallen below 60 in the region, regardless of official protection being granted in Colombia in 1997. Despite the downward spiral of the Orinoco crocodile, there is still much natural beauty in the area and some hopeful signs of a possible recovery. This is due in large part to the dedicated efforts of conservation biologists in the region.

Rafael Moreno-Arias is a Colombian biologist who was inspired by an undergraduate course in the Amazon rainforest, where his interest in crocodiles and other reptiles was kindled. In graduate school he focused on population dynamics, which drew the attention of Dr. Maria Cristina Ardila, then director of Estación de Biologia Tropical Roberto Franco of Universidad Nacional de Colombia, a facility founded for the reintroduction of Orinoco crocodiles. At Roberto Franco, Moreno-Arias worked with a team of scientists to reintroduce the imperiled crocodile in Colombia.

Moreno-Arias described a challenging and beautiful place to work in the Colombian Orinoco region, where a decade ago paramilitary groups and guerrillas were fighting for control. Suspicious of biological equipment such as GPS or radio transmitters, the combatants often interrogated the biologists. Once on a nighttime survey of a lake, the government bombed a nearby rebel group. Moreno-Arias told me by email of the region referred to in Colombia as the llanos, saying it's a joy to work there. "A savannah landscape with very small and perfectly shaped hills, where you can see easily cool animals such as the cougar or the giant anteater. Rivers are another world and there are three types: transparent water rivers coming from savannahs, black water rivers coming from forests and, white water ones coming from the Andes. All of the 'Llanos' rivers are surrounded by gallery forests."

Orinoco Crocodiles (*Crocodylus intermedius*) in Villavicencio, Colombia. (*Creative Commons*)

Today the Colombian government is focused on making peace deals with rebel groups and it's easier for biologists or tourists to get to the region. This sort of easy access is a double-edged sword: it also allows in more poachers, loggers, and commercial fishing concerns.

When the region became easier for biologists to work in, Moreno-Arias and his team were surprised by the abundance of white and dwarf caimans but the less than encouraging populations of Orinoco crocodiles. Due to the decline of the reptiles, a reintroduction program was started.

In a scientific paper published in 2020, Moreno-Arias and his colleague María Cristina Ardila Robayo describe the results of observing four Orinoco crocodiles released in 2015 and outfitted with satellite transmitters. The movements of the animals were monitored until 2018. Detailed data collected from such research makes the success of future releases more likely. The adult crocodiles were found to have large home ranges of 16 to 55 square kilometers, the males having the larger ranges. In the rainy season the males tended to travel, exploring greater areas, while the females stayed closer to one spot.

Numbers like these give the bare parameters needed for Orinoco crocodiles, South America's largest predator species, to survive. It will take some level of dedication in Venezuela as well as Colombia for the crocodiles to live as they once did. Not only space but tolerance are needed. The biologists for their part are optimistic, as evidenced by the name of their paper, "Journeying to Freedom: The Spatial Ecology of a Reintroduced Population of Orinoco Crocodiles (*Crocodylus intermedius*)."

Across the border in Venezuela, the same crocodile has a similar journey to make. As in Colombia, the transition from local groups hunting the Orinoco crocodile for food or religious purposes to hunting for the skin trade pushed by global economics devastated the population. Also similar to Colombia, Venezuelan attempts to protect and restore the species are hampered by a dysfunctional federal government. The Venezuelan conservation program for the Orinoco crocodile began in 1990 and centers on captive breeding programs at five breeding centers. Over the last thirty years, the program has released 10,699 crocodiles at fifteen locations. Unfortunately, oftentimes the impact of these reintroductions on the population of crocodiles hasn't been assessed. A survey carried out in 2020 found 260 crocodiles spread over fourteen different locations. Dr. Alvaro Velasco, who headed up the survey, told me in an email that this represents four new wild populations of Orinoco crocodile. Although he sees this as a success, he also told me that people still hunt the crocodiles out of fear and eggs are collected as food. The main obstacle for greater reintroductions is lack of money.

Velasco told me he's planning on surveying another location in 2021—the Arauca River, which forms the border of Venezuela and Colombia. Although there is officially no cooperation between the two nations, work has been carried out cooperatively there before, and Velasco hopes to survey the Colombian side of the river.

Just as the population of the Orinoco crocodile seems to be rebounding and conservation efforts bearing fruit, other crocodiles have even further to go. The Philippine crocodile (*Crocodylus mindorensis*) is the most critically endangered crocodile in the world, with less than a hundred adults in the wild. Some of the last remaining populations can be found in the northern Sierra Madre Mountains.

The Kalinga, an indigenous people of the Sierra Madre region of the Philippines, traditionally consider the crocodiles their ancestors. Traditional healers are said to have the power to control the reptiles or even turn into a crocodile during a trance. Other peoples in the Philippines have different traditional views of the crocodile. Dutch biologist Merlijn van Weerd told me in an email that the traditional beliefs seem to share elements of fear and reverence for crocodiles and a general attitude allowing humans and crocodiles to coexist: "Without discarding the fact that crocodiles are potentially dangerous, there is a common paradigm that if you do not harm a crocodile, the crocodile will not harm you and there is acceptance of crocodiles in the environment, even in areas shared with people."

This attitude has degraded throughout time with views brought from Spain with colonization; to the Spanish, crocodiles were simply monsters to be killed at first sight. Hunting and thoughtless killing shrank the population, making encounters with crocodiles less common. With fewer crocodiles and the influence of exploitation and media from America, traditional beliefs continue to diminish to this day, replaced by western views of crocodiles. The decline in traditional culture is linked to the decline in the numbers of Philippine crocodiles.

When van Weerd arrived in the Philippines in 1999, he had been trained as an ecologist, with some field experience in Cameroon and Mozambique, but had never set foot in Asia. It was to be the adventure of a lifetime. He was given a "simple and overwhelming" task—to map the biodiversity of Northern Sierra Madre Natural Park, a place he calls one of the last wildernesses of the Philippines. He also set about training locals in biological surveying methods.

Less than three months into his initial job, van Weerd was given a baby crocodile that fisherman Samuel Francisco turned over to his colleague, community organizer Tess Gatan-Balbas. Knowing next to nothing about crocodiles, van Weerd consulted the research library and identified the animal as the Philippine crocodile. Until that point, biological surveys hadn't identified the endemic crocodile in that part of the Philippines at all.

In fact, a lot of information was lacking, van Weerd told me: "Described in 1935 by Karl Schmidt of the Field Museum in Chicago from a specimen collected in 1929 on the island of Mindoro, this crocodilian species was among the least known and studied in the world." In 1999 there had been only one survey of the Philippine crocodile conducted almost two decades earlier in 1981, and the surveyor, American herpetologist Charles Andy Ross, didn't even visit northeast Luzon where the Sierra Madre lie. Ross concluded that the species was on the brink of extinction, and southeast Luzon wasn't included on range maps.

Despite the gap in official scientific knowledge, van Weerd, driven by curiosity and together with his team, interviewed fishermen and found several pockets of surviving crocodile populations. Unfortunately, these populations were outside of the Northern Sierra Madre Natural Park. The Dutch government extended van Weerd's original contract into 2003 and he continued to work with crocodiles. The original funding ran out but van Weerd stayed on, moving to work at Leiden University and continuing his involvement with research and conservation in the Philippines at the University's field station. Teaming up with the coordinator of the field station, anthropologist Jan van der Ploeg, and with help from his former research team, van Weerd wrote a conservation leadership program grant and established an organization known as Crocodile Rehabilitation, Observance and Conservation (CROC). Later CROC was institutionalized as "Mabuwaya," a contraction of Mabahay (Long live) and Buwaya (the crocodile) in Tagalog.

Since 2015, Merljin van Weerd has been CEO of Mabuwaya, co-managing the organization with Filipino COO Tess Gatan-Balbas. All together Mabuwaya and its international team have worked hard to promote local awareness and appreciation for the Philippine crocodile as well as create sanctuaries for them. The

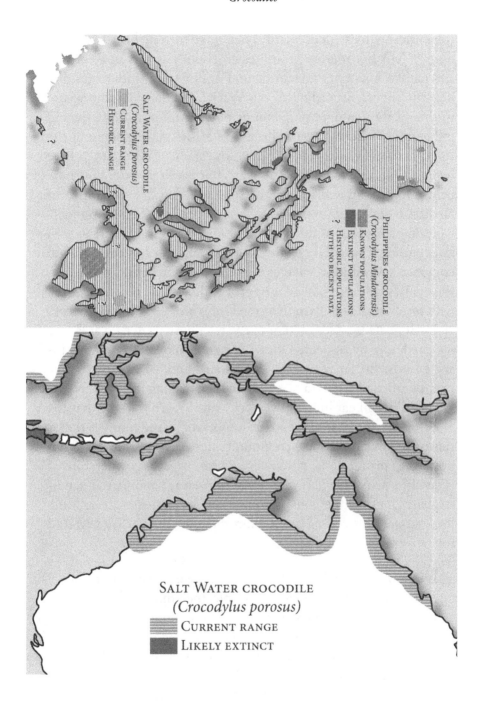

SALT WATER CROCODILE
(*Crocodylus porosus*)
CURRENT RANGE
LIKELY EXTINCT

organization doesn't necessarily encourage turning back to indigenous beliefs but merely promotes crocodiles as part of a cultural and natural history to take pride in. For now some indigenous belief still lingers, according to van Weerd: "In San Mariano where we found the remnant populations of crocodiles in 1999, the old indigenous belief systems still played a role among some of the Agta and the Kalinga people. Even now, some of the old folks here believe that crocodiles have a magical or mystical side. But these beliefs have long ago started to erode as a result of the influx of farmers from other provinces looking for land in San Mariano."

Using the place of the crocodiles in culture and nature as well as promoting peaceful cohabitation, Mabuwaya has been able to convince several local villages to set aside some land for the reptiles. They've established eight crocodile sanctuaries negotiated with local farmers to have their own rules and varying in size from "[a] half hectare lake to 10 km of river." These protected areas are watched over by respected local "Bantay Sanktuwaro," or sanctuary guards. Buffer zones are also established, so that the native prey of crocodiles have a place to flourish, making it less likely that a crocodile will eat human livestock. Van Weerd told me that the negotiation process is perhaps as important as the reserves themselves. Involving the local community in decision making and negotiating protections empowers them to take ownership of crocodile protection. In this way, Mabuwaya pioneered a new strategy of crocodile conservation, one concerned with building local respect instead of profit from the animals. Van Weerd told me,

> It is not necessarily a prerequisite to have a financial incentive to conserve crocodiles, as people, including poor farmers in a developing country such as the Philippines, can also conserve crocodiles or nature in general for its intrinsic value, or out of a sense of pride, or out of appreciation of the beauty of nature, or a sense of responsibility. I find it a rather arrogant and perhaps colonial thought, that only rich Western people can appreciate nature for its beauty because we don't

have to worry about our dinner, while poor farmers are only thinking of how to earn a living. . . . I also find the argument "when it pays, it stays" overly simplistic. There is so much more to why people appreciate the environment or nature and are willing to put effort in conservation than just monetary or utilitarian values.

I am not against creating non-destructive monetary incentives for conservation, but when there is a unilateral focus on creating financial incentives as a prerequisite for support to crocodile conservation (or other species or nature in general), then I think indeed this could be counterproductive, as an internal motivation to conserve crocodiles for intrinsic values is much more powerful and sustainable.

In the initial stages of Mabuwaya there was great success. An estimated population of twenty crocodiles in 2000 grew to more than one hundred in 2015, but there have been setbacks. The number today is down to eighty animals, partly due to bad storms and partly due to human killings.

Some projects also didn't turn out as planned. Fifty captive-bred crocodiles were introduced to Dicatian Lake in 2010, but the introduction was a failure. Three years later the crocodiles had all disappeared, mostly dying of starvation. The animals hadn't been trained to hunt and the habitat wasn't great for them either. But a lot was learned about crocodile reintroduction from these mistakes, and van Weerd is still hopeful for more crocodiles in the Northern Sierra Madre of the Philippines in the future.

San Mariano is the large municipality filled with the Sierra Madre Mountains, river valleys, and fast-flowing streams. The higher reaches of the mountains maintain relatively pristine tropical forests, while the lower reaches are severely damaged by logging. The remaining permanent crocodile populations are found as far upstream as the reptiles can swim, but higher in the mountains (where the Natural Park is), the flow of the streams is too strong for crocodiles. Because of this, many crocodile populations are found near human populations. Inhabited by roughly 55,000 people living mostly in the main, synonymous village of San Mariano, the area has enough room for both crocodiles and human populations. After all, Philippine crocodiles make snails a large part of their diet, including the golden apple snail, an agricultural pest, which should help farmers. Not only that; the crocodile is a smaller species that won't attack humans unless provoked. Unfortunately, for crocodiles to coexist with people, there must be understanding. Van Weerd told me that some people who don't agree with crocodile conservation will kill the animals on sight, even if it's illegal.

Despite the struggle and setbacks, what Mabuwaya has done is establish one of the first community based crocodile conservation programs of its type. Instead of creating a wall of separation between crocodiles and humans, the organization has promoted coexistence between two groups that have always lived together. This approach is perhaps more challenging but it also brings rewards of its own, allowing the crocodile its natural place in human culture.

For now this approach to crocodile conservation is working in the Philippines. In 2005, about six miles of Dinang Creek was declared a crocodile sanctuary, along with approximately ten feet of buffer zone on both banks. The creek held six human households in 1999, and today that's grown to nearly a hundred households. Monitoring still finds crocodiles in the area and even one to three nests per year. How long human populations can swell without destroying crocodile populations is unclear. The key seems to be gaining local support. If humans love a crocodile, reintroduction and protection are possible. Respect for these animals is more important than financial gain. In the end it's about showing people the intangible benefits of living with crocodiles. Van Weerd said that it's good if a community profits financially from the crocodiles, but having real respect for them is more important. This is an idea that the rest of the world and other crocodile conservation organizations can learn from, and some are. Projects protecting Siamese crocodiles in Cambodia, gharials and muggers in India, and dwarf and slender-snouted crocodiles in West Africa are using methods first laid out by Mabuwaya. Organizations protecting Morelet's and American crocodiles in Belize are doing likewise, and many other projects are using some of the same methods.

When I visited Florida, I came to the end of the Everglades, where fresh water meets ocean, looking for crocodiles but also to share a piece of the world with them. Paddling through the water, against tide and wave, watching mangroves crawling with crabs, I was simply happy knowing American crocodiles were there too. In the same way, I am happy knowing I share the planet with Orinoco crocodiles and those of the Philippines, Nile crocodiles and Australia's "saltie." Like all life, they deserve our respect and even our reverence.

– nine –

GHARIALS

THE FATES OF GHARIALS (*Gavialis gangeticus*) throughout their range and the people living near them are braided together like river channels, entwined with the other, yet each its own thing. To see a bit of both, I went to Nepal with a friend, former zookeeper and current fossil preparator Matt Seney, to see one of the few remaining populations of the critically endangered gharials.

Kathmandu was not a promising start. As I landed at Tribuhavan International Airport, the view of snow-topped Himalayan peaks was soon obscured by the haze of winter smog. Crossing the Bisnumati River on a footbridge to visit Swayambhunath Temple revealed a weak brown thing choked with all manner of trash below. Walking anywhere in Kathmandu requires jumping out of the way of oncoming traffic from motorcycles and cars to rickshaws, oxcarts, and bicycles.

Cocooned in the darkness by the constant blare of Bollywood music punctuated by musical horn blasts, we took a sixteen-hour bus ride into the Terai. The Terai is a low elevation plain area of sal forest, tall grassland, savannas, swamps, and small farming communities. On clear days, the Siwalik Hills—foothills of the Himalaya—stand vivid against bright blue skies to the north. The rivers here are clean with a slight turquoise hue, contrasting sharply with the brown sludge cluttered with trash seen beneath bridges in Kathmandu. This vast area stretches into India and makes up about 23 percent of Nepal's total land mass, varying in elevation from about 220 to 984 feet above sea level. The landscape brings to mind the classic sub-Saharan Africa ecosystem complex. Asian elephants and rhinoceros share the area with Bengal tigers. Four species of deer range from the nearly omnipresent spotted deer (*Axis axis*)—a small species that may remind North Americans of fawns—and the hog deer (*Axis procinus*) to the elusive barking deer (*Mantiacus muntijak*) and the largest species, the reddish colored sambar (*Russ unicolor*). The Terai is also home to the infamous mugger crocodile and the rarer gharial.

The Terai itself was sparsely inhabited before the 1950s, the main population was then the indigenous Tharu people, rumored to be malaria resistant. (A study published in the *Annals of Tropical Medical Parasitology* in February 1988 supported the idea that the Tharu are indeed resistant to malaria.) A government malaria eradication program in the area led to a massive influx of people from the surrounding hills. Today roughly 15 million people, more than half of Nepal's population, live in the Terai. Along with the people came larger-scale agriculture and development, destroying forests and marring river banks. The effects weren't good on the wildlife, including gharials. It was impacts like these that led to the establishment of Royal Chitwan, Nepal's first national park, in 1973. Now simply Chitwan National Park, its location relatively close to Kathmandu makes the park a thriving hub of tourism, complete with shops, westernized restaurants, and rows of hotels. Bardia National Park is more remote, less developed, and wilder. Bardia also just boasted the first verified gharials hatched in the park since 1982, although hatchlings were seen just outside the park in 2016. If gharials were successfully breeding in Bardia, it would broaden Nepal's breeding population into two populations in two parks—Chitwan and Bardia. It would mean eggs in more than one basket.

Gharials, arguably the oddest living crocodilians, and one of the largest, are hard to mistake for anything else. Adults can measure

eleven to twenty feet long, but their heads are strangely disproportionate to their bodies.

The gharial snout is a long, thin, needle-nosed shape lined with
a hundred sharp, interlocking teeth angling to the outside of the
jaws. The narrow snout reduces fluid resistance, allowing faster
head movements under water. With a quick swing of the head and
a snap of the jaws, gharials efficiently capture aquatic prey. During
early development the snout of the gharial starts out long and thin,
becoming proportionally shorter and thicker with age. Juvenile
gharials are eager to snap up frogs, insects, and other delectable
tidbits, but by the time they reach adulthood fish are the main staple. The fragility and narrowness of the gharial's jaws make killing
and eating a human, or other large prey, impossible.

The end of the snout of adult male gharials is even more
unique, the nostrils are surrounded by a bulbous growth called a
ghara, which is mostly made of cartilage. This ghara gives gharials
the distinction of being the only living crocodilians with sexual di-
morphism, meaning the females lack this strange appendage. The
ghara is probably used by males to amplify buzzing sounds that
are apparently enticing to females. It's also useful for blowing sexy
bubbles under water during courtship.

Gharials are the most water-dependent species of crocodilian—
crocodiles, alligators, and caimans are able to "high walk," lifting
their bellies off the earth to move with fully erect legs for short
distances. Sometimes crocodiles can walk longer distances to find
water or even hunt prey on land. Gharials can only manage a mea-
ger belly slide across sand, pushing feebly with their limbs in a maneuver that looks quite exhausting. Without the presence of water,
any great journey is impossible for gharials. This sort of special-
ization may make human-driven changes in river habitats especially threatening.

Once gharials swam in the Indus River of Pakistan as it splashed
down from the Tibetan Plateau. Gharials shared the sacred
Ganges River with river dolphins (*Platanista gangetica*) as it flowed
through both India and Bangladesh. Gharials were found in the
Irrawaddy River of Myanmar. They lived in the kingdom of

Top: A female gharial (*Gavialis gangeticus*) basking on the banks of the Babai River, Bardia National Park, Nepal. Bottom: A male gharial with the distinctive 'ghara' on its nose in Bardia National Park captive breeding facility, Nepal. (*Author*)

Bhutan. Historically, gharials were the most common crocodilian within their northern Indian subcontinent range. That historic population has been devastated and even now as the population slowly recovers, there are only approximately six hundred adult gharials in the wild living in about 2 percent of their once large territory. A current distribution map shows a scattering of small blobs representing isolated populations. Roughly 77 percent of the total gharial population is found in one location: National Chambal Sanctuary in northern India. The rest of the wild gharials live in a handful of places in India and Nepal, some with lingering hope for full recoveries, others less so. In Bangladesh, a small population is reportedly hanging on, but its viability is doubtful. Gharials are extirpated in Bhutan, Pakistan, and Myanmar.

Years of being hunted for skins and getting tangled in fishing nets have taken a toll. Males have been killed disproportionately to have their distinctive nasal "ghara" and penises used in traditional medicine. Competition with humans for a shrinking population of fishes leave more gharials threatened. The steady encroachment of development and human occupation of gharial habitat constitutes one of the most entrenched and ongoing threats to gharial survival. In India and Nepal, these threats are part of the ongoing drama of politics, people, and wildlife; gharials are just one actor among many.

All poaching is taken extremely seriously by Nepal, whose tiger population has nearly doubled from an estimated 121 tigers in 2009 to around 235 wild tigers in 2018. Military guards check your paperwork as you enter Bardia National Park. The soldiers politely stand on the porch of a wooden building, talking with local guides. The men (and a few women) in camouflage uniforms and carrying assault rifles make the park's militarization obvious. Other guard posts are scattered throughout the jungle within. Military patrols roam the forest to secure the park. A guide told me he once had to run with his guests to a military post to escape elephants that trampled their camp at night.

Bardia National Park, by all accounts, is a few decades behind the now crowded Chitwan National Park. Both parks require that the visitor be accompanied by guides, and camping inside Bardia is extremely expensive. A gharial biologist of NGO Biodiversity Conservancy Nepal, Ashish Bashyal, recommended the lodge and guiding service Mr. B's Place, an unassuming little hotel a short walk from the park entrance.

The paving stone pathway leading around the courtyard to the hotel rooms is patterned after the shores of a local lake, and the rooms are each named, not numbered, for mountains in western Nepal. Mimicking the local Tharu culture, the concrete bungalow rooms are painted a clay color, with raised patterns of stylized an-

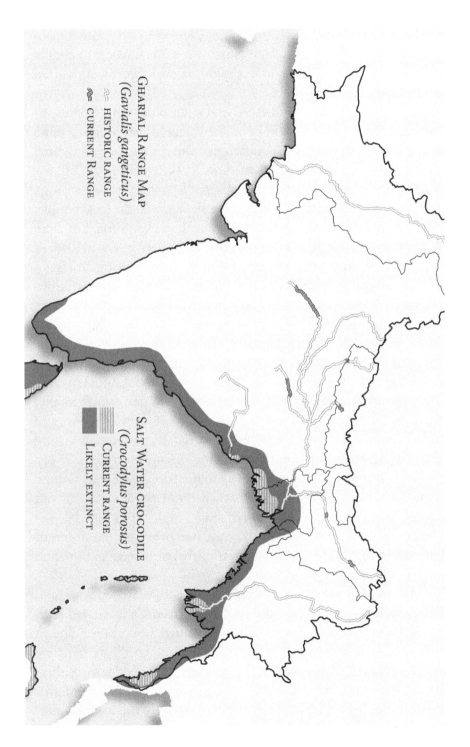

GHARIAL RANGE MAP
(*Gavialis gangeticus*)

≈ HISTORIC RANGE
≈ CURRENT RANGE

SALT WATER CROCODILE
(*Crocodylus porosus*)
CURRENT RANGE
LIKELY EXTINCT

imals, geometric designs, and people. Crocodiles with tiny bits of mirror for eyes lay next to elephants with wild trunks, and people carrying heavy loads on their shoulders and tigers with raised stripes stare from the walls.

Mr. B himself is a round-faced and stout older gentleman with thick glasses and a large smile, who has a long history working close to the land in Nepal. Mr. B at different points in his life has counted tigers in the jungle for conservation work, tracked wildlife for tourists, and owned his own lodge. He ran from his first simple hotel with his wife and children to hide from elephants in the local temple. The true passion of Mr. B's life is birds and other wildlife. Guiding, Mr. B told me, must come from the heart. It was Mr. B and his staff that made possible my trips into the jungle looking for gharials.

The morning came clear and cool the day of our first trip into the forest. I waited by the fire, sipping milk tea as Matt packed his own bag in the room. From where I sat, I could hear the crank of an engine trying to start punctuated sometimes by pauses, or by the sputtering grumble of the jeep coming to life. Eventually the coughing rumble became a steady growl and we climbed in for a drive toward the Babai River. After a turn from pavement to a dirt track in the forest, the jeep suddenly died. The two guides and driver leapt from the vehicle, talking excitedly in Nepali, lifting the hood and bending toward the engine, wrenches in hand. Eventually the car started again and we lurched along our way, only to turn back toward the hotel, at which point the engine cut out again. The guides—Bibek and Krishna—explained to us that another vehicle was already on the way, borrowed from a different lodge. In a short time, a new jeep with a driver arrived and the first jeep was taken back to Mr. B's Place.

The drive took us past small mud huts with thatched roofs and concrete brick houses painted in lively patterns and roofed with steel. Street dogs and domestic buffalo milled around the edges of dirt roads and women in bright harem pants and long hanging tunic tops carried bundles of firewood and vegetables atop their heads. Eventually we arrived at a long bridge spanning the Babai River at the edge of the park. Near the bottom of the bridge, mugger crocodiles swam along with one gharial. An enormous soft-shelled turtle looking to be two or three feet wide quickly dived, disappearing into the murky water. In the morning when we first arrived, the air was too cool for the crocodilians to lay sunning themselves on the sandy banks of the river. After a few photographs and a conversation between our guides and the park guards, we were ready to walk into the jungle.

The trail started as a partially overgrown two-track road into the forest. Following a ridge, quickly we descended, walking over small hilltops and slogging across loose river rock and sand. Obvious tiger footprints pressed into the earth were pointed out to us, in our guides' excited but hushed voices, as if the cats would overhear. Elephant tracks were nearly shapelessly round but delicately textured and impressive in their size, as if tree trunks had been walking. Nothing was taken more seriously, though, than the rhinoceros tracks. Elephants can't run for very long due to their enormous size and a lucky human can outrun one, but a rhino can easily chase down a person and kill them. Krishna told me that if a rhino charges, running in a zig-zag pattern, dropping a hat or backpack as a distraction, or climbing a tree are your best options. The walking sticks the jungle guides carried were also used to smack an angry rhino on the snout: a terrifyingly thin last resort. Sometimes you can hide on the other side of a large tree, dodging quickly around the trunk to keep it between you and the animal as a rhino charges.

Our journey loosely followed the bottle-green Babai River, slipping deeper into open forest at times and walking through tall dry grassland and crossing the river at others. The water was cool and clear but not unpleasant in the sunshine of a warm day in what counts for the cold season of the subtropical Terai. We stopped our walk and had a lunch of fried rice and vegetables washed down by boxes of mango juice at a place called Kalinara. In the shade of a jungled hill, we sat on a sandy bank, watching the far shore, a place where gharials are sometimes seen basking in the sun. We ate quietly and talked in whispers, but after waiting an hour, nothing larger than a bird made an appearance.

The trip back was made more exciting when we saw a small herd of spotted deer fleeing up a short slope near the river. Another time we saw a sambar, the park's largest deer, crossing the river in front of us in a spray of water. As the sun sank lower in the sky, we were coming close to the bridge we started from when Bibek froze in front of me. Ahead of us an elephant stood across the trail we were walking, looming like a brick wall among trees. Bibek turned slowly back and whispered "run!" We sprinted as a group down the path. Pausing for a bit allowed me to take a quick photo of the elephant before we veered onto a thin mud trail through the jungle and quickly jogged along the river to get past the elephant. The elephant trumpeted loudly and the guides told us she was gathering the herd to her. Adrenaline pumped into my body as we ran and later became giddy with relief.

This hike told me more about what it was like to walk the path my ancestors must've trod, to travel through a land filled with many dangerous animals that could easily kill a person. Crocodiles are also one of those animals. It's less common than with Africa's Nile crocodiles or Australia's famous "salties," but muggers do sometimes kill people, and less often eat them.

At the bridge again, before being ushered into our borrowed jeep I got a quick glimpse of gharials below, laying on the now cooling sand next to mugger crocodiles. The day was tiring but also exciting. I had thought that getting a better view of a gharial, some real time to watch the animal in the wild, was fairly easily accomplished. The next few trips into the jungle shook this illusion. We saw mugger crocodiles, elephants, and rhinos, and Matt and I even climbed to the top of a shaky wooden wildlife viewing tower mere moments after a tiger was glimpsed by others. It would be days waiting by rivers and sitting out cloudy weather before I'd see another gharial.

After a week of hiking through the jungle and a four-wheel drive journey along a river to look for crocodiles, we had our most successful trip so far. The day was cold and overcast, weather conditions that made it pointless looking for gharials on the sandbars where they lay in the sun for warmth. We'd planned an ambitious trek along and across a river in a far-flung corner of the park where Bibek, one of the more experienced guides, had seen baby gharials before. Now that plan for the day was shot. Instead Matt and I climbed onto the back of motorcycles, I riding behind Bibek, Matt behind Krishna.

The ride on the motorcycles was eye opening. The roads quickly changed from asphalt to dirt to gravel and back to asphalt, sometimes without reason. Honking horns seemed to be more of a courtesy notice that you're about to pass rather than an expression of unbridled disapproval and are used liberally. We'd come upon a small group of kids on bicycles, and our guides would honk and pass them on the right. When a black street dog started to come onto the road, Bibek honked and the dog paused as we passed. Slow tractors took up most of the road, leaving only a narrow shoulder to pass in, and the guides honked as we threaded our way between the chugging tractor and a small knot of ducks eating at the road's edge. Honks let the numerous pedestrians know to stay put as we zoomed past children riding bicycles or walking to school. We jostled through dips in the dirt road, bounced over gravel, and on our return trip, forded a river, slowly, so as not to splash, Bibek raising his legs above the water level. Once we rode down a dirt road between fields only to find that it ended near a house. An old man stepped to the door, standing between a child and a goat to laugh at us turning around, exchanging words in Nepali with our guides.

After the motorcycle ride, we arrived at a bridge over the Babai River, the departure point for our first trip. We stepped from the bikes, stretching our limbs—numb from cold and tight from clinging desperately to the rear handholds. As our guides rode to the far end of the bridge to park, Matt turned to me, his reddish hair pushed back from the wind, his face a vibrant pink from the cold, "That's the dumbest thing I've done since I've been in Nepal, and I've accidentally bought pot."

We both laughed at the joke. Earlier in the trip at a bar and restaurant with traditional clay walls Matt was smoking a cigarette when the bartender asked if he wanted to buy "smokes." We both thought he was selling local cigarettes. We only saw our mistake later when a bag of dried green plants and rolling papers were presented.

The Babai bridge turned out to be the perfect place to see gharials on a cloudy day in December. A small sandbank near the river was empty of all crocodilians, true enough, but both muggers and gharials were easily spotted in the shallow water over other submerged sandbars. After four long visits at the bridge, during my whole stay, I never saw any sign of an adult male gharial in the area.

That first day, we watched rather informally for a while, asking the guides about the gharials, muggers, and other wild animals we saw. The gharials seemed more active than the muggers, gently moving across the submerged bars, using their feet, plumes of sand filling the water behind. Two of the first three we saw quietly disappeared into the deeper water, and others came and went as we watched. Some of the muggers moved around, using their powerful tails to swim short distances, but mostly they sat still in the cold water.

The bridge itself is also a barrier, featuring a sharp concrete slope where a sheet of water rolls over and back into the river; this is segmented by concrete buttresses jutting out into the stream. The bridge necessarily represents a boundary between different breeding populations of gharials and mugger crocodiles; none of the crocodilians here could get upstream. Leaning against the buttresses were impressive logs—tree corpses—complete with the broken remnant of root systems. On one log a bright tricolor common kingfisher (*Alcedo atthis*) sat looking over the water for prey, periodically flying before returning to his perch. On another log, a pond heron (*Ardeola grayii*) made the delicate, deliberate steps his kind uses while hunting frogs; as usual, his neck was pulled in, and today he looked hunched against the cold. House swifts (*Apus nipalensis*) on wing darted above the water, searching for insects. Downstream dark-colored cormorants with snakes' necks sat on rocks midstream with wings outstretched, hoping in vain for sun near a gangly black stork (*Ciconia nigra*) and a flock of white egrets.

Two gharials bask near a mugger crocodile (*Crocodylus palustris*), lower left, Bardia National Park, Nepal. (*Author*)

As we watched Matt said, "Taking into account that I've counted some more than once, we've seen more than ten individuals."

One of the challenges of wildlife surveys is not counting the same animal twice. Some researchers have clipped scutes from the tails of captive bred gharials so they could be recognized when returned to the wild, but the animals we were looking at had few distinguishing features. There easily could've been ten gharials milling around below us—or six or seven. On different days, I was only able to count five animals at any one time.

Distinguishing gharials from muggers was quite easy though. Not only do gharials have the distinctive narrow, needle-nosed snouts, the gharial has a beautiful bluish greenish color highlighted by dark tiger stripes. As gharials grow older, their color becomes more uniform but they remain distinctly lighter than muggers. The muggers with their broader, stout jaws looked uniformly darkly colored from above. Most of the animals we saw were adults, with the exception of a three-foot-long juvenile. As we stood, eyes on the river, the guides talked and laughed together in Nepali and Krishna handed out a snack of hard-boiled eggs, collecting the shells in a small plastic bag.

A raft of smooth-coated otters (*Lutrogale perspicillata*) moved through the river in graceful arcing dives, and later a pair of spotted deer splashed across the water further downstream. Large fish swam near the barrage, appearing to be two feet long; Krishna told me these were the golden mahseer (*Tor putitora*). Fly fishermen travel from all over the world to be photographed with this fish before releasing them as regulations require. The guides told me that between the Karnali and Babai Rivers, there are 121 species of fish. It's easy to see why gharials would find a home in this place.

On another day I borrowed a rusty green single-speed bike with brakes that only slightly slowed the contraption. As I rode, the bike seat tilted backward, becoming increasingly uncomfortable. My knees developed a pain I'd never felt riding my mountain bike back home. A four-hour round trip delivered me again to the bridge overlooking the Babai River after the fog and clouds of the morning had given way to clear skies and warm sunshine. There on the sandy bank gharials basked, huddled in a group with a small mugger. Larger adult muggers seemed to form a different group close by. After watching for a while, a big mugger rushed one of the gharials as she lay meekly on the sand. The startled gharial thrashed her way into the river quickly as the mugger crawled over her, mouth agape. The other gharials and the small mugger all retreated in a flurry to the water. Slowly the animals repopulated the shore and continued as if nothing had happened. Though fights between adults may be rare, muggers sometimes eat young gharials. Fatalities in gharial young are very high. Sometimes even adult gharials are badly injured by muggers.

Biologist Ashish Bashyal later told me that he's seen as many as three male gharials near the bridge I'd been watching. Of these three, one was translocated to Chitwan to bolster the breeding population there. One seemed to be missing, perhaps moving elsewhere on the river. The third male gharial near the bridge died.

I walked from my room to the elephant breeding facility near Bardia to talk to Dr. Chitra Khadka, the veterinarian who'd done the autopsy on the gharial who died near the bridge. Khadka had worked for national parks in Nepal for twenty-four years—nine spent at Chitwan, the remainder at Bardia—and he now works at the elephant breeding center.

Dr. Khadka was a large man with fingers like calloused sausages and a smile that told me he was happy to help but not quite sure why I wanted to talk to him. We sat outside in plastic chairs, near the empty elephant stables where the animals are chained to stout wooden poles at night. I could hear a jingle of metal somewhere but didn't see where it was coming from. It was a cold, cloudy day and a group of men sat huddled around a small campfire not far off.

Khadka told me that just two days earlier, he'd been involved in rescuing a baby rhino that was injured by a tiger. Men on nine elephants had to surround the bleeding rhinoceros calf to safely catch it in a net, a tricky maneuver under any circumstances. Most of Khadka's experience is working with mammals—rhinos, elephants, tigers—not crocodiles, he told me. But he helps where he can.

The male gharial that died was large, he estimated fifteen feet long. The beginning of the animal's problem seemed to be a tail that was bitten by a mugger. The tail became infected and the gharial had a hard time catching food. The gharial also had a prolapsed penis, a condition Khadka had seen a few times in gharials during his career but, interestingly, never in muggers.

Crocodilian penises are bizarre. Permanently erect, the penis waits to be pushed out of the cloaca when needed. A rush of blood does slightly change the shape of the penis but muscles also work to protrude the organ. With the prolapsed penis of the gharial, the penis is permanently extended outside of the cloaca.

Wildlife experts from Chitwan National Park did their best in attempting to capture and treat the gharial, but it was obvious that their efforts were stressing the animal too much and they had to stop. Eventually, the unfortunate gharial starved, unable to catch food. Like in any population, some animals die; others are born.

The next place Bibek and another guide, Arjun, took us to was where Ashish Bashyal had discovered around a hundred baby gharials, living in a crèche. The trip started with a long bus ride to a small town on the eastern edge of Bardia National Park and a stay in a modest hotel with the two guides. An early start the next morning had us walking through the jungle along an old jeep trail, which quickly dwindled away after we passed the military checkpoint. We were just crossing a cold river under clouds when we saw a male elephant far off in a haze of fog near the edge of thick jungle. We carefully moved far wide of the elephant and scrambled over boulders for an hour or so, on the edge of a steep riverbank, to avoid encountering any elephants up close. As we neared the river where the babies had last been seen, gharials and muggers lulled on the sand across the water from us. Moving a bit closer startled them into the stream, and we sat down among the rocks and tall grasses to wait for their return.

Slowly gharials and muggers alike swam back to their spots in the sun. A male gharial stretched in the shallow water near a sandbar, his head lifted high, his tail resting on the sand, backlit with sunlight. This was the only adult male I would see during my time in Bardia. Female gharials crawled laboriously onto the shore on both sides of the river, laying side by side with muggers or quietly floating in the water. All the gharials I could see were adults. We waited for an hour, ate a simple lunch, passing fruit and packages of chips and cookies back and forth. We watched. I snapped photos and stared through the binoculars. I couldn't see any of the hundred young gharials that hatched here.

Ashish Bashyal later told me over Skype that the survival rate for gharials is incredibly small—maybe 2 or 3 percent live to be adults. Perhaps monsoonal rains washed the infants downstream while the adults took refuge in smaller tributary rivers. Perhaps some of the young gharials were eaten by muggers or other predators. No one knows for sure. Also uncertain is the role of the hydroelectric and irrigation project being built upstream.

Before retiring to the hotel room the night before, I went for a walk with guides Arjun and Bibek. We stood on a bridge over the Babai for a while and Bibek pointed down a road, indicating the lodgings for the workers and engineers completing the Bheri Babai Diversion Multipurpose Project (BBDMP) set to be finished within a few years. The idea is to change the natural fluctuation of the river from flood during monsoon and trickle during dry season to a year-round dependable water source. The government hopes that the project will supply year-round irrigation to 51,000 hectares of farmland and create 46 Megawatts of hydroelectricity annually (conservatively, enough to power about 34,500 American homes). No one knows for certain how the project will impact the gharials just downstream.

Bashyal told me that many common people think the project will help gharials, giving them more ability to move through the river. This is possible, he concedes, but there are also potential concerns. The first problem is that the Babai River is a warm river, and the Bheri is a cold river originating high in the Himalaya. So, as water from the Bheri is diverted through a tunnel and into the Babai, the river's temperature will change. The change in water temperature might change gharial basking and swimming behavior, causing them to spend more time warming up on the sand than usual. With colder water, the sand along the riverbanks might also cool, causing changes in gharial nests or increasing failures.

The diversion is also sure to introduce new species from fish to plants to microbes into the Babai River, each representing unknown consequences. Meddling so much with a complex ecosystem is a messy thing to predict, as too many variables create uncertainty. The same is true perhaps of the fate of the gharial. As human populations swell, massive infrastructure and intensive agriculture increase. Along with these come pollution, habitat disturbance and destruction, and incidental killing. Whether there is room for any wild gharials in the Indian subcontinent depends on whether humans have the ability to let some things alone, something we have yet to prove ourselves capable of. I was still thinking of these things when I left Bardia and continued on my trip.

In Sauraha, a tourist town on the outskirts of Chitwan National Park, I met a man named Tika. While I was at the hotel restaurant, sitting at a table outside waiting for my dinner, Tika arrived and introduced himself. He was a heavy-set older gentleman with a careful, intelligent way of speaking.

Tika had worked as a guide for several years, now he manages the hotel I stayed at and trains nature guides. He told me with some pride that he's been watching birds for forty years. Much earlier he worked at Bardia, he told me, in the old days when there was only one lodge.

For someone who's worked as a guide, Tika has an interesting perspective; he told me how trash from the trekking industry connects to gharials. Businesses in the mountains catering to tourists collect plastic trash with little infrastructure to take care of it. During the monsoon season, trash washes down from the mountains and ends up in the lowlands (averaging 1,362 feet above sea level in Bardia and 1,500 in Chitwan) where gharials live. He also spoke of the growth of hotels around Bardia and Chitwan, how more and more people are here, "looking for something." The phrase made me cringe a bit internally. *I suppose this is why I'm here too.* But Tika is right; he quickly pointed out the number of people selling their guiding services on the street, in hotels, everywhere. For a white foreigner, someone is always trying to sell you something on the streets of Sauraha. "Maybe you've met some of them." He said this with a knowing smile.

The government, he told me, doesn't regulate tourism enough; it's a capitalist free-for-all, allowing an incoming flood. What he was saying reminded me of a conversation I'd had with a guide inside Bardia two days earlier. It was raining and I sat with my guides inside a wildlife viewing tower near an older German woman and her own guide, a man whose name I didn't catch. The guide was telling me how in parts of India, you see a tiger calmly napping surrounded by twenty jeeps filled with excited tourists snapping photos. *It's not even special anymore* he seemed to be saying.

Tika also pointed out the dangers of having more people in parks with dangerous animals. In the United States, he said, you

Tourists enter boats to leave Chitwan National Park as mugger crocodiles and gharials, left, bask unnoticed nearby. (*Author*)

have alligators and there are signs warning people about them, yet every year someone gets killed. It's not true that every year someone gets killed by a gator, but his point was nonetheless valid. I thought of hearing a talk from a park ranger at the Grand Canyon who'd rescued a woman who'd hiked for miles down a trail wearing high heels. The problem is really one of a population of people disconnected from nature, trying to reconnect without knowing how. With more people taking up more space and smaller numbers of wild animals, the problem will only grow. There are some organizations in Nepal trying to correct or at least mediate the problem.

I met with Santosh at the National Trust for Nature Conservation (NTNC) building at Sauraha, just outside of Chitwan National Park. Santosh is a thin man with a serious but kind air, a conservation officer for NTNC. He ushered me up the stairs to a part of the building that seemed empty except for his large office in the corner. There was a comfortable orange sectional sofa stretched next to his desk, a small glass table sitting in front of it.

On Santosh's desk was a laptop plugged into an ethernet cable, a printer, paperwork in stacking plastic trays. Near where I sat on the sofa two books were piled one on the other, *Pangolins: Science, Society and Conservation* was below *Birds of Shunklaphanta National Park*.

Santosh told me there were many threats to gharials. Crocodilians are often caught in fishing nets, so his organization is piloting the creation of fish-farming ponds in local communities to remove this threat. Poaching was once a problem for almost all of the wildlife in Chitwan, so beyond military patrols, NTNC started community-based anti-poaching units at Chitwan and other parks; I had heard about these earlier at Bardia. The idea is for local volunteers to patrol their own communities and become invested in the local wildlife personally. This program has been successful for tigers, rhinos, and elephants, and recently the anti-poaching units have been trained to monitor sections of rivers and report any problems gharials or other aquatic wildlife are having. Poaching isn't much of an issue for Nepal's crocodilians anymore, but if a gharial gets caught in a net, it's a problem authorities might be able to mitigate. A threat that is harder to solve is that of human disturbance of habitat. Santosh told me that part of the trouble is that the Narayani and Rapti Rivers, those that gharials live in near Chitwan, don't flow through the heart of the park. Instead, they form the boundaries of the park, with one side protected, yet the other often heavily used by people.

As I went for a walk through Sauraha, what Santosh had told me was glaringly obvious. The day before, I had been heading toward my hotel in the late afternoon when a man asked me if I wanted to see a rhinoceros. Surprised, I assumed he was trying to sell a tour. No, he explained, there's a rhinoceros just down this trail across the river, he pointed for me. People swarmed down the trail along a channel of the Rapti River; mostly Nepalis on vacation with a smattering of European tourists. I walked along with the crowd until I saw a huddle of people with their phones out whispering "gaida," which means "rhino" in Nepali. Looking across the river it took me a while to find the animal, but its back was exposed above high grass just across the water from us. It felt as easy as seeing an animal in a zoo and not much more satisfying.

In the river between us, a mugger crocodile swam lazily, not garnering much interest from the crowd. On other days on the sandbars in town, just across from where wooden canoes sit tied to the banks near a row of restaurants, crocodiles sunned themselves. A large mugger especially caught my attention; he looked potentially dangerous. In Bardia, I'd heard stories of a girl who'd been attacked by a mugger while she was washing in a canal years earlier, luckily the girl survived with no major injuries, but it brings to mind the possible threat. Gharials sometimes came and basked on the same sandbar.

Walking outside of town toward Chitwan's elephant breeding center, a simple footbridge set on concrete footings crosses another channel of the Rapti. There people herd domestic water buffalo into the waters to drink or simply to get them across. When I arrived an older woman was washing her hair in the waters just to the side of the bridge. Feeling embarrassed as an intruder, I turned away and moved off to give her privacy. After a short time of dawdling, the woman walked away, putting her hair up as she moved. I walked down the stream where she'd been, looking at the banks on both sides, which were all vegetated, no gravel, no sand. *Not good for basking*, I thought, remembering that adult gharials use almost exclusively sandy banks. As I turned to leave, I spotted a small mugger crocodile sitting on the grassy bank across from me, mouth open in the warm weather. A mugger this size is no threat to people, but it's easy to imagine a different animal capable of killing a person or a small buffalo so close to villagers going about their daily chores.

Part of the problem for gharials is they can't adapt as well as muggers, which are more generalists. Instead, gharials are quite dependent on high sandy banks for laying their eggs and for fish to eat. Muggers aren't doing well, either, but they've been able to use their more generalized niche to their benefit. When people mine river banks for sand, muggers move to other banks; gharials simply fail to breed. When people catch too many fish, muggers eat turtles, deer, birds, stray dogs; gharials simply starve. This is how gharials went from being more abundant than muggers to less abundant as both populations suffered losses.

On my last day in the lowlands, I took a long bicycle ride with a guide through a wetlands known as Ten Thousand Lakes to the gharial breeding facility inside Chitwan National Park. As we reached the edge of the park, we crossed an especially high bridge over a river. We paused on the concrete bridge and my guide told me that a few decades earlier, visitors were poled across the river in boats. Below in the river, gharials lay stretched on a sandbar in the sun. Half a dozen females lay contentedly warming their bodies. Their heads were raised, as if reaching for the sunlight glinting off their scales.

Inside the breeding facility itself, chain link fences are planted in short concrete walls, the tops covered with netting in the pens where smaller animals are kept. Protected this way from birds and other predators, the crocodilians are kept until they're old enough to have a good shot at survival in the wild. As I moved through the facility, the size of enclosures progressed until large gharials, almost ready for release, luxuriated near concrete pools of water. I was happy that so many gharials were alive, but I couldn't help but be struck by the wrongness of the situation. These animals are kept well fed in clinical pools because we humans continuously fail them. These failures endanger the survival of a species. Gazing close at the captive animals, I thought of the contrast with the gharials just outside the park in the river. I wonder if this is how it must always be. Must a wild animal always lose some freedom to survive side by side with human "progress"?

Weeks after I returned home, I got an email from Ashish Bashyal, along with a photo of a depression in the sand. The gharials were digging trial nests at the same place he'd found hatchlings the summer before. There was hope that wild gharials inside of Bardia were still making a place for themselves. Only time will tell how gharials will fare.

– ten –

The SERPENT *in the* GARDEN

SOME OF OUR MOST INSTINCTIVE FEARS could be the shadows of our "former selves"—cautionary emotions left over by evolution from the dangerous world inhabited by our ancestors.

I have a memory from when I was a young kid growing up in Wyoming. Throughout the western United States, rivers have been dammed and the cool reservoirs created are popular places for recreation during the hot summer months. Swimming in the dark, muddy waters of Keyhole Reservoir in eastern Wyoming was a treat. Jumping with a splash from a motor boat my father borrowed, my brother and I would swim in circles, far from any shore. Slowly though, treading water would become a little unsettling. The water was dark and I couldn't see my own bare feet churning beneath me. Who knows what could be swimming down in the unfathomable depths of the water? Of course such fears are misplaced (at least in Wyoming), and even at a young age I knew it. Mostly I swallowed my misgivings and ignored the creep of goosebumps that weren't all about water temperature. As I lay in the warming sun on the boat, aquatic horrors evaporated and inevitably the cool water called me back again. Some of our deepest fears are irrational.

In Madagascar, a place with only one species of poisonous snake, a type of sea snake, people, even far from the ocean, are generally terrified of serpents. At the research station where I volunteered, I caught a beautiful boa by hand near a campsite. Carrying her back to the open air kitchen, I expected some people to be excited to see the reptile. The locals were appalled, backing away from me quickly as I showed off the boa. This fear of snakes might be reinforced by local culture, but it can't be rooted in an individual's negative memory of a venomous snake bite. Even those of us who love snakes can sometimes be unreasonably startled by them.

I don't generally consider myself especially fearful of any reptiles, but Erin, my wife, loves to tell a story of me jumping ("flying" in her words) off a trail in Ecuador's cloud forest as a non-venomous snake surprised me by slithering quickly down the trail in our direction. Charles Darwin himself owned up to an uncontrollable reaction to a snake under harmless conditions, writing in *The Expression of the Emotions in Man and Animals*: "I put my face close to the thick glass-plate in front of a puff adder in the Zoological Gardens, with the firm determination of not starting back if the snake struck me; but as soon as the blow was struck, my resolution went for nothing, and I jumped a yard or two backwards with astonishing rapidity."

However laughable such leaps of fear may be, it seems that the dread of animal attacks is deeply imbedded in Western culture, and perhaps in humanity itself. Few things capture the collective imagination like the story of a human being killed, or even worse, eaten by a wild animal.

In 2016, Lane Graves, a two-year-old boy from Nebraska, was playing on a beach area at a Disney resort in Florida when an alligator lunged out of the water and grabbed him in its mouth. Lane's father tried to fight the alligator and wrest his son from the jaws, but later said another alligator attacked him, dividing his attention. The first alligator got away with the little boy. Eventually Lane's body was found—dead of drowning and wounds from the alligator—in the water nearby. The father needed stitches and antibiotics from his own reptile-induced injuries. News like this seems to get a disproportionate amount of public attention.

Attacks by alligators that seem to be hunting their victims are the things of collective nightmares. The alligators involved in the attack were killed, just as have 240 other "nuisance alligators" found on Disney resort properties, yet this was said by Disney to be the first serious alligator attack on their property. Alligator attacks aren't as common or dangerous as crocodile attacks in other parts of the world.

The late Dr. Val Plumwood, Australian environmental philosopher, survived an attempted predation in Australia's Kakadu National Park on a canoe trip during the 1980s by a saltwater crocodile (*Crocodylus porosus*). Plumwood borrowed a canoe to explore East Alligator Lagoon on a day when a warm drizzle became a constant rainfall.

Encountering Australia's largest and most dangerous (nonhuman) predator floating in the channel she was paddling, Plumwood tried to steer the thin canoe past the crocodile only to have the animal ram her boat. Again and again the "saltie" smashed into the fiberglass hull. In desperation, Plumwood tried to climb into an overhanging tree to escape, but when she pulled her legs from the boat, the crocodile lunged and grabbed her by the crotch. After surviving two death rolls and finally pulling herself up the riverbank, Plumwood walked back toward the ranger station, bandaging an injured leg on the way. Writing in her essay *Being Prey*, which was part of the book *The Ultimate Journey: Inspiring Stories of Living and Dying*, Plumwood explained how what she viewed as the horror and denial we feel at being prey items is wrapped up in Western cultural trappings. "In the human supremacist culture of the West there is a strong effort to deny that we humans are also animals positioned in the food chain. This denial that we ourselves are food for others is reflected in many aspects of our death and burial practices—the strong coffin, conventionally buried well below the level of soil fauna activity, and the slab over the grave to prevent any other thing from digging us up, keeps the Western human body from becoming food for other species. . . . Horror and outrage usually greet stories of other species eating humans."

TEARS *for* CROCODILIA

Perhaps denial of predation is simply another manifestation of our deeper fear. Interestingly the reluctance to accept the possibility of modern humans and our ancestors as regular prey items spills over from common people to professional anthropologists. In *Man the Hunted: Primates, Predators and Human Evolution*, authors Donna Hart and Robert W. Sussman describe the hesitancy of some of their fellow anthropologists to consider the impact of predation on early humans: "Many scientists will turn ghastly shades of red when arguing against creationism and for evolution, yet they want to hang onto some special classification for modern humans, early hominids, the great apes, and even primates in general as too smart to be prey animals. Surely, they insist, at least humans . . . had to be in control of their environment—they couldn't have been at the mercy of 'dumb animals' that ate them right, left and center."

The denial that sometimes other animals kill and even eat humans can lead to tragedy, as in the case of Lane Graves. This denial is perhaps a leading reason tourists will snap selfies with large and dangerous bison (which are herbivores but still sometimes kill humans), bears, or even crocodiles without apparent fear. It's why people persist on feeding alligators in spite of warning signs.

Despite our collective amnesia, it's hard to deny that some level of fear still lingers when we encounter even the possibility of a dangerous animal. Anyone who's spent many nights alone in the forest has felt unnerved, as if being watched. The knowledge of the proximity of large predators changes how you perceive a place. Seeing a mountain lion track pressed into fresh snow or mud on a trail makes one watchful, quiet, careful. When working on Afognak Island, a place where Kodiak brown bears (the largest brown bears in the world) were regularly encountered, I was always thinking about the bears. Swimming in oceans where sharks may be or standing on a riverbank in crocodile country feels different, more intense, than a swimming pool. These fears are easy to deny when we are safe in a resort, a building, in a city surrounded by metal and glass and the hum of electricity and human voices, but you'll find they're very real when you're alone in a hammock in the Amazon or West African rainforest.

These tingles of fear are not very helpful in the modern daily life of Westerners. It would be much more useful for survival to be afraid of driving in heavy traffic than of meeting a reptile. It may be wariness of animals is a remnant from older times when everyone faced the possibility of being hunted. Predation certainly has an impact on prey species—if an antelope is caught by a lion, it loses its life; if the lion loses the prey, the big cat only loses a meal. If our ancestors were eaten by crocodiles, even occasionally, it certainly had a bigger impact on us than the crocodilians. Scientists have begun to look at the role crocodilian predation may have played for our ancestors.

Anthropologist Dr. Jackson Njau is a scientist now based in the United States with field work in Tanzania, a nearly perfect place for his research. Njau has compared ancient hominin fossils to modern crocodile kills to ask the question whether crocodiles preyed on our ancestors. Growing up in Tanzania, a place famous for discoveries of early human fossils, Njau told me he became interested in the deep roots of the human species when he was young, influenced by his archaeologist uncle Amini Mturi and school trips to museums.

Jackson Njau followed his budding interest in anthropology to college and out into the field where he worked on digs in the famed Olduvai Gorge. Starting at Olduvai, Njau told me he began thinking about what the modern African landscape can tell us about our early human origins and questioning the standard scientific narrative: "I began to critically think about some of the longstanding hypotheses about the origin of hominin behavior . . . in light of just simple observations of wildlife and predator behaviors on modern African semiarid savanna landscapes."

Njau was lucky enough to live in a place where wildlife and fossils were both abundant. The two seemed to inform each other and naturally raised questions. These questions followed Njau to graduate school, where he considered the struggle between modern humans and crocodiles for resources like water, especially during dry seasons. How did crocodiles impact early humans? There was already some tantalizing evidence that early humans had been killed by crocodiles, but no one had any idea how common it was. In 1960 Mary and Louis Leakey uncovered the remains of a *Homo habilis* foot. The foot of the early human is eerily similar to the bones in your own foot—nicely articulated cuneiform and ankle bones leading to mostly complete metatarsals except for two that are broken and sharp.

Njau and his professor, Dr. Robert Blumenschine, were some of the first to look closely at the bite marks crocodiles make on their food. Observing the leftover bones from captive crocodile meals, they noticed the pattern was distinct. With mammal predators, teeth are used to dismember the prey and break bones open to eat the marrow. With crocodiles, the prey animal is swallowed more or less whole and the bite marks are incidental but apparent. Njau compared the grooves made by modern crocodiles to those found on the *Homo habilis* ankle.

Gouges on the ankle are the same size and shape of crocodile bite marks found on the modern bones of prey. This first scar on an ankle was just the beginning. There was more evidence hidden in research collections, but some of it had been misinterpreted for years. What were thought to be 2.5 million-year-old cut marks on remains from Ethiopia are now confirmed as more crocodile bite marks. As Njau looked more closely, the more he realized this foot bone was only one small piece of a greater picture showing the threat of crocodiles to our hominid ancestors. Njau found that the "home bases" of early hominids, the places they centered their lives around, were also uncomfortably close to crocodiles:

> When I started to look at Olduvai fossils I realized that many of these purported "hominin home bases" contained also dangerous aquatic species like hippo and crocodile remains. Most significant was the presence of many crocodile shed teeth in these sites. Crocodiles shed mature teeth repeatedly during life. My studies in Serengeti show that shed teeth concentrate in the pools where crocodile feed and live. I suggested that crocodile would have posed great danger to hominids in these "home bases," and there were much safer

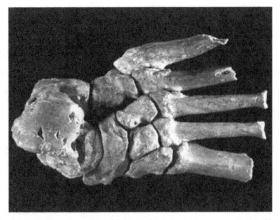

This is OH 8, a fossil discovered in 1960 in Tanzania in a research effort led by Louis Leakey. This specimen is the foot and ankle of a *Homo habilis* with marks that match the bite marks of a crocodile and the heel bitten off. OH 8 was found near a lake with crocodiles. (*Copyright Dr. Jackson Njau, used with permission*)

places on the landscapes for the breeding hominin groups to socialize than in these open and dangerous landscapes on the ancient Olduvai lakeshore. Through my taphonomic study [taphonomy is the science of what happens to a body after death—decomposition, fossilization, digestion of bones, etc.], which was controlled by crocs experimental feeding, I developed criteria for recognizing crocodile bite marks and damage to bones during killing or scavenging. Unfortunately, I found that some of the hominin bones contained crocodile bite marks.

What Dr. Njau discovered is something we often try to hide in modern Western society, the fact that humans are sometimes just another prey species. Much of the early work on human fossils ignored the evidence of bite marks by crocodiles and other animals. There is now clear evidence that our early ancestors were attacked and eaten by large cats, canines, crocodiles, and even large birds. It may be that certain fears are inherited from our long history of being another item on the menu.

Our fear, no matter how small, of wading into dark waters with a hidden bottom, may be a shadow of our history with crocodiles. We see this shadow of our past in the cultural importance of crocodiles. Powerful and dangerous forces were often deified—volcanoes and lightning were given personhood in the form of gods by many cultures. Crocodilians too gained mythical importance, partly because we feared and wished to appease them. Before we could invent complex systems of worship or predator control methods, our ancestors simply reacted to predation like any animal would. Certain adaptations allowed our lineage to survive predation by crocodilians as well as many other fierce beasts.

We humans seem weak and small in comparison to creatures like crocodilians with large muscular bodies and sharp teeth designed for killing. We aren't entirely helpless though. Like every other animal on earth, we've adapted due to the pressures we've faced over time. We ourselves have a suite of anti-predator traits honed and reinforced by encounters with crocodilians and other dangerous animals.

To stand upright, as we do, is to see our surroundings more easily. Having eyes five or six feet off the ground may allow a person to see a crocodile laying carefully in wait amid a cluster of vegetation that a rabbit might miss. If you notice that crocodile, you undoubtedly appear bigger than you are, towering over the reptile from its perspective. Even an animal that could in reality easily eat you might be confused into estimating you as too large to swallow. Being on those hind legs does something else special for humans—it leaves our hands free for other things. It's a pretty simple thing to pick up a rock at the edge of the pond and toss it toward the crocodile to scare a potential predator away. A move that's a little more advanced is to carry a spear and take the predation to the aquatic ambusher itself.

Of course to do things like design a spear and learn how to use it, you need to have some intelligence, a trait humans are quick to associate with themselves. Intelligence also allows greater degrees of communication. People can explain to their children, in detail, the dangers of crocodiles or where a specific crocodile is laying in wait for them.

To communicate with each other, we need to live in groups. Sociality is seen as potentially an adaptation to predation as well. It means more eyes, more ears, more chances someone in the group will spot a potential danger and raise the alarm. Being social is one of the traits that makes us human, though we share it with most other primates. All of these traits are essential to us as humans, and to some degree or other, these traits may have been influenced by our past interactions with dangerous predators, including crocodilians. Evolution is complex, and it's impossible to say with certainty that predators created evolutionary pressure for these traits, but it's certain that these traits serve us when we encounter a creature ready to eat us. For every case of a child that is killed by an alligator or crocodile, there are many stories of someone who survives an attack or even a crocodilian that considers a person too intimidating and doesn't attempt a predation at all.

When I was in Nepal, I heard the story of a small girl that went to a canal to collect some water. A mugger crocodile (*Crocodylus palustris*) lunged up and grabbed her arm. Luckily, family members nearby were able to literally pull the girl from the crocodile's jaws. The fortunate girl survived with nothing more than nasty scars due to the help of her family. This isn't that unusual of an outcome.

In the aftermath of Lane Graves' death, Disney World initially claimed he was the first child attacked by an alligator. Another man contested that claim, sharing with the media the story of his own attack at Disney World and how things might've been different for Lane Graves with a bit of luck.

Paul Santamaria was eight years old when, oblivious to a seven-and-a-half-foot-long alligator in the water nearby, he was feeding ducks at a pond in Disney World. Suddenly the animal burst from the surface of the pond and grabbed the child's leg. The alligator shook her head and tried to pull Santamaria into the water. Initially he remembers being in shock, he told New York's *Daily News*, "I wasn't screaming at first. I had to process what was happening, that I was being attacked by an alligator. It was shock at first, and then it triggered me to call for my brother and sister."

TEARS *for* CROCODILIA

It was calling for his brother and sister that saved Paul's life. His sister Carolyn was twelve and his brother Joseph Jr. was ten; together the siblings grabbed Paul's arms and engaged in a deadly game of tug-of-war. Joseph grabbed sticks and stones to hit and throw at the alligator, and Paul started kicking with the one leg outside the animal's mouth. Together it seems the children intimidated the alligator into releasing Paul, who in the end suffered nothing more than a lingering fear of water after recovering from his wounds in the hospital. As unlikely as it seems, sociality and being able to grasp with hands while standing on two feet can sometimes save a child attacked by a crocodilian.

In 2017, Rudy Francis, an animal expert at a zoo in Borneo, was also the unlikely survivor of a crocodile attack. Francis was feeding a crocodile when the animal grabbed him by the arm and pulled him into the water for an immediate death roll. After losing his arm, Rudy Francis was again seized by the leg. Similarly to Paul Santamaria, Francis called for help, in his case from his coworkers. Rudy Francis had his coworkers pull, which caused him to also lose his leg to the crocodile but allowed him to survive.

Others have survived crocodile attacks by gouging the animal's sensitive eyes causing them to release, a method hard to carry out without some sort of fingers. In fact, most human survivors prevail over attacking crocodiles with very human survival techniques. Indeed, it seems possible that we've been in an evolutionary arms race against crocodilians and other predators. Of course technology like guns, large motorized boats, and even warning signs and fences often make our most basic survival adaptations a moot point, but we shouldn't forget that, until recently, those were all we had. Intelligence, bipedalism, and sociality to some degree or other may all have been gifts to us from as unlikely as it seems, predators.

No one would question that the speed of an antelope or deer is related to the speed of cheetahs or wolves and a history of being hunted. So too, we should be able to embrace the idea that some of our adaptations, and even our fears, have evolved in response to predation.

In a brief paper, famous orangutan biologist Biruté Galdikas and Carey Yeager described the case of a crab-eating macaque being preyed upon by a crocodile and observed that since crocodiles are in decline, this was probably once a more common occurrence. The scientists also noted that it's possible that crocodile predation has impacted the macaque's anti-predator behavior. Two years later, Galdikas reported a crocodile predation upon a proboscis monkey in the same area, again noting the possible importance in the monkey's evolution.

Interestingly, a paper published in 2017 found that crocodiles in Malaysia (*Crocodylus porosus*) tended to rest in the same type of areas monkeys used to spend the night. Crocodiles actively sought out places where trees hung over the water, the same areas macaques liked to sleep, ironically, to perhaps avoid terrestrial predators. This correlation, along with the observations of crocodile predation on monkeys, seems to suggest not only that crocodiles may influence the behavior of monkeys but that monkeys may also influence the behavior of crocodilians. It's easy to see how this might have been the case with our distant ancestors as well. Today, we continue to influence each other but perhaps in a more lopsided way.

When it comes to us and crocodilians, predation goes both ways, but humans now kill far more crocodilians each year than crocodilians kill humans.

As much as crocodiles may have in part offered our ancestors the bite of fruit that opened our eyes and remade us as humans, we play a role in shaping the future lives of crocodilians as well. We're pressed up to each other like puzzle pieces fit together. Eating and being eaten creates an intimate relationship between beings. Although when we consider this, it's good to remember that a crocodilian's basic natural history, including predation, arose long before modern humans walked on the earth, and we ultimately are late comers fitting ourselves into a pre-made order.

What do we make of this relationship? In his book *Feral: Rewilding the Land, the Sea and Human Life*, author George Monbiot suggests that some people love wildlife that are perceived as dangerous for the very same reason others fear them. Our deep sense of our past in the danger of a wild animal, and much of the malaise common in modern Western society is due to what Monbiot calls "ecological boredom." Perhaps the case can be made for some deep value being found in crocodilians because a few of them, at least, are still fearsome or dangerous to us. On some level this means that we and crocodilians are one—we are both beings capable of impacting the other, viewing and shaping the other.

The hard part of this view is that people, Westerners especially, are generally in the habit of viewing the natural world as a backdrop, tool, or sometimes inconvenience to human activity. Even many conservation-minded individuals tend to think of trees, animals, minerals, and other parts of the "natural" world as "resources." It's entirely different to consider a relationship of give and take between a human and a nonhuman. This interactive view of humans and nonhumans is more common in other cultures beyond our narrow Western perspective. It's something anthropologists have started to pick up on recently.

Anthropologist Eduardo Kohn describes his goal of creating an anthropology "beyond the human" in his paper "How Dogs Dream" as well as in his book *How Forests Think*. In "How Dogs Dream," Kohn describes the views of the Runa people of Ecuador on nonhuman life: "according to them, all beings, and not just humans, engage with the world and with each other as selves—that is, as beings that have a point of view. Runa ways of knowing others, then, are predicated on what I call an 'ecology of selves.'"

A similar idea is also expressed by ethologist Jakob von Uexküll who presented a world where interactions between organisms weren't mechanical but arose from the "umwelt" of each animal involved. This is an idea that other animals are, like humans, "selves." This concept is just as applicable and potent for crocodilians as it is for dogs, dolphins, parrots, or chimpanzees. If crocodilians are indeed selves, as I believe the evidence overwhelmingly indicates, this is a crucial detail to consider in human-crocodilian interactions, even conflicts and predation.

An attack by a crocodilian might be a terrible ordeal for a human, but it's likely to turn out much worse for the reptile in the end these days. Our long history with crocodilians has created a range of cultural responses from awe at the majestic creatures to a deep and abiding desire to exterminate them. Beyond culture, evolution seems to have imbued us with fear and antipathy toward predators of all sorts. Few people, whatever their cultural background, will argue against killing a crocodilian that has made an attempt at eating a human being.

Beyond revenge killing or attempts at predator control, humans kill crocodilians for hosts of reasons. Death by the hands of humans has had an enormous impact on modern crocodilians. Our evolution may have been partly shaped by the avoidance of toothy crocodile jaws, but the ecology, distribution, and behavior of many crocodilians are influenced by our behavior in turn.

One study from 1998 looked at the impact of human disturbance on the behavior of two caiman species (*Caiman crocodylus* and *Melanosuchus niger*) in Ecuador. The researchers captured, marked, and released caimans in some of the ponds they were surveying but not in other ponds. After returning for another survey days later, they found fewer caimans in the ponds where the animals had been captured and tagged. The upshot is that capturing and tagging the caimans resulted in caimans hiding from their would-be human assailants. In the ponds where caimans were merely surveyed by spotlight, the animals were still readily observable, not having learned to be afraid of scientists. It's not a stretch to think that hunting likewise makes a crocodilian more wary of predation. Indeed, there is much anecdotal evidence that alligators in the American South make themselves more scarce in areas where they're hunted.

Until relatively recently, crocodilians weren't intensively hunted but only killed as a minor food source, ritualistically, or when perceived as a danger to humans or livestock. Global economics and the use of crocodilian skin in fashion has driven much of the hunting. Indeed, in Mexico, the Mayan went from rarely hunting crocodiles to a well-established "lagartero" culture of sophisticated crocodile hunting practices in a short time. Crocodiles are not usually hunted primarily for meat but instead for skins, even now. Hunting is also used directly as a management tool, along with farming.

In 2008, a strange population of African dwarf crocodiles (*Osteolaemus tetraspis*) was discovered living in caves in Gabon off a diet of bats, the reptile's skin bleached a strange orangish color. Genetic research showed that the crocodiles were on their way to becoming a new species. The researchers suggested that crocodiles might've taken up life underground at least part of the time, due to pressure from human hunters.

Together, intensive hunting and especially farming of crocodilians has changed their world, and possibly begun a fundamental shift, an "unmaking" of them as wild animals and remaking of them as something akin to domestic creatures with artificial habitats, artificial selection, and even artificial insemination.

Another problem is that the market for the skin of crocodilians is constantly in flux, supplying riches to farms in some years and very little income in others. In a word, crocodilian skins are luxury. No longer are crocodilians a primal force in our lives but merely a fashion statement. In this way, we are remaking animals that might've helped make us in the first place.

In most parts of the world, crocodilians seemed to have gone from a revered and ancient creature, important to the history and lives of humans, to a cash crop in a short period. It's good to remember, however, that before the rise of global economics, crocodilians were, in some places at least, gods.

eleven

GODS *and* DEVILS

WHEN I WAS AT ARANSAS, I heard a story. A family had been pic-
nicking at a table near a slough. An alligator rose from the slough
and in a high walk slowly ambled towards them. The family wisely
moved away from the alligator, relocating at a farther table. The
alligator in turn lay down on the grass near the table, seemingly
unconcerned.

It's a mundane story, but it says something small, if obvious,
about the human perception of alligators and other crocodilians—
we respect, or at least fear them. As I've already discussed, many
crocodilians have the ability to literally consume an adult human.
Of course seeing any animal through human culture is seeing them
through glass darkly, but it's also a way to see ourselves clearly. Crocodilians and humans have shaped each other through evolution and
behavior. By looking at the rough edge of our culture torn to fit with
crocodiles jaws, we glimpse something eerie and essential.

The stream of fear that flows through our consciousness splits
and meanders, welling up in a number of different ways. The
source of awe or worship on some level is fear. This is revealed
most familiarly in the phrase "God fearing," which only makes
sense when you equate fear with awe or worshipfulness.

TEARS *for* CROCODILIA

Temples in ancient Egypt were built for Sobek, the crocodile god. The god himself was depicted sometimes as a man with a crocodile head, sometimes as a crocodile, and sometimes closely associated with other gods such as Horus, the better known falcon-headed god. Fierceness was clearly an aspect of Sobek, an aspect that the Egyptians must have wanted to harness or at least placate with their worship—the fierceness not just of the Nile crocodile but also of the Nile itself. The temples must have been dark, terrible places even when filled with worshippers. Deep within the dim stone temples, live crocodiles were kept as deities manifest, adorned in jeweled splendor and fed choice foods.

Another channel that fear flows into is an urge to control. The power of lightning is terrifying, but if you control that power, it is the magic of nighttime lights and television and the cellular phone. Rituals surrounding Sobek were not just about showering the crocodile god with adoration; as with most religion, it was also about obtaining favor and invoking the god.

Southwest of Cairo, the city of Faiyum is located in the basin by the same name. There is a dry hollow flooded into an oasis by the Nile River when its banks occasionally overflow. Faiyum lies on the shores of this lake, a desert city near water, a place the Greeks once called Crocodoliopolis. With a population of less than half a million, the city is dwarfed by Cairo but contains the desert-dried ruins of temples, writing, and the dead, comprising a history that extends back at least three thousand years.

On December 3, 1899, British papyrologists Bernard P. Grenfell and Arthur S. Hunt arrived at a site outside of Faiyum to begin an excavation that would stretch into the early part of the next year. The researchers had been hired by the University of California at Berkeley to gather material for the university's collections. The work must have been rough; the researchers were based in large, hot, canvas tents, the digging was done by shovels and other hand tools.

The excavation was focused on finding papyrus to glean what written historical records had survived. By modern scientific standards, the focus solely on papyrus was very unscientific and perhaps

The Temple of Kom Ombo photographed in 1903. This temple was built as a double temple dedicated on one half to Sobek, the crocodile god, and to Horus on the other half. Three hundred crocodile mummies were found in the vicinity of the temple. (*New York Public Library*)

destructive. In a little more than a week the expedition cleaned out 150 graves of their written records, showing little interest in other artifacts or the human remains.

Eventually the site of the dig was discovered to be known as Tebtunis, a town with its center marked by an impressive limestone temple to a crocodile god, Soknebtunis or "Sobek Lord of Tebtunis." The temple was originally approached by a ceremonial processional walkway lined with statues of lions and sphinxes. First constructed between 305 and 285 BCE, the temple was completed and expanded beyond its original plans roughly two hundred years later. Impressive gates lead to a courtyard, with the temple and other buildings in one complex. It was here that crocodiles were buried in a special graveyard or even an exclusive tomb, depending on the importance of the individual animal.

The town of Tebtunis, including the temple to Sobek, was full of papyri: Grenfell and Hunt found as much paper in a month as a typical year of excavation yielded. Today, some researchers have guessed that as many as 100,000 papyri—one fourth of all papyri known from Greco-Roman Egypt—have been discovered in the Tebtunis region. After Tebtunis, the two men turned south to the necropolis—city of the dead—to search for papers found in the coverings of mummies.

Instead of golden masks like that of King Tutankhamen, lower castes of ancient Egypt were sometimes buried with death masks made of cartonnage: a material consisting of glue and papyrus scraps, something akin to papier-mâché. Just like with modern papier-mâché, the scraps of papyrus sometimes contain tidbits of current events. Other pieces of paper show up amid the layers of linen wrapped around the mummies, crinkled into balls much as modern newspaper might be used to protect fragile glassware sent through the mail. Written in black ink on brownish paper carefully cleaned to be read by researchers, papyrus scraps found on mummies have proven to be receipts and pieces of contracts as well as fragments of Homer, biblical texts, and histories. Researchers even announced in 2012 that they found pieces of the oldest known gospel of Mark in an Egyptian death mask's cartonnage. Looking through the wrappings and masks of mummies is a bit like searching through someone's recycle bin to learn about their life: time consuming and only occasionally enlightening.

Looking for the tiny insights revealed in scraps of paper recycled for mummification, Grenfell and Hunt were drawn to the potential library of papyrus scraps represented by the necropolis. Ferreting about for human mummies, one of the workers dug into a row of mummified crocodiles. Frustrated at finding what was then thought to be archaeologically useless, the man smashed a crocodile to pieces. To everyone's surprise, the crocodile was wrapped in papyrus similarly to his human counterparts. The rest of the season was dedicated to excavating the crocodile cemetery next to the human one. Of the thousand crocodile mummies found, only thirty-one were mummified with discarded papyri.

A wooden mask with gold leaf decoration for a crocodile mummy, Late Period-Ptolemaic Period (525–30 BCE), Fayum, Egypt. Masks such as these were placed on the heads of sacred crocodile mummies prepared from animals which had been worshiped as deities in life and mummified after a natural death. Alternatively, more expensive votive offering crocodiles may have sometimes been adorned with masks as well. (*Metropolitan Museum of Art*)

The many strange gods and burial practices are part of what make ancient Egypt such a fertile place for the imagination. Human mummies have long been held in horror and fascination by the Western mind. Even in the ancient world, Roman senators visited Egypt as tourists to view "labyrinth" tombs and observe rituals at crocodile cult temples. The reality of animal mummification in Egyptian culture was a far greater enterprise than most casual readers understand.

Cats were raised in large numbers to be made into mummy offerings to the cat goddess Bastet. Ibises likewise have been found mummified and interred en masse, as offerings to the ibis-headed god of magic, wisdom, and the moon, Thoth. Pet baboons and dogs were mummified, apparently to be reunited with loving owners after death. Crocodiles were mummified in large numbers for various reasons. The different cults of worship came and went according to trends, as denominations in modern religions gain and lose popularity with the times.

During the Greco-Roman period in Faiyum, Sobek and other crocodile gods were of great importance. Like different manifestations of the Virgin Mary in Catholicism, it seems that different gods associated with crocodiles were the embodiment of different aspects of the same deity.

In worship of Sobek and other similar gods, crocodiles were, as mentioned earlier, sometimes kept bejeweled in a temple, offered the best of foods, and generally adored. Herodotus wrote that sacred crocodiles wore earrings and bracelets and were fed bread and meat. Strabo describes the crocodiles being fed honey mixed with wine. When these crocodiles died, presumably at a ripe old age, they were duly mummified and interred as deities, in a special tomb.

Other crocodiles were apparently hatched and kept in captivity solely to be killed and mummified, when they were perhaps only a foot long and maybe a year or less old. These crocodiles were raised in nurseries with features recognizable to modern crocodile farmers today. These tiny crocodile mummies were sold as votives to the worshippers to be left to the crocodile gods as gifts. Even mummified crocodile eggs were apparently used as votive offerings. This commercial enterprise was an important piece of the economy of ancient Faiyum and is part of the obvious nuances of how individual crocodiles were actually treated by worshippers.

Some crocodile mummies have been found as adults with babies attached to their backs as they would be found in life; another realistic mummy was discovered with young held protectively in her mouth. Crocodiles were clearly closely observed by those preparing their mummies.

I asked Michal Molcho, a historian who did her PhD on crocodile worship during the Greco-Roman period of Faiyum, some questions about the worship of crocodile deities. Molcho told me in an email that it can be hard to tease out the exact meaning of the crocodiles to ancient Egyptian supplicants:

Small juvenile crocodiles were killed and mummified to become votive offerings to Sobek. This example is dated, ca. 400 BCE–100 AD. (*Metropolitan Museum of Art*)

I think it's a bit difficult to really be able to say what a god meant to people—even today, it is hard to describe what deities mean to worshippers. I think we can say that the crocodiles were both manifestations of the gods and a symbol of the god, so for example, specific, sacred crocodiles were kept in the temples and treated as gods, but the crocodiles bred for mummification were not treated that way, but used as symbols of the god, and given to him in veneration. In other animal cults, such as that of the Apis Bull, we know that specific animals were chosen as the sacred animals based on certain unique physical attributes (a mark, etc.) and that only they were sacred.

Interestingly there are actually two species of crocodiles that live in Egypt, the well-known Nile crocodile (*Crocodylus niloticus*) and the smaller, more docile West African or "sacred" crocodile (*Crocodylus suchus*). Only the smaller crocodile was kept in temples, suggesting that the Egyptians were aware of the difference between two crocodiles that were once considered by modern science to be a single species.

It's thought that due to the sacred crocodile's calmer nature it could be kept in a temple with less danger to worshippers and priests. Despite a preference for a peaceable nature, danger was probably one of the elements that made the crocodile fascinating to the Egyptian imagination. In a paper published as part of her thesis in the *Journal of Egyptian Archaeology*, Michal Molcho quoted Scottish Egyptologist Angela McDonald: "The crocodile symbolizes raw power, context determines whether this is negative or positive."

Or as Molcho wrote herself, "The crocodile, one of the most iconic features of the River Nile, was an important element in the lives of the ancient Egyptians who resided alongside its banks. This fierce animal dominated the waters of the Nile, but its presence was viewed not only as dangerous and threatening, but as representing life and fertility as well, as it was seen to be emerging from the river which was regarded as Egypt's source of life. This duality in the perception of the crocodile as a great natural power of which to be thankful as well as wary, was subsequently realized in the various cults with which it was associated."

Without fully understanding the complex view of crocodiles in the context of the cult, it's easy to see that the physical power and danger of the actual animal was part of the draw. Crocodiles waiting patiently by a river to catch and kill cattle was a common depiction on tomb walls in the Old Kingdom, and the prowess and strength of hunting crocodiles was often mentioned in ancient Egypt, in both papyri and inscriptions.

The potency of the crocodile wasn't only associated with physical violence or bodily protection; the ancient Egyptians also called Sobek the "lord of semen" and associated him with fertility. Sometimes crocodile penises are used in folk medicines for male virility. One common potion was a powdered crocodile penis mixed into honey. Even today, a common brand of Egyptian honey features a label with a crocodile. In her essay "Crocodiles: Guardians of the Gateways," Egyptologist Salima Ikram tells how this association probably comes from the large number of eggs that crocodiles lay as well as the fact that crocodile penises can measure nearly a meter in length. In one Egyptian myth a king turns into a crocodile to steal wives, a nod to the sexual potency of the reptile.

The ancient Egyptian human relationship with crocodiles was far from straightforward, and even ambivalent. Tombs from the sixth dynasty of Egypt have been found illustrated with herdsmen using spells to keep crocodiles away from their livestock. A passage from the Egyptian Book of the Dead also contains a spell to fend off crocodiles in the underworld.

Late in Egyptian history, people who were eaten or even attacked by crocodiles achieved a semi-divine status. This may be due to an association with the sun god or because the crocodile was considered a sacred animal in some parts of Egypt.

When Christianity came to Egypt during the Coptic period of the fourth to seventh centuries, crocodiles maintained their importance, if in a different way than in the ancient Egyptian religion. Abba Bes, a Coptic priest, was said to have rid his region of Egypt from crocodiles through prayer. The wooden door of one of the churches of the Monastery of Abu Sefein, in Old Cairo, was once adorned with crocodile skin. It's uncertain whether the skin was merely decorative or served the purpose of protecting the wood. It seems likely, however, that the skin was intended to ward off evil. Other Coptic churches have studs covering their doors, giving them the appearance of crocodile skin, perhaps with the same purpose. Crocodiles were thought in ancient Egypt to always know how high to place their nests and avoid flooding. Because of this, some placed a crocodile above a doorway to protect the home or perhaps a church from flooding.

Even today, Egyptologist Salima Ikram writes that a taxidermy crocodile can be found hanging inside the doorway of the Café El-Fishawy in Cairo, attesting to the continued presence of crocodiles as protectors. Although many no longer remember the origins of crocodiles as protectors or potion ingredients, they linger in modern Egyptian culture. The remnants of crocodilian spirituality can in fact be found throughout Africa and the world.

Some major world religions have sacred places dedicated at least in part to living crocodiles. Mor Sahib is a crocodile claimed to be eighty-seven years old living in a pond near a shrine in Pakistan. Here the Sheedi community comes to offer the crocodile sweets and pieces of goat meat in ancient rituals with unclear origins. Songs are sung in African languages that many of the Sheedi (whose ancestors migrated to Pakistan long ago) no longer speak.

The Sheedi are Muslim, and the crocodile is not considered a god but still important to the sacred site.

In the northern part of Madagascar, the village of Anivorana has a myth: An old man shuffled along a cracked dirt trail into the village. It wasn't much—just some small huts made with split bamboo walls and thatched in palm leaves. The man was thirsty. Nearing the open entrance to the first hut, the old man called out for water in a raspy, dry voice like an old leaf. The thin wooden door swung shut, propelled by unseen hands. At the next hut the old man came to, the door was already closed but voices could be heard inside. Again the old man asked if someone inside could give him a sip of water. The voices from the hut quieted and, after a long pause, the old man wobbled on, leaning into a worn stick he carried.

The old man teetered against his stick, making his way along the dusty path leading through the village asking everywhere for a simple cup of water to slake his thirst on a hot day. Everywhere the man asked, he was ignored until he came across a small child playing in front of a hut. The old man, in near desperation, asked the child for some water. Unsurprisingly the child turned and quickly darted into the doorway of the nearest hut. The old man heard a woman's voice scolding or comforting the child. The man paused, swaying against his stick for stability. Soon a young woman, the mother of the child, came from inside the home holding a small gourd full of cool water. The old man took the water quietly and swallowed the liquid with long slow slurps. When the man had drank his fill, he passed the gourd back to the young woman and spoke to her quietly, "Since you helped me, I offer you some advice: when your baby cries tonight, take your children together and leave this village immediately. You can return the next morning when the rain stops."

The young woman turned away for a second as one of her children ran past her, bumping her legs. When she turned back, the old man was gone. The woman shivered but tried putting the old man out of her mind, returning to her house with the half-empty gourd of water.

Crocodile amulets from Madagascar, used to give safe passage over rivers to the wearer. (Musée du quai Branly, Paris)

That night, the rains started gently, little more than a soft mist, and the young woman lay down, falling easily into a peaceful sleep. As the night wore on though, thunder started to growl overhead and her smallest child woke in a panic and started screaming through her tears. The young mother remembered the old man's advice and she quickly gathered her children to her and walked away from the village, mud sticking to their feet in the dark.

The night was a miserable one spent huddling beneath jungle trees and rock ledges, the rain keeping them all awake, wet and cold. More than once the woman wondered if what she was doing made sense. More than once her children pestered her for a reason they were there, something she couldn't easily give. Every time she doubted, the woman thought of the way the old man who moved so slowly had seemingly vanished in the blink of an eye, and she shivered. Still, when the sun peeked over the horizon, the young woman was more than happy to finally return to the village.

At first, she couldn't believe what she saw. The woman had to trace and retrace the paths back to her village until she was certain she was at the right place. Where once there was a small cluster of huts and people, there was now a pond full of crocodiles. The old man (who was a sorcerer) had taken his revenge on the villagers by giving them what he had asked for—water. The sorcerer had also turned the people of the village into crocodiles.

This story is my own retelling of a myth from Madagascar. People living near a pond in the northern part of the country consider the crocodiles of the pond their ancestors. Today, the villagers sometimes call upon the crocodiles to answer prayers, chanting a request while throwing the reptiles offerings of meat. If the meat is eaten by the crocodile it is seen as a commitment by the crocodile (and thus ancestor) to answer the prayer. In this way the bond between crocodiles and humans is maintained with a sort of reciprocity of payments for services.

Some Malagasy tribes afford the same funeral rites to crocodiles as they do to people. Other people in Madagascar variously believe that their chiefs are descended from crocodiles or that evil people are reincarnated as crocodiles or snakes. As with many things, a certain set of beliefs involving crocodiles is not universal in Madagascar. When I visited the island nation as a reforestation intern, I learned that in some places the eerie-looking aye-aye (a nocturnal species of lemur) was thought of as a harbinger of evil, other groups considered the primate to be a reincarnated ancestor. A dislike of crocodiles makes a certain amount of sense in Madagascar, yet in some regions the fear of crocodiles is described as extreme and superstitious.

The grouping of snakes and crocodiles together for being reincarnations of evil people in Madagascar is interesting. The inherently dangerous crocodile contrasts strongly with snakes in Madagascar, which as I mentioned has no venomous or dangerous snakes at all. The Ekoi of West Africa associate snakes and crocodiles closely as well, with snake cults closely related to the crocodile.

The Shona people, a Bantu ethnic group of southern Africa, liken their chiefs to crocodiles. The chiefs sometimes swallow gas-

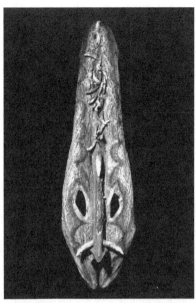

Crocodile mask from Papua New Guinea. Crocodiles represent ancestral spirits among some people of Papua New Guinea, especially along the Sepik River. (*Brooklyn Museum*)

trolith stones to ritually become crocodiles. During initiations to chiefdom, a man sometimes spends a night in a hut with a crocodile. The Thonga people of southern Mozambique believe that a chief swallowing a gastrolith along with certain drugs can lead to the premonition of his own death.

In Papua New Guinea, along the Sepik River, various groups use the crocodile as their totem. Similarly to the people of northern Madagascar, they feel a kinship with the amphibious reptiles. In the male initiation into manhood, boys are ritualistically scarred with cuts that are said to represent crocodile bite marks. The blood loss incurred during the ritual is said to be the loss of the last female blood: a ritualistic way to sever a boy from his mother and bring him into manhood.

The scars also create the effect of the rough scales and scutes of crocodile skin. Thus through ritual a boy is consumed by the crocodile and reborn as a crocodile man. The ritual seems to not only recognize the killing power of the crocodile but also acknowledge the intimacy of being consumed by another. The cuts are often patterned into shapes of vaginas and breasts as well. Interestingly, the scars are only a small part of a larger ordeal. Boys who would transform themselves into crocodile men go through weeks of isolation living in the ritual "crocodile nest," an area created by a temporary wall built around a spirit house. The scarification ritual occurs while the boys sit on overturned canoes with elaborate crocodile faces carved into their prows. Each boy leans back between the legs of an elder, who carves the markings into the boy's skin—traditionally with sharpened bamboo but now sometimes with razor blades; the position of boy and man represents the older giving birth to the younger. After the initial scarification, the ritual goes on much longer, with boys dancing and being beaten by the older men. Boys are covered head to toe with clay and have a piece of rope tied around their necks. The boys are force-fed four meals a day of fish, sago, and other foods meant to make them gain weight and appear like a crocodile with a swollen belly full of food. Not until night are the boys allowed to return home to sleep—only on their bellies—but not to be seen by women or children. The ritual ends with the best known symbol of rebirth in the West: a dip into the river, a baptism into life as a crocodile man.

This ritual links reproductive power to crocodile spirits, similar to the potency and fertility ancient Egyptians accorded to crocodiles. In fact, among the people along the Sepik River, it is said that only senior crocodile spirits give birth to children as well as crocodile men. Women are seen as just the agents *for* birth rather than the agents *of* birth. The ritual can be seen as a way in which men have stolen reproductive powers from women, since men are the only conduits of the crocodile spirit powers. It perhaps even hints at a spiritual connection between sexual orgasm and death. During sex, a man's penis is engulfed in a vagina in a similar way to being swallowed. Crocodiles literally swallow humans, and symbolically swallow men before they're reborn as "crocodile men." Thus the myth acknowledges the place of death within life. Rebirth is achieved through being consumed entirely by the other, even if only through ritual. The power of life is controlled through the power of death. The crocodile is the agent of both.

Some of the Larrakia people of Australia consider the saltwater crocodile (*Crocodylus porosus*), which they call "Dungalaba," a totem animal as well. Much of the cultural importance of the crocodile and even language has been lost, unfortunately.

Further south in the central part of Madagascar, the people living near Lake Itasy, not far from the capital city of Antananarivo, have a slightly different conception of their relationship with the crocodile. Once a year the people call to the crocodiles to renew an agreement. The people warn the crocodiles that as many people are killed by crocodiles, that many of the reptiles will be killed in turn. The well-intentioned crocodiles are asked to not interfere, as they are meant no harm. This means that crocodiles are also not killed except to enact "justice" against them for breaking a truce.

The idea of a general truce between crocodiles and humans is a common idea shared among cultures that grew up near crocodiles. It's also a common theme among peoples who share the land with other dangerous animals. For example, Indigenous people in Siberia believe that when a person is killed by a tiger, the victim is often thought to have in some ways broken an agreement between tigers and humans.

The idea of a crocodilian killing a person being a part of justice is very common. *Eyelids of the Morning,* by Alistair Graham and Peter Beard, is a classic book on the relationship between native peoples and crocodiles living on Lake Rudolf/Lake Turkana in northwest Kenya. The book notes that the locals act unconcerned about the threat of crocodiles, assuming that they kill only evil people.

Fishermen in the upper Congo have been observed calmly going about daily tasks in close proximity to crocodiles, claiming that "real" crocodiles don't attack people. Only a witch transformed into a crocodile represents a danger. In many parts of Africa, the distinction between dangerous "were"-crocodiles (akin to werewolves) and harmless normal crocodiles is often made.

Among the Nuna people of Burkina Faso, mythology represents crocodiles as spiritual and sometimes benevolent creatures. The mask, left, shows a crocodile above a hornbill (bird). Crocodiles such as the one carved into this nineteenth-century door, right, often represented political power and authority for the Baule people of Ivory Coast. (*Brooklyn Museum*)

Lake Victoria once held the famous Lutembe, a sacred crocodile. Trials by ordeal were sometimes held with Lutembe acting as omniscient judge. It was thought that Lutembe would only assault a guilty person; if a person offered to the crocodile was attacked and eaten it was considered to be both judgment and sentence.

The idea that crocodiles could be closely related to groups of people or could mete out justice is a very odd thought to most Westerners. It's important to realize that these views come from peoples with long histories of interactions with crocodiles, something that European cultures lack. Crocodiles for many are a very normal part of daily life, even now. Westerners have a way of artificially separating ourselves from the "natural" world in an attempt to feel superior to it and in some cases justify our destruction of it. To many other groups of people, including those closely associated with crocodiles, there is a very different vision, and being human and non-human are not so very separate. Beneath the strange rituals, crocodile gods, temples, and superstitions, I believe there is a hard kernel of truth many Westerners never have to face.

In "A Cultural Herpetology of Nile Crocodiles in Africa," a paper published in *Conservation and Society*, herpetologist Simon Pooley notes that the Wapokomo people living on the banks of the Tana River in Kenya are said to be fearless of crocodiles, explaining to researchers a sort of reciprocity: "we eat each other."

This simple statement seems to point to a strange paradox. Crocodilians and humans are bound together by a simple ecological interaction that is painful to acknowledge: Crocodilians sometimes eat people. People today, in contrast, raise alligators, crocodiles, and caimans to be turned into battered and fried nuggets, handbags, and novelty tourism items. In a strange way, the commercialism of the crocodile stems from the animal's status as sacred. When crocodiles were worshipped in Egypt, an entire industry raised them in captivity only so they could be killed, mummified, and offered in worship to crocodile gods. Yet the ancient Egyptians—for all the control they exerted over the lives of individual crocodiles, both worshipped and sacrificed—acknowledged the intrinsic power of the crocodile.

The power of crocodilians is the power of death. This power also offers humans one significant gift: through death we can find unification. When someone is eaten by a crocodile and digested, part of that person literally becomes one with the crocodile. Westerners sometimes seek "oneness" with nature as a mystical quest. It needn't be so complicated. To become one with nature, all that is needed is to acknowledge the power of death and succumb to it, something we must all do. Death is followed by consumption, if not by a reptilian predator than by tiny invertebrates, bacteria, and fungi. Full recognition of the crocodile is a recognition of this universal truth: in the end, we're always eaten.

Paradoxically the power of death is related to the power of life. A crocodile is not just a destroyer to be feared but a powerful being

Golden crocodile funerary pendant from the Kingdom of Baule (Ivory Coast). Pendants such as these are associated with ancestral spirits and kept hidden until important events such as funerals where they are displayed. A widow wearing a pendant such as this one may represent the end of her period of mourning. Crocodiles are associated with Queen Abra Poku, founder of the Kingdom of Baule. (*Cleveland Museum of Art*)

to be respected in her own right. This seems to be the essence of crocodilian worship the world over. With the rare possibility of an adult human being eaten by a crocodilian, a rather visceral and stunning opportunity of coupling with nature is on offer, for the steep price of life. Of course consumption by a crocodilian was and is a very real threat, yet also very rare. Being swallowed by an animal is largely symbolic. The historic fear and hatred of crocodilians can be seen as a fear and hatred of submission to wildness in all its forms. Unfortunately, wildness is something modern conservation ethics have still not fully embraced.

$\mathcal{The}$ (ALMOST) LOST WORLD of CROCODILIANS

WHEN, ROUGHLY 95 MILLION YEARS AGO (mya), crocodilians with modern body plans made their first splash in history, the earth was a much warmer and more climatically homogenous place than it is today. The difference in average temperature between polar regions and equatorial regions was less than half of current numbers. Through the Eocene (65.5 to 56 mya) the temperatures remained relatively warm, which is why a crocodilian fossil (*Borealosuchus sp.*) I prepared was pulled from a quarry in Wyoming rather than Georgia or Texas. Crocodilian fossils have been found as far north as 50°N latitude, the equivalent of crocodiles living in what is now Maine or Frankfurt, Germany. Northern crocodile fossils are, themselves, important evidence supporting the idea of a more equitable past climate.

The amiable temperatures allowed crocs to spread into a larger percentage of the earth's surface than allotted to them today. As the planet dried and cooled, the range of crocodilians has shrunk to their current tropical and subtropical habitats. People like to live in and visit these same areas—warm places with waterfront views. We like to swim, scuba dive, or simply drink away warm evenings on booze cruises. Warm areas are also big draws for wildlife tourism, with abundant wild animals from fishes to birds and much more in between. Some tourists even pay to interact with crocodilians.

Frolicking in swimwear is a favorite pastime for many but it comes with a price. What now seems like a pristine beach may once have been a coastal mangrove forest cleared by a local resort. Locally caught seafood served at that same resort might be netted with dolphins or sea turtles drowning as bycatch, or cause smashed up reefs and continually shrinking fish populations. Wetlands are drained for development. All of this drives us inexorably into conflict with wildlife, including crocodilians. Habitats are being destroyed at alarming rates by growing local human populations and the influx of large numbers of tourists and multinational industry, evaporating crocodilian habitat even further as the planet warms once again.

Despite our proclivities for warm and wet, most native haunts of crocodilians are unappealing to many Westerners, at least in how we portray them. Dismal, dark, fearful swamps full of mud and shadowy trees draped in eerie moss is what most think of. Historic attempts to literally "drain the swamp" and even the phrase itself point to the western antipathy toward wetlands.

Swamps, marshes, and bogs don't capture the Western mind like mountains, clear rivers, or the sea. As Barbara Hurd wrote in her book, *Stirring the Mud: On Swamps, Bogs and Human Imagination*: "To love a swamp, however, is to love what is muted and marginal, what exists in the shadows, what shoulders its way out of mud and scurries along the damp edges of what is most commonly praised."

Because of the under-appreciation of bogs, swamps, marshes, and other wetlands, and greedy human desire for heat, water, and "usable" land, there has been a historic tendency to cultivate, change, destroy, or "make something" of many crocodilian haunts. In China, the alligator habitat has been mostly swallowed whole by the unending expansion of agriculture and other human sprawl.

The Everglades, often thought of as a last American refuge of swamp lands or marsh, is much and permanently damaged by human meddling. Once water in southern Florida flowed from the Kissimmee River to Lake Okeechobee and southward in a slow-moving mass covering 11,000 square miles. This unchanneled water supported a patchwork of ponds, sawgrass marshes, hardwood hammocks, sloughs, and forests. Through the terrible history of southern Florida, slaves and Native Americans have sought refuge in the Everglades, Ponce De León quested for riches and the fountain of youth, and much of what was there has now been lost forever. Today, Big Cypress Swamp is a last holdout of hydrologically undamaged south Florida habitat; the rest of the Everglades is choking on what's left over after the Army Corps of Engineers and big agriculture has their share of water. The scale of what was destroyed throughout the southeastern United States can be seen in the slivered remnants of what still is.

Dark coastal forests of mangroves with fishes breeding about their roots and tree crabs (*Aratus pisonii*) scuttling through their canopies were sawed down. In their place perfectly groomed beaches with unobstructed views and strategically placed palm trees were created as "natural" areas for recreation. Sawgrass prairies filled with vast sheets of moving water where ibis and great blue heron stalked frogs among the sedges and among hunting alligators have shrunk. Channeling and draining in southern Florida has converted wetlands into a landscape of monotonous fields of sugar cane, further polluting the remaining ecosystems with agricultural run-off. A Florida guidebook proclaims, "the Everglades also embraces more than 7 million residents, 50 million annual tourists, 400,000 acres of sugarcane."

The Everglades have been so desecrated that in her book, *Ill Nature*, author Joy Williams goes so far as to write,

> That the Everglades still exists is a collective illusion shared by both those who care and those who don't. People used to say that nothing like the Everglades existed anywhere else in the world, but it doesn't exist in South Florida anymore ei-

ther. The Park, which millions of people visit and perceive to be the Everglades, makes up only 20 percent of the historic Glades and is but a pretty, fading afterimage of a once astounding ecosystem, the remaining 80 percent of which— drained, diked, and poisoned—has vanished beneath cities, canals, vast water impoundment areas, sugar cane fields, and tomato farms . . . one hour from Miami, has become a horror show of extirpated species. On land, a water park with no water; at sea a sick marine estuary turning into a murky hyper-saline, super-heated lagoon.

It's hard to say if the remnants of the Everglades will be damaged even more into the future or if this is even possible; the park and other public lands in theory protect at least a remnant portion of the once much greater ecosystem. These remnants in Florida and other areas are not nearly enough to contain growing alligator and crocodile populations completely, even if they were maintained in pristine condition, which is far from the case.

Poaching led to a crash in alligator numbers followed by a subsequent rebound. Approximately two thirds to 80 percent of the Everglades ecosystem was destroyed, along with much of the rest of the southeastern wild landscape. Alligators with populations now returning toward normal often spill out of the remnants of their "wilderness" homes into what has become golf courses, gardens, canals, farms, and other places where a small contact with a human is often a death sentence.

Even American crocodiles, considered vulnerable under the International Union for the Conservation of Nature, are still subject to government control and the whim of human caprice. After living at Dry Tortugas National Park in Florida for almost fourteen years, the single crocodile in residence was removed from the park for visitor safety and forcibly relocated to a remote part of Everglades National Park. This despite the fact that there's never been a reported human death caused by an American crocodile in the United States. The animal merely followed tourists, behavior almost certainly created by visitors ignoring rules prohibiting the feeding of animals. When it comes to humans or wildlife paying the price for the behavior of foolhardy people, the animals are always charged more. Such intolerance of crocodiles (as with alligators) and their habitat is unfortunately the norm.

People and crocodiles are increasingly jockeying for space, even in parks. Now approximately 25 percent of the U.S. American crocodile population lives in the cooling canals of Florida's Turkey Point nuclear power plant nestled between Biscayne National Park and Everglades National Park. Turkey Point is actually quite hard to visit, and despite requesting permission months in advance from two different people, I couldn't enter the nuclear plant to personally report on the crocodiles there. Ironically, these crocodiles may be safer than those in places like Dry Tortugas National Park (or Everglades)—at least they're not threatened by tourists.

Despite the historic destruction and ongoing threats, many argue that there is still an abundance of beauty and wildlife to be found in the Everglades, though less so than in historic times. I remember distinctly Zach Piotrowski, my supervisor at Aransas National Wildlife Refuge, telling me that the Everglades are *wild* with something of a fierce pride in his voice, recalling his time as a ranger there.

Everglades restoration efforts are also under way, starting in earnest at the end of the Clinton administration and initially backed by such odd bedfellows as Al Gore and Jeb Bush. The efforts still rely on enormous engineering projects and concessions to agriculture, however. To my mind, the restoration plans are more a model of compromise to big money than a model for future conservation. The future of the Everglades is uncertain; for now, some beauty lingers in remnant animals and plants.

Southern Florida is still a place where you can find human solitude in the company of a diversity of wildlife. People flock to the Everglades to canoe through green waters past quiet alligators or to catch sight of rare tropical birds. Whether the Everglades survive or not, the expansion of infrastructure, pulled along by human population growth, will leave less room for crocodilians everywhere.

The same is true in Nepal. Standing on the bridge overlooking the Babai River near Bardia, observing gharials, I saw a panoply of other wildlife using the river. One day, I saw the beautiful common kingfisher, with his bright turquoise wings and brown head fly over the water looking for a meal. Dark cormorants stood on rocks in the water, wings spread in the crooked fashion peculiar to them. Impressively large golden mahseer (*Tor putitora*) swam in the clear water next to even larger turtles. On a log balanced against the buttress of the bridge, an Indian pond heron (*Ardeola grayii*) with its brownish body moved in careful jerks toward the water and sat quietly watchful with neck pulled in as if against the cold. At other times I watched otters move across the river in fast, graceful leaps, arching their bodies out of the water just to splash back in. Spotted deer and sambar drank and crossed in big, obvious splashes. Of course, gharials swim in these waters, bask on the sand bars, eat, drink, mate, sleep, and dream in this place. Mugger crocodiles hunt, doze, and guard their young. Places like these have in recent history been strangled with pollution, their shores ravaged for gravel mines. More and more people live in and visit gharial habitat. Where langur monkeys in jungle trees once looked down on rivers, tourists peep from hotel rooms on irrigation canals. So-called ecotourism is a double-edged sword everywhere in the world, but it's far from the only cause of habitat destruction globally.

When I asked biologist Matt Shirley about the impact of habitat destruction on crocodiles in Africa, he assured me the damage is already done and most habitat is already destroyed. Still, Africa is a historic home to great numbers of crocodiles and some surprisingly unique crocodile environments. The whole continent bears the marks of crocodilians.

Strangely, West African crocodiles (*Crocodylus suchus*) even lived in the Sahara, a place now known for sand dunes that was once wetter. Stranger still, small numbers of these crocodiles are there even today.

Unlike American alligators that have been found in the Grand Canyon and wandering residential lawns in Phoenix, these crocodiles are leftover natives to the area, not later transplants. Over its seven-million-year history, the Sahara region has fluctuated in humidity and the desert has expanded and contracted—moving like blowing sand. When the Sahara goes through a drying period, as it is now, populations of animals requiring large amounts of water shrink as if evaporating under a relentless sun, along with their water sources.

Until the early twentieth century, crocodile populations were widespread at scattered water sources in the North African desert. As a product of a hotter, drier climate and human persecution, crocodiles have been eradicated throughout much of the region. Small "gueltas" or oases—pockets of water that remain after seasonal rivers dry up—are the last few refuges of Saharan crocodiles.

Guelta D'Archei of the Ennedi Plateau of Chad is a guelta in a region of strange mushroom-shaped rock formations and deep orange sandstone canyons, reminiscent of Utah. The pools of the guelta are nestled into the rocks of the desert where petroglyphs show how human life has changed along with the climate. An early period of pastoral cattle herding was replaced by a culture revolving around horses, and finally desert-tolerant camels became the main livestock two thousand years ago.

Today, dung from camels and other animals left in the guelta seems to allow algae and fish to live where little nutrition is likely to wash into the pools. The crocodiles in turn have made the fish a staple of their own diets, supplemented by whatever else they can catch from the shore. Of course, this is an atypical arrangement; more crocodilians live in rainforests and expansive wetlands than in desert pools. South and Central America are also home to an abundance of crocodilians under more "normal" conditions.

The tropical parts of the Americas and Caribbean regions (called neotropics) include some of the most biodiverse ecosystems on the planet; they're also habitat for several crocodilian species. The dense vegetation, infectious diseases, poisonous snakes, and other dangers not fully understood by the first Westerners to encounter them have long worked in the favor of preserving tropical habitats such as the Amazon. Settlements like Fordlandia, in which

Henry Ford attempted to build a working factory and village in the Brazilian Amazon based on U.S. standards, ultimately failed. Unfortunately other destructive forays into the neotropics are having an impact on the ecosystems and wildlife including the crocodilians that live there. Carlos de la Rosa, aquatic biologist and former director of La Selva Biological Station in Costa Rica, told me that neotropical habitats can be extremely fragile despite their bristling dangers:

> "One thing I worry about in particular is the general lack of knowledge about the fragility of these ecosystems and these species. While caimans and crocodiles seem magnificent and powerful, they are no match for us humans and our massive disturbances of ecosystems. Mining for minerals, rocks, and sand, extraction of water from rivers and streams, dikes and dams, pollution from agricultural runoff, sewage, and garbage, all work against the survival of these magnificent wildlife. We have too many humans on the planet now for us to be careless about nature and other creatures."

There is one thing in common between the Sahara and the neotropics where de la Rosa works—the water levels change radically from one time period to the next. Many forests in South America and other parts of the tropics flood; depending on the season, where once you walked on foot, you may float between trees in a canoe, watching for swimming sloths. There are even whole forests that float in South America; rafts of buoyant vegetation that support copses actually move with the water current, much like floating mats of vegetation in Okefenokee Swamp in the United States. The undulating rainforest waters blur what we imagine is a solid line between wetland or river and terrestrial habitat. With this blurring it becomes even more obvious that the crocodiles and caimans that live in the neotropics are not just part of rivers, lakes, and swamps; they are a part of the rainforest engulfing these things as well. As a piece of the greater ecosystems of the new world tropics, crocodilians are not only important predators but also important prey.

In the expansive wetland of the Pantanal (largest in the tropics), caimans are one of the jaguar's favorite foods. This is the best place in the world to see the big cats hunting along riverbanks, and some tour operators guarantee their visitors jaguar sightings. It may be surprising, but in the Pantanal, predation accounts for over 60 percent of caiman deaths. In the jungle, caiman are just another snack, but being food for other animals points to the important ecological role the reptiles play. The more species that eat you, the more biodiversity you support. This interconnectivity also highlights the fragility of the whole. Harm to a caiman can also hurt a jaguar. Rainforest destruction doesn't stop at the banks of a river and poisons won't stay just in water. Crocodilians are, like all life, deeply imbedded and dependent on everything else. This ecology is more important than any individual, yet it is made of individual lives enmeshed in a physical environment.

The ecology of crocodilian habitats and the complex interplay of physics, evolution, and just plain life, creates strange self-organized systems that sometimes seem alien to the unknowing visitor. The Okefenokee National Wildlife Refuge in Georgia is also one of those strange places.

Before being preserved as part of the largest black water swamp in North America, Okefenokee was logged for cypress and channels dug in attempts to drain the land. Much better preserved than the more famous Everglades, Okefenokee still bears the scars of human intervention.

It was when I visited Okefenokee as a child that I saw my first wild alligator—a quietly floating primordial beast that was branded into my memory as I stood staring at it in a light rain from a boardwalk. The name Okefenokee is possibly derived from a Native American phrase meaning "trembling earth." The translation, whether accurate or not, is appropriate. In places the land of the swamp is nothing but a thick floating mass of moss, which you can step on, jump on, and feel actually tremble beneath your feet. Growing in earth that can barely be considered earth, plants receive much less nutrition than in many other places, and some make up for it the same way animals do, by consuming prey. This is the bizarre adaptation of the carnivorous pitcher plants and bladderworts which grow in Okefenokee and other parts of the south.

The trumpet pitcher plant (*Sarracenia spp.*) is a vibrant, gaudy thing with a modified leaf swollen to the point that it resembles a flower—green with red speckles, like the wing of a strange butterfly. Above the mouth of the "flower" hangs a trap door, leaving the mouth of the pitcher invitingly open. Enticing aromas draw in flies, bees, or whatever insect is attracted. At the lip of the plant, the insect slips or sticks in waxy deposits and inevitably slides deeper into the yawning vegetable chasm. Hairs point downward, directing the insect past the point of no return. In the bottom of the "pitcher" the insect is in a vat of digestive fluid where in thrashing agony, the plant "eats" its prey. Another pitcher plant, the parrot pitcher (*Sarracenia psittacina*), is curved and shaped like the head of a parrot; small false exits draw the helpless insect deeper into the plant with promising pricks of light. The bladderwort (*Utricularia spp.*) has flowers reminiscent of snapdragons or orchids. The strange bladders actually suck water and aquatic prey into them when triggered by movement. Some bladderworts consume prey as small as rotifers: nightmares when spied beneath a microscope with their "wheeled" heads full of beating cilia, pulling any water creature into their relentless jaws crunching like a beating heart.

Carnivorous plants are common in wetlands, especially in tropical and subtropical areas. Acidic waters and thin soils are good places for supplemental flesh; surely crocodilians would agree. The Venus flytrap (*Dionaea muscipula*) I remember feeding bits of hamburger to as a child is native to the Carolinas of the southern United States. The same habitats that draw crocodilians also created the carnivorous plants, and the same threats to one often plague the other. Some pitcher plants, like crocodilians, are often threatened because their wetland homes are being drained by human avarice. In the same way that humans hunt crocodiles for their skins, people also remove wild plants from their homes, not necessarily killing them but leaving an ecological hole in the wild

"Arthur" a large American crocodile in a group named with a King Arthur theme. The big male basks near a water hazard at a golf course in South Carolina. Despite being captured and tagged before, Arthur defies researchers with his failure to fear humans. (*Author*)

nonetheless. Of course crocodilians and carnivorous plants are just two of the vast array of creatures that share warm wet places the world over.

It's estimated that over two thirds of all the world's biodiversity—that is, plants, animals, fungi, and the rest—live in tropical regions. Crocodilians of course stray from purely tropical areas to the subtropics as well, thus increasing the amount of biodiversity the group as a whole interacts with.

The big reptiles play a role in the tropics and subtropics of the Americas, Africa, Asia, and Australia, linking in a very real way their fate with the fate of forests, rivers, marine coasts, lakes, and other wetlands all through the earth's warm central beltway. These latitudes of wild warmth and wet are also a playground for the rich and powerful and home to some of the world's poor and desperate. Increasingly wetlands are drained and become something else. Considering this problem is how I ended up on golf courses in South Carolina, collecting data on alligators.

The coast of South Carolina is a maze of different islands, many of them gated communities complete with private golf courses. With their water traps and hot humid weather, these artificial green spaces are perfect habitats for American alligators. When I arrived in Beaufort, South Carolina, the October weather was mild—in the seventies with slight wind and light cloud cover. I was welcomed as a biology research volunteer and settled into a house at the edge of the forest that first night. The next morning brought the first day of alligator urban ecology research.

I came here to volunteer as a field technician for Anje Kidd-Weaver, a PhD student at Clemson University on her last season of doctoral field work. Kidd-Weaver's research looks at strategies of mitigating alligator-human conflict and the related issue of how alligators respond to the approach of humans as well as novel objects. I helped her perform alligator personality tests of a sort.

Driving across the bridge to Fripp Island and its golf courses, we passed a small pod of dolphins swimming with dorsal fins flashing above the sea on the right and a fluffy osprey perched on the railing to the left. On the golf course the grass was bright and well groomed. Golf carts coursed with a quiet electric hum down thin asphalt ribbons and across wooden bridges over dark waters. Dense copses of trees and shrubs hedged the green playing fields. Wood storks huddled in branches and great blue herons picked their way through the water. On the banks of the water hazards, alligators lay basking in the sun. Surrounding the courses are rows of large second homes and manicured palm trees. It's a surreal world, almost a fantasy kingdom in which the alligators have taken on the role of dragons.

The research involved such odd experiments as driving a garish blue and orange remote control toy SUV toward a basking alligator and watching for a response. I also simply walked towards alligator(s) until the animal(s) moved, or I was on the cusp of being uncomfortably close, a human-reptile game of chicken. The last move was casting a yellow rubber ducky—more at home in a bathtub—into the water next to a floating alligator with a fishing rod or sometimes a hookless lure.

An alligator is approached by a remote control car during behavioral research on a golf course in South Carolina. (*Author*)

I made a mistake on my first day while casting the rubber duck. A small alligator swam quickly toward the floating toy, and before I could reel it in, the reptile ferociously seized the yellow bird in her mouth. We didn't want the gator to eat the rubber toy. I struggled to pull the duck back, keeping tension on the line, waiting for the moment that the alligator might open her mouth. The struggle ended when Kidd-Weaver took the reel from me as the alligator drew near shore. I then drove the remote control car towards the gator, and the animal opened her mouth in fear or aggression and released the duck. She retreated, hissing, deeper into the water.

Such is the absurdity of encountering a prehistoric creature in the groomed sports-scape of a modern golf course. It's important to consider alligators in these landscapes as well as the more "wild" habitats, because golf courses aren't going away any time soon. The southeastern United States, especially, has an abundance of these resorts. Southern Florida—said to have the highest density of golf courses in the world—is also a hot spot for human-alligator conflict. Data on how alligators react to the presence of humans and our technology is useful in shaping plans for future landscapes shared between humans and alligators. Research and mitigation may be the best we can muster, since real self-control is lost to us *Homo sapiens* entirely. The research I volunteered on was aimed at contributing to our understanding.

Toward the end of my time volunteering on Anje Kidd-Weaver's project, she drove us on a detour between two golf courses. We passed through an area full of million-dollar homes, surrounded by a small remnant of forest—oaks hung with moss, wrapped in vines and dappled with ferns growing from their bark, palm trees, thick bushes. On the other side of the road, the green tangle of forest was still largely intact, but wooden posts marked the area as lots owned but not yet developed. Around a corner was a pond, behind which a mansion was under construction. As men worked on the house suspended from a bucket lift, Kidd-Weaver told me this pond was where a large alligator once lived. The animal was found dead with a nail driven partly into his head. Kidd-Weaver speculated, with sadness in her voice, that one of the construction workers could've killed the animal. As we drove away and talked about the destruction of the island's forests, she told me that recently a healthy population of bobcats has been seen there, but she doesn't know what's supporting them. We discussed how the remaining trees, the alligators, and the bobcats give the unknowing homeowners a small illusion of an intact ecosystem. I realized then, that this place, all of the golf courses we've visited, are microcosms of the whole world. Everywhere crocodilian habitat is being eaten up by houses, golf courses, farms—in short, us. We save small parks, forests, and riverways while ignoring the true impact of our global economic system and growing consumption. The lucky global rich get to live on golf courses without realizing the forests may, in the near future, not exist at all.

Worldwide, humans will soon be running out of water. The earth is getting hotter. More land will be used up by agriculture to feed a growing population and a growing hunger for a Western diet. Wetlands will be drained, rivers will be rerouted. The major tributary of the Amazon River is set to be dammed. Rivers important to gharials in Nepal are also being reconfigured for humans

An alligator is caught with a "noose" to tag and collect data during research on a golf course in South Carolina. (*Author*)

with no regard to wildlife. Nearly all of the Chinese alligator's habitat is lost forever. The future for crocodilians may look more like the ponds in a golf course, or a farm, than the expansive wetlands they've enjoyed so far, unless we can control ourselves.

The last day I helped on alligator research in South Carolina was spent catching alligators to tag them. Part of the rationale for the exercise was that alligators that are caught will have negative associations with humans and avoid them, Anje Kidd-Weaver's preliminary data supports this idea, although her full conclusions aren't released as of the writing of this book.

Catching and tagging alligators is brutal work. A weighted treble hook is thrown over the alligator floating on the surface of the water and reeled back. When the hook connects with the reptile, it's jerked sharply to seat the hook. Mostly the hook sank into the scutes on the back, but during my day of alligator catching, I saw it hooked in feet and just behind the jaw as well.

The unluckily snagged crocodilian is reeled in where people on shore wait with snares—cable loops attached to bamboo poles or PVC pipe. The snares are snugged around the angry reptile's neck and she's pulled ashore to be further violated. A towel is thrown over the alligator's eyes to calm her and two people sit on her back and tail, her mouth is taped shut so that biologists and volunteers aren't bitten. Measurements are taken and then the tagging begins. The tagging is as rough as anything else: a hole is drilled through a scute on the tail and the same tag used for the ears in cattle is punched into the tail, the number and color of which is duly recorded. Then as an added measure, in case the tag is lost, scutes are cut in a prescribed pattern; marking the animal with literal scars. The black scutes, once cut, reveal startling white flesh oozing droplets of crimson beneath.

I kept remembering the groaning of one alligator in a voice of low thunder as her scutes were cut and the way she thrashed afterward. My mind kept circling back to it and feeling a stab of guilt. It wasn't my project, yet I participated willingly in the catching. A thought occurred to me later that night. The alligators living in the water hazards of golf courses inside gated communities are captive animals. Instead of being dragged from the wild and shut behind fences, the fences were built around them as they stayed in place. They're not fed by a zookeeper, but they're tagged and catalogued with the same devices punched into the ears of so much mooing livestock. Their young are captured and put into glass aquariums inside nature centers to be viewed for a while by curious golf community residents.

After we were finished with catching alligators, Kidd-Weaver and two of the others involved in catching showed me a small outdoor enclosure where young alligators are soon to be kept. It was a perfect square of wood with a small pond in a corner. An elevated wooden walkway hugged it on one side for people to watch from above. I wondered if any of the alligators on the golf courses could be considered truly wild, or, were they something else entirely? With an increasing human population pushing against potentially dangerous animals like alligators, it's not easy to come up with a satisfying and practical solution. Our golf course research has its place, but the importance of this work seems like an unfortunate necessity born of the world we now inhabit.

If the alligators conditioned by tagging are less likely to approach human golfers, it's a good thing. Better to harass and invasively handle an alligator than to kill one who's taken an unhealthy interest in people.

Yet it's important to consider the context and realize that this work is made necessary as the consequence of human greed and overreach. The alligators we encountered were living on golf courses that until recently were undeveloped forest on undeveloped islands. The wildlife only come into conflict with humans in these places because humans came into conflict with them first—by destroying their habitat. By encroaching on their homes and building lavish mansions, clubhouses, golf courses, and nature centers. The primeval world once ruled by crocodilians is quickly being chewed up by asphalt, condos, grass, and putting greens. What's left is degraded by agricultural runoff and crowded with tourists keen to ride a fan-powered swamp boat on an hour-long tour. This is what remains of the almost lost world of the crocodilians. It's no longer a world ruled by reptiles, now it is to us that the decision falls to how much of the planet we'll share.

A 2020 paper based on spotlight surveys of the lower St. John River system in Jacksonville, Florida, found that alligators can live in urban areas. Disturbingly, the paper also found a distinct lack of adults in the alligator populations of Jacksonville, suggesting that the larger alligators are removed by hunters and as nuisance alligators. It seems there's enough room for a few crocodilians, even within big cities, if we are able to tolerate them, but we don't readily tolerate any animals deemed remotely threatening.

– thirteen –

A **FUTURE** *for* **CROCODILIANS?**

VIOLENCE TOWARD CROCODILES AND ALLIGATORS is very much in vogue. People for the Ethical Treatment of Animals (PETA) have recorded videos of workers at skin farms in Vietnam sawing crudely into the necks of crocodiles and jamming steel rods through the incisions of the still living animals' hides and into their spines. On screen, the crocodiles, with their powerful jaws taped shut, kicked their legs feebly in exquisite pain.

Experts have pointed out that these crocodiles will likely live for hours after the initial gashes into their necks due to their unique physiology. In other crocodile farms the animals are electroshocked in an attempt to stun them before this procedure. The result is still a long and painful end.

Before being killed, crocodiles and alligators in farms such as these are kept in tiny concrete pens, some of them so small that an animal's tail curls against one wall while the snout is pressed into the opposite wall. A warren of these tiny concrete cells resembles something of an unnatural hive of strange, scaled, giant insects—unmoving, trapped.

These farms raise crocodiles for skins sold to the likes of Louis Vuitton, maker of high-end clothes and accessories, including crocodile skin purses. Others sell their hides to be crafted into fancy boots, belts, watchbands, and more. Crocodile or alligator farms can be found in North America, Africa, Asia, and Australia. In some of them, animals are also displayed for the public in a zoo-like setting where you can munch on gator nuggets while watching a man in a cut-off T-shirt wrestle an alligator. Meat is a less valuable byproduct created by raising animals for skins, but crocodile farming is still a profitable, if unstable business. It's also a business backed by many government and NGO programs—crocodilian agriculture is part of the machinery of modern conservation.

Conservation is not what many people think it is. Its central tenets are sometimes counterintuitive and seemingly at odds with one another. No one else has quite embodied the paradox at the heart of conservation like U.S. president Theodore Roosevelt. He laid the foundation of federal land conservation in the United States, setting aside wildlife reserves for birds, creating the United States Forest Service, and making national parks an American institution.

Roosevelt also loved killing individual animals as much as protecting natural habitat and certain species. Before boosting a captive bison breeding program at the Bronx Zoo, Roosevelt traveled to the windy prairies of the Dakotas to hunt the shaggy beast. One bison he shot at 325 yards without killing; the injured animal was never found. In another instance, Roosevelt was hunting for black bears in the cane brakes of Mississippi; when an assistant found a bear, he tied it to a tree for the president. Encouraged to shoot the restrained bear, Roosevelt refused, considering it unsportsmanlike. What is often left out of this famous story is that Roosevelt did in fact kill the bear, with a knife rather than a gun, as an act of "mercy." It seems what the president was most concerned about was his own sense of personal honor rather than the well-being of the bear.

On safari in Africa after his presidency, Roosevelt and his son Kermit together killed 512 large animals, contributing to 11,000 specimens the expedition sent to the Smithsonian, including plants, insects, and other smaller animals. Of this number, Teddy Roosevelt killed one crocodile himself and Kermit killed three. On this rich man's hunting trip requiring five hundred porters over twelve months, Roosevelt did some very unsporting things. Many of the animals were shot repeatedly from extremely far distances. Sometimes Roosevelt would let someone else finish off an animal he injured with a first shot. Lord Cranworth, a Kenyan, whose business outfitted the expedition, was unimpressed by the "slaughter," asking, "Do these nine white rhino ever cause Roosevelt a pang of conscience or a sleepless night?" Roosevelt himself, in the book *Theodore Roosevelt on Hunting*, wrote, "Game butchery is as objectionable as any other form of wanton cruelty or barbarity; but to protest against all hunting of game is a sign of softness of head, not of soundness of heart."

Other historic conservationists have also been engaged in killing wildlife, for recreation or study. John James Audubon was enthusiastic about shooting birds, including those he famously painted. Aldo Leopold was a hunter; Charles Darwin, Alfred Russel Wallace, and their contemporary scientists often killed specimens for science. Today, many scientists, including conservation scientists, still collect specimens by killing them. Conservation organizations also often promote sportsmen as their natural champions. Hunting and killing for conservation is not often something the general nonhunting population considers.

For many, it seems that public opinion has moved away from this Rooseveltian, bloodthirsty sportsman's attitude. From 2011 to 2016, surveys by the U.S. Department of the Interior have shown an increase in wildlife viewing of 20 percent while during the same years, hunting dropped by 2 million participants in the United States. Meanwhile Burger King and Carl's Jr. offer vegetarian burgers as regular menu items; fur clothing and accessories are seen by a growing number of people as poor taste and bad moral judgment. Even as many fear nature deficit disorder in youth and worry about the accelerated shrinking of natural landscapes, it may seem Americans have become more compassionate toward nonhuman animals aside from pure environmental concerns.

Often this change in attitudes toward animals is seen as a view centered in an urbanized environment where the creatures most often encountered are cats and dogs kept in confined quarters at home, not a view based on close contact with wild animals or indeed scientific knowledge. This soft-hearted animal welfare sentiment is at odds with the mainstream crocodilian conservation of today as much as with the Rooseveltian conservation ethic of the past.

Most conservation is concerned with the survival of species and ecosystems, and not so much about the welfare of individual animals. In mainstream crocodilian conservation, managed hunting and farms that raise animals for food—or more commonly, skins—are often used as tools. Within farms, the wild animal populations are bolstered, by a percentage of captive hatched crocs that are returned to their native habitat. The rest are bred for more young—or slaughtered for skins. The system works because in the wild, despite careful mothering, only a small percentage of young survive to adulthood. A much larger number of animals hatched in captivity will grow to maturity, leaving a fraction that can be "harvested" without impacting a wild population. It also makes crocodilians into money-making machines, things to value economically, not intrinsically. This, many crocodile researchers believe, is a good way to maintain populations of unpopular reptiles.

Matthew Shirley, a scientist with well over a decade of crocodile research experience, mostly in Africa, explained crocodilian conservation to me over the phone. Shirley echoed Theodore Roosevelt when he told me people who don't agree with crocodile farm conservation aren't very smart:

> Most people don't try and understand something they don't inherently understand. . . . This concept of killing something to save it is a bit of a challenging thing to wrap your mind around. . . . We harvest these animals and all of a sudden people have money and with that money they improve their lives and they're less in contact with these animals. The less

in contact with these animals, the less conflict they have, the less conflict they have, the less they're motivated to kill them . . . they're conserving habitat, they're protecting species and the cycle ramps up.

This conservation model is based on the idea of sustainable use, where some crocodilians are killed, mostly for their skin but also for food, in a carefully managed way. Done well, as it has been implemented in the United States and Australia, for example, sustainable use seems to have allowed wild populations of alligators or crocodiles to recover. The key is creating a financial incentive to protect both habitat and wild animals. Shirley told me that in the 1950s there was a real possibility alligators would go extinct in the United States, and populations were so low in some areas it was a challenge to find even one animal. Legal protections and human populations moving from rural toward urban living are part of the impressive recovery of alligators. This success story Shirley told me entirely depends on sustainable use:

> In places like Louisiana you have private land owners who specifically manage their land for alligator habitats so they can increase alligator production and the alligator egg harvest. Well, when you're managing habitat for alligators, you're also managing habitat for fish and birds and everything else and carbon stocks, air quality, water quality. These complicated, intricate connections are what makes it work and the vast majority of naïve or ignorant or just plain dumb public, all they see is just the body of a bleeding dead animal twitching from neural reflex and they say there's no way you're saving this animal with that sort of inhumane and barbaric treatment.

A more palatable application of sustainable use conservation is the U.S. Forest Service system. Visitors may not realize that many national forests are logged but often in managed ways that ensure forests always remain. Instead of merely clear-cutting entire regions,

Alligator heads for sale in New Orleans. Despite the recovery of the American alligator (*Alligator mississippiensis*) as a species, individual animals are raised as livestock and treated as disposables in part of a luxury goods and tourism industry. (*Pictures at Sea/Creative Commons*)

only relatively small areas are generally cut and seedlings established to replenish the forest. The very basic concepts are the same for crocodilians as they are for pine trees, but it's not all just basic concepts.

Details are important for this type of conservation to be carried out successfully. In South Africa, according to Matthew Shirley, key elements of the strategy are missing from government management programs. Instead of eggs being collected in the wild and hatched in captivity where some young are destined to be slaughtered and others returned to the wild, all of South Africa's skin trade is from captive-bred animals. This creates no incentives to protect either habitat or wild crocodiles, and the populations of South African crocodiles are in decline.

Chinese alligator conservation has a different but similar problem. Separate from any skin farming operation, the government of China for a long time paid local farmers for eggs collected in the wild to be hatched in captive breeding programs. No thought was given to Chinese alligator habitat because the government seemed to find the situation hopeless. The end result in China is that there are more alligators in captive breeding facilities than in the wild and few places left to reintroduce captive animals to.

Mismanagement can be a problem for crocodilians, but there are also risks and problems involved with no management, especially as human populations boom right next to crocodilian habitat. According to Shirley, there's very little research and almost no management at all for crocodilians living in West and central Africa where he does most of his field work.

The west African dwarf crocodile (*Osteolaemus tetraspis*) is the most harvested crocodilian in the world outside of a management program. Highlighting the lack of knowledge is the fact that African dwarf crocodiles have been split into three species since the last conservation assessment by the IUCN. This means that for the dwarf crocodiles as a group, the last international population assessment is more than ten years out of date and considered three species as one. For west African dwarf crocodiles, it means the species has never been assessed for its conservation status officially. The unfortunate present state of west African dwarf crocodiles is mirrored in the regrettable pasts of many other species. It's a history some of which I've already covered in this book but worth revisiting. At one point every crocodilian in the world was hunted without any management plan—for meat, for skin, for fat.

The hunting of crocodilians has a long and global history, but it seems that the commercial skin trade started in North America with alligators. Alligators were first killed in great numbers for their skin and meat in Louisiana in the 1800s. During the American Civil War, desperation and lack of resources led the Confederate Army to use alligator skins for boots and saddles. The techniques of the times made the alligator leather wares weaker and less waterproof than cow and other skins.

Still, the unique look and exotic nature of alligator skin for belts, saddle bags, and mostly footwear resulted in more commercial hunting in the wake of the war. During this time, commercial

Two crocodiles strung up by hunters in Australia circa 1920. It was the unchecked slaughter of wild crocodiles such as this that so diminished wild populations world-wide. The apparent human callousness and colonial attitude demonstrated here continues to negatively impact crocodiles in the wild and in farms. (*Aussie~mobs/Creative Commons*)

tanneries in New York, New Jersey, and Europe developed new techniques that made alligator skin more viable for use in clothing and accessories.

Alligators were always hunted in the American South for food, but now their fat literally greased the machines of the industrial revolution. As demand for the luxury skin increased and piled on top of other alligator uses, thousands of the reptiles were slaughtered. Soon, the supply couldn't keep up with demand. With the growth of the skin trade, crocodiles in Mexico and Central America were increasingly hunted for skins as well. As with any luxury good, the demand for crocodilian skins dropped off during times of economic scarcity, such as during the world wars and the Great Depression.

After World War II, the economic boom led again to people buying handbags, shoes, hat bands, and belts made from crocodilian skin. Nile crocodiles (*C. niloticus*) were gunned down in Africa, and Australia's "salties" (*C. porosus*) were targeted for their especially fine skins. By the late 1950s even black caimans (*Melanosuchus niger*) in the Amazon basin were being hunted to meet the world's greedy hunger for luxury leather.

Demand kept up through the 1970s, the end result being a severely depleted population of crocodilians worldwide. As black caiman populations shrunk in the Amazon, even smaller caimans with their bonier bellies, which produce lower quality leather, weren't safe from the orgy of death. Some crocodilian species were extirpated from parts of their range, while others were severely reduced. Through some miracle or perhaps because of the crocodilian's famed ability to survive, no known species was quite pushed to extinction anywhere in the world, though that event may be close at hand now. Eventually people and governments noticed the steep decline of crocodilians and took action.

In 1969, the American alligator gained federal protection. In 1972 Australia prohibited trade in crocodile skins, so while hunting remained legal the motive of legal profit was removed. Other nations followed suit. In 1979, crocodiles were added as appendix I of the Convention on International Trade of Endangered Species of flora and fauna (CITES), an international agreement on animal trade. At first they were protected by strict restrictions on trade of the animals and their body parts. Soon, however, the idea of farming took root. More than a desire to simply protect crocodilians as *wild animals*, this was a way people could make a profit and protect their *investment* (in the form of an animal) from mismanagement. This idea of treating a wild animal or plant as a resource to be utilized wisely, rather than a collective of individuals, is at the heart of sustainability. An article in the *New York Times* on January 18, 1970, highlighted this new way of thinking about crocodilians in a headline, "One Way to Halt Poaching—Gator Farming."

The *Times* piece discussed Cecil Clemons, owner of Gatorama, a Florida roadside attraction where captive alligators and croco-

Crocodile

AMAZING VALUE

11/9

At 11/9, two styles—a crocodile and calf Handbag, and
crocodile and crocodile calf
"Zipper" Bag. Price, 11/9

17/6

At 17/6, two styles — a
vagabond style Handbag of
crocodile and calf, and an
all-crocodile "Zipper." 17/6

Carriage paid by

FARMER'S

Advertisements such as this one promoted the crocodilian skin industry. Unregulated hunting of crocodilians devastated many populations. Later carefully regulated farming caused (and continues to cause) enormous suffering to individual animals and a loss of autonomy for populations. (*Aussie~mobs/Creative Commons*)

diles still live in pens for the viewing enjoyment of tourists, decades later. In the article Clemons's idea of farming alligators for their skins as a way toward conserving them put him at odds with most conservationists of the day, as the journalist observed: "Conserva-tionists have shown little enthusiasm for alligator farming, insist-ing that the creature should remain in its natural state in the wilds. Many conservationists would rather destroy the market for alliga-tor products."

In 1970 when the piece was written, alligators were still strictly protected. The article did mention that some mainstream conser-vationists of the time favored alligator farming but emphasized they were a minority. The (then) few in favor of farming are the conservationists who won the scientific consensus over time, partly at least, because of appeals from those who profited directly from selling crocodilian skins.

By the late 1980s, forty countries embraced commercial use of crocodilians in some form or other, as part of their conservation programs. We may be living in a time of widespread veggie burgers, but we're also living in a time of intense, industrial animal agriculture, including crocodile farming. Many scientists I talked to point out commercial farming as key to the success of alligator and other crocodilian conservation projects. The first alligator farms in the United States, however, were founded over one hundred years ago, near the beginning of the alligator's precipitous decline. Alligator numbers were on the rise before mainstream conservationists fully embraced farming, and not all scientists are quick to give farming credit for crocodile conservation. Merlijn van Weerd, the Philippine crocodile conservationist, seemed to doubt farming was necessary for crocodile conservation, writing in an email:

> Crocodile farming has been presented as a conservation activity, and in some cases it has helped to ease pressure on wild populations who are not hunted anymore, or by providing incentives to protect wild crocodiles. I think you could ask the question though if crocodile farming was really necessary for this. . . . Croc species that have made spectacular comebacks in the wild have done so mainly as a result of a shift in public opinion and government protection, for example saltwater crocodiles in Australia and alligators in the USA. . . . Both species are also farmed, but crocodile farming and conservation in the wild are not operationally or financially connected in these countries, apart from conservation breeding to reinforce wild populations (a practice technically unrelated to farming of crocodiles for use). I don't see why you would need to use a crocodile for its skin or meat to conserve it.

The history of crocodile farming in the United States seems to bear out van Weerd's criticism. The first known alligator farm, in Palm Beach, Florida, was opened in 1891 by "Alligator Joe" Campbell. This pioneering farm was successful enough that it inspired Campbell to open a second operation in Jacksonville soon after. Later in St. Augustine, Felix Fire and George Reddington

A man walking an alligator on a leash at an alligator farm, circa 1900. Alligators have often been treated like domestic animals at farms, especially in the past. Sometimes young guests of farms were even allowed to ride the animals. Such treatment is not only unlikely to be appreciated by the animals, it also perpetuates a misguided perception of alligators and other crocodilians. (*Fae/Creative Commons*)

started an alligator farm and tourist attraction, buying up Campbell's and others' alligators. After a change in name, the St. Augustine attraction eventually became what is today the St. Augustine Alligator Farm Zoological Park, a modern and accredited zoo. By the time conservation efforts for alligators were picking up in the U.S. and conservationists were turning to raising alligators for skins, the idea spread to Australia, where conservationist Dr. Grahame Webb modeled his own crocodile farming after alligator farms in Louisiana.

Grahame Webb perhaps best embodies the general view of many conservationists today when it comes to farming crocodilians. Webb has been working in reptile research since the 1960s and has focused on crocodiles since the 1970s. Webb grew up in Australia, arguably one of the most exciting places in the world to study reptiles, especially crocodiles. In an email, he told me he's always been interested in hunting, fishing, anything involving nature. Now in his early seventies, his enthusiasm for zoology was evident: "I went to university to do agriculture and only then found out that 'zoology' was a career! You could work with animals 100 percent of the time, asking as many questions as you wanted and do research to answer them—I couldn't believe it. So got seriously into research and field work and was happy to work long long hours seven days a week. It was a privilege society had bestowed . . . not simply a career."

The year after finishing his PhD, Webb began working with crocodiles in Australia's Northern Territory, a place with no university at the time. Financially it was easier for him to work on his own with a small team to collect basic biological information on crocodiles, much of which was missing at the time. He told me his main interest in those years was basic research, not management. Management came later, when the population of saltwater crocodiles was about 30 to 40 percent recovered. As crocodile populations grew and their threat to human interests became more evident again, support for the animals was quickly disappearing. Grahame Webb and his team turned to sustainable use of crocodiles, basing their management plan on the management of alligators in Louisiana, which he says is still the best blueprint. It's this model that has led to the modern state of crocodilians in many parts of the world, but the idea of farming crocodiles has deeper roots in history and philosophy.

The sustainable farming model of crocodile conservation reduces individual wild animals to not just farm animals but consumer products like scaly handbags. This truth is muddled by the fact that many crocodile farms, including Webb's Crocodylus Park, are also places where visitors can view live animals, much like a typical zoo. The crocodiles, cut off from their wild habitat, are consumed intellectually through voyeurism first, before they're consumed as fried nuggets and fancy belts.

The sort of reduction of an animal to a machine to be manipulated for human use, even in the name of conservation, has its basis in the thinking of the likes of philosopher René Descartes, perhaps best known for his contributions to mathematics and his famous saying in Latin, "Cognito, ergo sum" (I think, therefore I am). Descartes also believed animals were mindless automatons, and he dissected live dogs whimpering and thrashing without anesthesia. In *Crocodile Undone: The Domestication of Australia's Fauna*, author Marcus Baynes-Rock acknowledges Descartes' role in popularizing this view of animals as unfeeling robots: "[Descartes] sought to separate his humanity from earthly life, his ideas from history, and . . . his very thinking from his corporeality. He set the ego apart from all else and reduced other animals to machines that showed motility only in response to the knives of anatomists."

Baynes-Rock also notes that historian Donald Worster suggested this way of disassociating one animal or plant from its greater ecosystem began long before Descartes, with the start of economic farming; other thinkers believe that this mode of thought began even earlier. Whatever the origin, removing crocodilians or their eggs from the wild for breeding programs to produce skin is based on the idea of crocodiles, alligators, and caimans as mere resources—as cogs in an economic machine. This thinking within conservation bares itself in terms such as "natural resource" applied to plants and animals as well as minerals and land.

In this view, no longer are crocodilians individuals entwined in a great ecological web of connection; instead, they can be removed, replaced, honed, for the enrichment of humans and the salvation of their own reptilian genes. The question becomes: at what point have we removed crocodilians from something essential to their very nature?

It's a hard question to answer, but it's good to remember that in some ways the farmed crocodilian species have fared better than many others still too rare in the wild to be farmed. In the case of many species, conservationists are currently working hard to simply build viable populations, and sustainable use is not even a consideration yet. One such animal is the Cuban crocodile (*Crocodylus rhombifer*).

The Cuban crocodile is a smallish species of crocodilian, the largest animals reaching only about eleven feet in length; seven feet long is more typical. Compared to the long-snouted American crocodile, the Cuban animal has a short, blunt nose bringing its head closer to that of an alligator. The crocodile is also strong-legged and the most terrestrial of all living crocodiles, able to actually gallop on land. The Cuban crocodile lives only in the Zapato Swamp of the island nation of Cuba and in Lanier Swamp on a smaller island off Cuba. This restricted distribution is the smallest of any known extant crocodilian species.

Zapato is the largest wetland in Cuba with 1,600 square miles, but only around three thousand "purebred" Cuban crocodiles live in the wild today, restricted to the southern part of the greater wetlands. Originally the crocodiles inhabited the even larger Zapata Peninsula, but hunting reduced their range by 30 percent.

Cuban crocodiles are more of a freshwater species than their American cousins, but occasionally an American crocodile will venture into the freshwater habitat of Cuban crocodiles. Interestingly, the two crocodiles freely hybridize, which is why I mention the "purebred" individuals. Efforts to save the Cuban crocodile also involve efforts to halt hybridization and maintain a pure line of Cuban crocs. Robin Moore, senior director of digital media with Global Wildlife Conservation, told me:

> The workers at the Cuban Crocodile breeding sanctuary, like Gustavo Sosa, who has been working there for more than 20 years, since he was 19, work incredibly hard. They care for more than 4,700 crocodiles at the sanctuary, and this requires a lot of maintenance and care. When breeding season comes they carefully incubate and hatch out eggs, weighing, measuring and tagging every hatchling. Natalia Rossi works with the Wildlife Conservation Society coordinating the release and monitoring of crocodile populations, and also developing educational materials to change perceptions to the country's top predator.

The goal of the breeding facility in Cuba is to breed captive crocodiles and release their young into the wild. In November 2019 I received a multimedia press release on the project with photos of Cuban female celebrities posing with young crocodiles about to be released. The breaking news was that ten young crocodiles from the breeding facility were just set free into the wilds of Zapato Swamp.

As much as helping Cuban crocodiles survive is admirable, the idea of separating two species that freely interbreed from one another smacks of its own artifice. Hybridization is actually an important part of normal biological evolution. Unfortunately, human interference has turned hybridization into a complicated conservation issue for many wild animals. Domestic cattle and wild bison have hybridized both in captivity and in the wild, something that would never have occurred without people importing cattle to North America. In many cases, hybridization places an equal threat to the less populous animal. The bison remains a good example of this. The much larger population of cattle than bison means that if the two bred without interference, the bison genes would become extremely diluted and "purebred" bison would be replaced by hybrids, a process known as genetic swamping. This hybridization may be a threat for Cuban crocodiles. However, American and Cuban crocodiles have interbred since before human interference and continue to do so. The issue is complicated by the fact that American crocodiles in Cuba have a unique set of genes compared to other American crocodile populations.

In its own way, breeding pure strains of a crocodile that so often hybridize without interference is asserting a type of control similar to domestication or breeding for skins. Asserting human control of crocodile breeding undermines their own wildness and self-determination. The question becomes whether conservation should uphold the integrity of biological systems or the idea of a species.

Still, there is a world of difference between captive breeding facilities like the one in Cuba or the gharial breeding facilities I visited in Nepal, and crocodile farms. In nonagricultural breeding facilities, the animals are kept alive and healthy for the propagation of their species and the release into the wild of their young. In crocodile farms, release of some amount of the young crocodiles is incidental and many of the crocodiles are killed for profit. Both facilities are considered part of conservation, much as hunting animals can be considered conservation if managed properly. This doesn't mean that the two are morally equivalent.

One expert I discussed farming with was very critical. Dr. Clifford Warwick, a veterinarian based in England, has spent a career investigating animal welfare as well as studying the captive treatment of crocodilians and other reptiles with an aim at minimizing cruelty. As an independent scientist Warwick has written over 150 scientific papers on topics ranging from zoonoses (diseases transferred from animals to people) to captive reptile care. Warwick is a staunch advocate for humane treatment. He told me in an email that sometimes his work can lead to exciting, if dangerous scenarios, "being shot at, stabbed, major brawls, car chases and such, while investigating animal dealers and farmers, but that was really the fun part."

Clifford Warwick has been open about his dislike for crocodile farms and their central place in many conservation frameworks. He's been quoted saying that there's not a lot he approves of in crocodile farming, when I asked him about this, he gave a more nuanced response. Warwick told me that he doesn't disapprove of farming *per se* but instead the cruelty and harm he often sees in crocodile farming. He compared farming crocodiles to cattle but said that there is a difference in cattle being domesticated while crocodiles are biologically wild. It's the wildness of crocodilians that makes them more prone to stress in captivity. Warwick observes that conservation efforts don't really need farms to succeed.

> I do not see farming any animal as a panacea for its conservation. Self-proclaimed "pragmatists" argue that farming is necessary to prevent inevitable over-exploitation. But that argument is an admission of lack of self-restraint, instead of simply saying such exploitation should be strongly prevented. If we were talking about people wanting to exploit a near extinct race of humans (e.g. an isolated Bornean tribe), we would not argue about farming them, we would just say "no." Simply because we can farm another species legally and make it socially acceptable, does not make it right. . . . I think croc

farming for "conservation" is a double-edged sword at best, and bogus at worst. The true conservationist would simply leave crocs alone, stop taking their habitat, and spend their time persuading people and governments to do the same.

A PETA spokesperson I emailed was even more blunt about using farming for conservation:

Killing an animal in the name of conservation is like selling a child on the black market to raise money for an anti-trafficking organization. The best way to promote conservation is to devote money and time to projects that protect animals' natural habitats—not by fueling the violent slaughter of animals. Wildlife farming can even increase the demand for these animals, prompting people to capture them in their natural habitat—and farms can act as loopholes for trading illegally caught wildlife.

As I was writing this chapter, an alligator farm was being implicated in an illegal scheme to sell flying squirrels captured in the wild as pets, showing that some alligator farms, at least, are not looking out for conservation efforts any more than they're looking out for the long lives of individual alligators. An undercover investigator for PETA painted a disturbing picture of the farm they investigated:

As I walked down the main hall in each warehouse there, I heard nothing. While each building contained dozens of small, dark rooms that confined a hundred or more animals each, the alligators made no noise. All I could see would be the reflection of light in the eyes of alligators languishing in the shadows of the rooms filled with murky brown water. The smell coming from these pits was overwhelming. Throughout the years of my career, I had become accustomed to the smell of animal excrement—however, I was not prepared for the smell of feces and feed rotting in water. The putrid rotted smell was so overpowering that it was difficult to stop my natural gag reaction, even though I am a seasoned investigator who has been able to handle even the stench of the most noxious pig farm.

The alligator and crocodile farms used to make fashionable skins and promote conservation for conservation's sake are often a type of hell for the individual animals found inside them. PETA investigations in 1995 found farmed alligators repeatedly beaten over the head with aluminum baseball bats before having their throats slit with switchblades. This type of slaughter sounds like it's carried out by mobsters more than farmers. The question for many remains, whether the ends justify the means. Clifford Warwick told me his own method for measuring the justification for treating an animal a certain way, and I think it's a good one.

When it comes to considering any animal, a starting point for anyone is to at least try to see the world from their perspective. For example, by learning about crocodilian mental, emotional, and environmental needs (for which there is a great deal of scientific information), we can appreciate that they are sentient, sensitive, animals with needs, wants and feelings. The fact that they are major predators must be separated from the individual and its own aspects of "self." If one can "put themselves in the croc's place" then whether or not we should be confining them to near-barren prisons for skin, meat and display, become easier to understand—and answer.

There are new and better ways of looking at crocodile conservation than the mainstream farming model. Some deep ecology philosophers call for a closer look at autonomy or wildness and its importance in wildlife preservation; meanwhile, some biologists have championed a new "compassionate conservation." In a *Bioscience* paper titled "Compassion as a Practical and Evolved Ethic for Conservation," Daniel Ramp and Marc Bekoff wrote, "The good news is that the asserted dichotomy between conservation and animal welfare has waned, and the unifying aim of reducing harm to nonhuman animals in both these disciplines has gathered momentum." In the same paper, the scientists point out that Aldo Leopold's land ethic espoused a more equitable arrangement of shared land between wildlife and humans, but all too often in implementation, the human view and economic concerns take precedent in decision making. The new compassionate conservation ethic pushes back against the self-proclaimed pragmatic approach, instead enshrining the intrinsic value of other individual organisms as important to conservation.

Although change is coming, it's coming slowly. Matthew Shirley told me he enjoyed working with crocodilians, partially because it allowed him more tools than working with many other animals. The subtext is that it's still largely acceptable to farm crocodiles in large numbers for conservation; this wouldn't be true for zebras. It's typical of humans, including scientists, to value more highly the lives of organisms that are more similar to us. When I was in my twenties, I helped in a few conservation or biology projects where killing insects was commonplace. I caught hundreds of butterflies, squeezing their thoraxes to crush them to death before putting their bodies into tiny envelopes in Africa. I was proud to catch a possibly new to science centipede in a cave in Arizona and drop the squirming animal into a vial of alcohol. I would never have done these things to a vertebrate animal, but from an objective standpoint it's hard to justify valuing individual insects less.

For me, it all boils down to simple empathy. It's easier to empathize with a puppy than it is a buzzing insect, therefore the outcry over wolf slaughter is greater than a carefully engineered attempt to eradicate the mosquito. The killing of one giraffe, Marius, in the Copenhagen Zoo when he was deemed surplus, predictably drew public outrage. Yet, the killing of thousands of crocodilians annually causes little outcry, simply because it's harder to empathize with a crocodilian and perhaps because it's commonplace. As Warwick seems to suggest, it's important to learn about crocodilians to develop empathy.

TEARS *for* CROCODILIA

There are many ways to engage with crocodilians, by visiting a museum exhibit or reading about them. The best way, though, is to visit a park or wildlife reserve where wild crocodilians live. Even if you don't see an alligator or a crocodile, seeing the beauty, challenge, and complexity of their world may perhaps help you understand a bit of their lives. The future for crocodilians, beyond bare survival, may depend on how well a self-proclaimed "clever" primate can see the world through reptilian eyes.

BIBLIOGRAPHY

CHAPTER I. CROCODILIANS IN STONE

Knapton, Sarah. "Giant walking crocodile terrorized earth before dinosaurs." *Telegraph*, March 19, 2015, https://www.telegraph. co.uk/news/science/dinosaurs/11482314/Giant-walking-crocodile-terrorised-Earth-before-dinosaurs.html.

Mayor, Adrienne. *Fossil Legends of the First Americans*. Princeton University Press, 2007.

Rivera-Sylva, Héctor E., and Frey, Eberhard. "The first mandible fragment of Deinosuchus (Eusuchia: Alligatoroidea) discovered in Coahuila, Mexico." *Boletín de la Sociedad Geológica Mexicana* 63, no. 3, 2011, 459–462.

Rivera-Sylva, Héctor E., Rodríguez-De La Rosa, Rubén, and Ortiz-Mendieta, Jorge A. "A review of the dinosaurian record from Mexico." In F. Vega et al. (eds.). *Studies on Mexican Paleontology*, Springer, 2006, 233–248.

Sankey, Julia T., "Late Campanian southern dinosaurs, Aguja Formation, Big Bend Texas." *Journal of Paleontology*, 75, no. 1, 2001.

Schwimmer, David R., *King of the Crocodylians*: *The Paleobiology of Deinosuchus*. Indiana University Press, 2002.

CHAPTER 2. OTHER BRANCHES OF THE TREE

Biello, David. "Mutant chickens grow alligatorlike teeth." *Scientific American*, Feb. 22, 2006, https://www.scientificamerican.com/article/mutant-chicken-grows-alli/.

Britton, Adam. "Frequently asked questions: How long can a crocodile stay underwater?" *Crocodilian Biology Database*, http://crocodilian. com/cnhc/cbd-faq-q5.htm.

Dinets, Vladimir. *Dragon Songs*. Arcade Publishing, 2013.

Durso, Andrew. "Tibetan hot springs snakes," May 15, 2013: *Life Is Short but Snakes Are Long: Snake Biology for Everyone*, http://snakesarelong.blogspot.com/2013/05/hot-spring-snakes.html.

Farmer, C. G. "Similarity of crocodilian and avian lungs indicates unidirectional flow is ancestral for archosaurs." *Integrative and Comparative Biology*, 55, no. 6, December 2015, 962–971, https://doi.org/10.1093/icb/icv078.

Kawagoshi, T., Nishida, C., and Matsuda, Y. "The origin and differentiation process of X and Y chromosomes of the black marsh turtle (Siebenrockiella crassicollis, Geoemydidae, Testudines)." *Chromosome Res.* 20, 2012, 95–110, https://doi.org/10.1007/s10577-011-9267-7.

Rafferty, A. R., Johnstone, C. P., Garner, J. A., and Reina, R. D. A "20-year investigation of declining leatherback hatching success: implications of climate variation." *Royal Society Open Science*, 4(10), (2017), 170196. doi:10.1098/rsos.170196.

"Reproduction." Crocodile Specialist Group. http://www.iucncsg.org/pages/Reproduction.html.

Rothe, Nina. "How do sea turtles mate?", July 26, 2018: Olive Ridley Project, https://oliveridleyproject.org/blog/how-do-sea-turtles-mate.

Scott, Graham R. "Elevated performance: the unique physiology of birds that fly at high altitudes." *Journal of Experimental Biology* 214.15 (2011): 2455–2462. Web. 7 April 2021.

Stevens L. "Sex chromosomes and sex determining mechanisms in birds." *Science Progress*, 1997; 80 (Pt 3):197–216. PMID: 9354761.

Stint, Eric. "Pond slider (Trachemys scripta)," originally published in the *Sonoran Herpetologist* 2005 18(6): 65–66, *Tucson Herpetological Society Webpage*, https://tucsonherpsociety.org/amphibians-reptiles/turtles-tortoises/pond-slider/.

Watanabe, Myrna E. "Generating heat: new twists in the evolution of endothermy." *BioScience*, 55, no. 6, June 2005, 470–475, https://doi.org/10.1641/0006-3568(2005)055[0470:ghntit]2.0.co;2.

"What causes a sea turtle to be born male or female? Most turtles are subject to temperature-dependent sex determination." NOAA Website, updated March 1, 2021, https://oceanservice.noaa.gov/facts/temperature-dependent.html.

CHAPTER 3. PHYSICAL ADAPTATIONS

Allen, V., Molnar, J., Parker, W., Pollard, A., Nolan, G., and Hutchinson, J. R. "Comparative architectural properties of limb muscles in Crocodylidae and Alligatoridae and their relevance to divergent use of asymmetrical gaits in extant Crocodylia." *Journal of Anatomy*, 225, 2014, 569–582, https://doi.org/10.1111/joa.12245.

Black, Riley. "Great galloping crocodiles!" January 13, 2015, *National Geographic*, https://www.nationalgeographic.com/science/phenomena/2015/01/13/great-galloping-crocodiles/.

Clarac, F., De Buffrénil, V., Cubo, J., and Quilhac, A. "Vascularization in ornamented osteoderms: Physiological implications in ectothermy and amphibious lifestyle in the crocodylomorphs?" *Anatomical Record*, 301, 2018, 175–183, https://doi.org/10.1002/ar.23695.

Dacke, C. G., Elsey, R. M., Trosclair, P. L. III, Sugiyama, T., Nevarez, J. G., and Schweitzer, M. H. "Alligator osteoderms as source of calcium." *Journal of Zoology*, 297 (2015): 255–264, https://doi.org/10.1111/jzo.12272.

Dinets, Vladimir, Britton, Adam, and Shirley, Matthew. "Climbing behavior in extant crocodilians." January, 25, 2014, *Herpetology Notes*, Vol. 7, 3-7. https://www.seh-herpetology.org/journals/herpetology-notes/back-issues/volume-7-2014.

Di-Poï, Nicolas, and Michel C. Milinkovitch. "Crocodylians evolved scattered multi-sensory micro-organs." *EvoDevo*, vol. 4, 1 19. 2 July 2013, doi:10.1186/2041-9139-4-19.

Florida State University. "Alligator's bite could lift a small truck." *Science Daily*, March 29, 2002, www.sciencedaily.com/releases/2002/03/020328073615.htm.

Handwerk, Brian. "Crocodiles have strongest bite ever measured, hands-on tests show." *National Geographic News*, March 15, 2012, https://www.nationalgeographic.com/news/2012/3/120315-croco-diles-bite-force-erickson-science-plos-one-strongest/.

Jackson, Kate, and Brooks, Daniel R. "Do crocodiles co-opt their sense of 'touch' to 'taste'? A possible new type of vertebrate sensory organ." *Amphibia-Reptilia* 28 (2) April 2007, 277–285, https://doi.org/10.1163/156853807780202486.

Kommanee, Jintana, et al. "Antibacterial activity of plasma from crocodile (*Crocodylus siamensis*) against pathogenic bacteria." *Annals of Clinical Microbiology and Antimicrobials,* vol. 11 22. 30 July 2012, doi:10.1186/1476-0711-11-22.

Merchant, M. E., Leger, N., Jerkins, E., Mills, K., Pallansch, M. B., Paulman, R. L., and Ptak, R. G. "Broad spectrum antimicrobial activity of leukocyte extracts from the American alligator (*Alligator mississippiensis*)." *Veterinary Immunolology Immunopathology* 2006 Apr 15;110(3-4):221-2288. doi: 10.1016/j.vetimm.2005.10.001. Epub 2005 Nov 18. PMID: 16298430.

Moskowitz, Clara. "Crikey! How crocs digest animals whole." *Live Science,* Feb. 4, 2008, https://www.livescience.com/2259-crikey-crocs-digest-animals.html.

Nagloo, Nicolas, Collin, Shaun P., Hemmi, Jan M., and Hart, Nathan S. "Spatial resolving power and spectral sensitivity of the saltwater crocodile, Crocodylus porosus, and the freshwater crocodile, *Crocodylus johnstoni*." *Journal of Experimental Biology,* 219, 2016, 1394–1404, https://doi.org/10.1242/jeb.135673.

Pilkington, J. B., and Simkiss, K. "The mobilization of the calcium carbonate deposits in the endolymphatic sacs of metamorphosing frogs." *Journal of Experimental Biology,* 45, 1966, 329–341 https://jeb.biologists.org/content/jexbio/45/2/329.full.pdf.

CHAPTER 4. INTELLIGENCE

Cesario, J. et al. "Your brain is not an onion with a tiny reptile inside." *Current Directions in Psychological Science,* 2020, 1–6, doi: 10.1177/0963721420917687.

Dinets, V. "Play behavior in crocodilians." *Animal Behavior and Cognition,* 2(1), 2015, 49–55. doi: 10.12966/abc.02.04.2015.

Font, E., García-Roa, R., Pincheira-Donoso, D., and Carazo, P. "Rethinking the effects of body size on the study of brain size evolution." *Brain, Behavior and Evolution*, 93, 2019: 182–195, https:// doi.org/ 10.1159/000501161.

Ngwenya, Ayanda, Patzke, Nina, Manger, Paul, and Herculano-Houzel, Suzana. "Continued growth of the central nervous system without mandatory addition of neurons in the Nile crocodile (*Crocodylus niloticus*)." *Brain, Behavior and Evolution*, 87, 2016, 10.1159/000 443201.

Pritz, Michael B. "Crocodilian forebrain: evolution and development." *Integrative and Comparative Biology*, 55, no. 6, December 2015, 949–961, https://doi.org/10.1093/icb/icv003.

Tisdale, Ryan K., Lesku, John A., Beckers, Gabriel J. L., and Rattenborg, Niels C. "Bird-like propagating brain activity in anesthetized Nile crocodiles." *Sleep* 41, no. 8, May 24, 2018, https://doi.org/ 10.1093/ sleep/zsy105.

Tosches, Maria Antonietta, Yamawaki, Tracy M., Naumann, Robert K., Jacobi, Ariel A., Tushev, Georgi, and Laurent, Gilles. "Evolution of pallium, hippocampus, and cortical cell types revealed by single-cell transcriptomics in reptiles." *Science*, May 25, 2018, 881–888.

CHAPTER 5. THE SOCIAL LIVES OF CROCODILIANS

Brattstorm, Bayard H. "The evolution of reptilian social behavior." *American Zoology* 14, 1974, 35-49.

Brien, M. L., Lang, J. W., Webb, G. J., Stevenson, C., and Christian, K. A. "The good, the bad, and the ugly: agonistic behaviour in juvenile crocodilians," *PLoS One*, Dec. 11, 2013; 8(12):e80872. https://doi. org/10.1371/journal.pone.0080872.

Britton, Adam. "Father and sons." *Crocodilians Natural History and Conservation*, https://crocodilian.com/cnhc/potm-oct00.html.

Budd, Kris, Spotila, James R., and Mauger, Laurie A. "Preliminary mating analysis of American crocodiles, *Crocodylus acutus*, in Las Baulas, Santa Rosa, and Palo Verde National Parks, Guanacaste, Costa Rica," *South American Journal of Herpetology*, April 1, 2015, 10 (1), 4–9.

Buffetaut, E. "Wounds on the jaw of an eocene mesosuchian crocodilian as possible evidence for the antiquity of crocodilian intraspecific fighting behaviour." *Paläontology*, Z.57, 143–145 (1983), https://doi.org/10.1007/BF03031756.

Bull, C., Gardner, Michael, Sih, Andrew, Spiegel, Orr, Godfrey, Stephanie, and Leu, Stephan. "Why is social behavior rare in reptiles? Lessons from sleepy lizards." *Advances in the Study of Behavior* (2017). 10.1016/bs.asb.2017.02. 001.

Chabert T., Colin A., Aubin T., Shacks V., Bourquin S.L., Elsey R.M., Acosta J.G., and Mathevon, N. "Size does matter: crocodile mothers react more to the voice of smaller offspring." Oct. 23, 2015, *Nature, Scientific Reports*, https://DOI.org/10.1038/srep15547.

Chabreck, Robert H. "Moisture variation in nests of the American alligator (*Alligator Mississippiensis*)." *Herpetologica*, 31, no. 4, 1975, 385–389. JSTOR, www.jstor.org/stable/3891524. Accessed 4 Apr. 2021.

Christian, K., Webb, G. J., McGuinness, K., Brien, M. L., and Lang, J. W. "Born to be bad: agonistic behaviour in hatchling saltwater crocodiles (*Crocodylus porosus*)." *Behaviour*, 150(7) (2013), 737–762. doi: https://doi.org/10.1163/1568539X-00003078.

Coombs Jr., Walter P. "Modern analogs for dinosaur nesting and parental behavior." *Geological Society of America Special Paper* 238, 1989, 21–53.

Dawson, John. "Egg Mountain, the Two Medicine, and the caring mother dinosaur." 2014, *National Park Service* webpage: https://www.nps.gov/articles/mesozoic-egg-mountain-dawson-2014.htm.

Dinets, Vladimir. "Apparent coordination and collaboration in cooperatively hunting crocodilians." *Ethology Ecology and Evolution*, 27, Jan. 7, 2014, 244–250, https://DOI.org/10.1080/03949370.2014.915432.

———. *Dragon Songs*. Arcade Publishing, 2013.

———. "Play behavior in crocodilians." *Animal Behavior and Cognition*, 2(1) (2015): 49–55. doi: 10.12966/abc.02.04.2015.

Drews, Carlos. "Dominance or territoriality? The colonization of temporary lagoons by Caiman crocodilus L. (Crocodylia)." *Herpetological Journal*, I, 1990, 514–521, https://www.researchgate.net/profile/ Carlos_Drews/publication/282676523_Dominance_or_territoriality_The_colonization_of_temporary_lagoons_by_Caiman_crocodilus_L_Crocodylia/links/5edbefbf92851c9c5e8ae806/Dominance-or-territoriality-The-colonization-of-temporary-lagoons-by-Caiman-crocodilus-L-Crocodylia.pdf.

Freimuth, Willie. "Paleontology—Egg Mountain, The Montana Geoheritage Project," https://serc.carleton.edu/research_education/mt_ geoheritage/sites/augusta_choteau/paleontology.html.

Gardner, M. G., Pearson, S. K., Johnston, G. R., and Schwarz, M. P. "Group living in squamate reptiles: a review of evidence for stable aggregations." *Biology Review*, 91, 2016: 925–936, https://doi.org/10.1111/ brv.12201.

Giddings, Lydia A. D. "Behavior response to juvenile distress calls as a measure of extended care in crocodilians." September 2019, University of Bristol master's thesis, https://research-information.bris.ac.uk/ws/portalfiles/portal/220685754/Behavioural_Response_to_J uvenile_Distress_Calls_as_a_Measure_of_Extended_Care_in_Croc odilians.pdf.

Jones, Ann. "Life, death and a sleepy lizard: one researcher's remarkable work on a monogamous blue-tongue." Australian Broadcast Network News, updated May 31, 2017, https://www.abc.net.au/news/ 2017-04-16/life-death-and-grief-of-the-sleepy-lizard/84422 52?nw=0.

Kofron, Christopher P. "Courtship and mating of Nile crocodile (*Crocodylus niloticus*)." *Amphibia-Reptilia*, 12 (1991): 39–48.

Lance, S. L., Tuberville T. D., Dueck L., Holz-Schietinger C., Trosclair III, P. L., Elsey, R. M., and Glenn, T. C. "Multiyear multiple paternity and mate fidelity in the American alligator, Alligator mississippiensis." *Molecular Ecology*, 18, 2009, 4508–4520. doi: 10.1111/j.1365-294X.2009.04373.x.

Lang, Jeffrey W. "Adult-young association of free-living gharials in Chambal River, North India." 2010, *Crocodiles: Proceedings of the 20th Working Meeting of the Crocodile Specialist Group of the Species Survival Commission of IUCN*, Manaus, Brazil, 142, http://www.iucncsg.org/365_docs/attachments/protarea/20th-4fc13431.pdf# page=142.

Lang, Jeffery W. "Social behavior," in *Crocodiles and Alligators*, ed. C. A. Ross, pp. 102–117. Sydney: Golden Press, 1989.

Murray, C. M., Crother, B. I., Doody, J. S. "The evolution of crocodilian nesting ecology and behavior." *Ecology and Evolution*, 2020, 10: 131–149, https://doi.org/10.1002/ece3.5859.

Ojeda, Guillermo N., Amavet, Patricia S., Rueda, Eva C., Siroski, Pablo A., and Larriera, Alejandro. "Mating system of caiman yacare (Reptilia: *Alligatoridae*) described from microsatellite genotypes." *Journal of Heredity*, 108, no. 2, March 1, 2017, pp. 135–141, https://doi.org/10.1093/jhered/esw080.

Oliveira, Deyla P., Marioni, Boris, Farias, Izeni P., and Hrbek, Tomas. "Genetic evidence for polygamy as a mating strategy in *Caiman crocodilus*." *Journal of Heredity*, 105, no. 4, July-August 2014, 485–492, https://doi.org/10.1093/jhered/esu020.

Rossi Lafferriere, Natalia A., Antelo, Rafael, Alda, Fernando, Mårtensson, Dick, Hailer, Frank, Castroviejo-Fisher, Santiago, Ayarzagüena, José, Ginsberg, Joshua, R., Castroviejo, Javier, Doadrio Ignacio, Vilá, Carles, and Amato, George. "Multiple paternity in a reintroduced population of the Orinoco crocodile (*Crocodylus intermedius*) at the El Frío Biological Station, Venezuela." *PloS One*, March 16, 2016, https://doi.org/10.1371/journal.pone.0150245.

San Diego Zoo Wildlife Alliance Library. "Nile crocodiles (*Crocodylus niloticus* and *C. suchus*)." Fact Sheet: Behavior and Ecology, Last update March 9, 2021, https://ielc.libguides.com/sdzg/factsheets/nile_crocodile/behavior.

Silveira, R. D., Farias, I. P., Magnusson, W. E., Muniz, F. L., Hrbek, T., and Campos, Z. "Multiple paternity in the Black Caiman (*Melanosuchus niger*) population in the Anavilhanas National Park, Brazilian Amazonia," *Amphibia-Reptilia*. 32(3) (2011), 428–434, https://doi.org/10.1163/017353711X587741.

Tucker, A.D., McCallum, H. I., Limpus, C. J., and McDonald, K. R. "Sex-biased dispersal in a long-lived polygynous reptile (*Crocodylus johnstoni*)." *Behavioral Ecology and Sociobiology* 44(2), 1998, 85–90.

Vergne, Amélie L., and Mathevon, Nicolas. "Crocodile egg sounds signal hatching time." *Current Biology*, 18, no. 12, June 24, 2008, R513–R514, https://doi.org/10.1016/j.cub.2008.04.011.

Whitaker, Nikhil. "Extended parental care in the Siamese crocodile (*Crocodylus siamensis*)." *Russian Journal of Herpetology*, 14, Nov. 3, 2007, 203–206, https://www.academia.edu/6729813/Parental_care_in_the_Siamese_Crocodile_Crocodylus_siamensis_.

CHAPTER 6. ALLIGATORS

Defenders of Wildlife. "American Crocodile and Alligator", https://defenders.org/wildlife/american-crocodile-and-alligator.

Louisiana Department of Wildlife and Fisheries. "Early Wild Harvest History," 2020, https://www.louisianaalligators.com/history.html.

Mendal, Abram, "The History of Alligator Skin Tanning." Dec. 7, 2012. *PanAm Leathers*, http://www.panamleathers.com/blog/bid/249454/The-History-Of-Alligator-Skin-Tanning.

Mississippi Wildlife, Fisheries and Parks. "The Recovery of the American Alligator in Mississippi", https://www.mdwfp.com/wildlife-hunting/ alligator-program/the-recovery-of-the-american-alligator-in-mississippi/.

Ouchley, Kelby. *American Alligator: Ancient Predator in the Modern World*. University Press of Florida, 2013.

Strawn, Martha A. *Alligators: Prehistoric Presence in the American Landscape*. Johns Hopkins University Press, 1997.

Stromberg, Joseph, and Zielinski, Sarah. "Ten threatened and endangered species used in traditional medicine." *Smithsonian Magazine*, Oct. 18, 2011, https://www.smithsonianmag.com/science-nature/ten-threatened-and-endangered-species-used-in-traditional-medicine-112814487/.

Thorbjarnarson, John. "Crocodile tears and skins: international trade, economic constraints, and limits to the sustainable use of crocodilians." *Conservation Biology*, 13, no. 3, 1999, pp. 465–470. JSTOR, www.jstor.org/stable/2641860.

Thorbjarnarson, John and Wang, Xiaoming, *The Chinese Alligator: Ecology, Behavior and Culture*. Johns Hopkins University Press, 2010.

Whyte, Chelsea. "New species of giant salamander is the world's largest amphibian." *NewScientist: Life*, Sept. 17, 2019, https://www.newscientist.com/article/2216451-new-species-of-giant-salamander-is-the-worlds-largest-amphibian/.

Wildlife Conservation Society. "Chinese Alligator", https://china.wcs.org/Wildlife/Chinese-Alligator.aspx.

CHAPTER 7. CAIMANS

Azevedo, Fernando, and Verdade, Luciano. "Predator-prey interactions: Jaguar predation on caiman in a floodplain forest." *Journal of*

Zoology, 286, 2012, 200–207, https://doi.org/10.1111/j.1469-7998.2011.00867.x.

Bontemps, Damien, Cuevas, Elvira, Ortiz, Eileen, Wunderle, Jr, Joseph, Joglar, Rafael. "Diet of the non-native spectacled caiman (*Caiman crocodilus*) in Puerto Rico." *Management of Biological Invasions*, 7, Jan. 1, 2016, 287–296, https://doi.org/10.3391/mbi.2016.7.3.08.

Campbell, David. *A Land of Ghosts: The Braided Lives of People and the Forest in Far Western Amazonia.* Houghton Mifflin Harcourt, 2014.

CBS News. "'Operation crocodile'": drug traffickers fed bodies of victims to reptiles, feds say." Feb. 28, 2019, https://www.cbsnews.com/news/operation-crocodile-puerto-rico-drug-traffickers-fed-bodies-of-victims-to-caimans-feds-say/.

Choi, Henry. "Paleosuchus palpebrosus," "Dwarf caiman," "Cuvier's smooth-fronted caiman." *Animal Diversity Web* (University of Michigan Museum of Zoology), https://animaldiversity.org/accounts/Paleosuchus_palpebrosus/.

Coto, Danica. "Puerto Ricans fight back against caiman onslaught." *Seattle Times*, Dec. 7, 2012, https://www.seattletimes.com/nation-world/puerto-ricans-fight-back-against-caiman-onslaught/.

Da Silveira, Ronis, E. Ramalho, Emiliano, Thorbjarnarson, John B., Magnusson, William E. "Depredation by jaguars on caimans and importance of reptiles in the diet of jaguar." *Journal of Herpetology*, 44(3), Sept. 1, 2010, 418–424.

Ecuadorian Biodiversity Project. "Documenting biodiversity in Ecuador." *Biodiversity Group*, https://biodiversitygroup.org/ documenting-biodiversity-ecuador/.

Kruckewitt, Joan. "Oil and cancer in Ecuador: Ecuadoran villagers believe high rates of disease are tied to petroleum pollution, a contention that Chevron disputes." *SFGate*, Dec. 11, 2005 (updated Jan. 15, 2012), https://www.sfgate.com/green/article/oil-and-cancer-in-Ecuador-Ecuadoran-villagers-2557444.php.

Linares, Francisco Watlington. "¡Santiago y a Ellos!: La Política Pública Del DRNA Contra Caimancito Centinela del Karso de Puerto Rico." *Revista de Administración Pública*, https://revistas.upr.edu/index.php/ap/article/download/307/295.

Rosolie, Paul. *Mother of God: An Extraordinary Journey into the Uncharted Tributaries of the Western Amazon.* Harper, 2014.

Somaweera, Ruchira, Brien, Matthew, and Shine, Richard. "The role of predation in shaping crocodilian natural history." *Herpetological Monographs*, 27, 2013, 23–51, https://doi.org/10.1655/herpmono-graphs-D-11-00001.

Torralvo, K., Rabelo, R. M., Andrade, A., et al. "Tool use by Amazonian capuchin monkeys during predation on caiman nests in a high-productivity forest." *Primates*, 58, 2017, 279–283, https://doi.org/10.1007/s10329-017-0603-1.

CHAPTER 8. CROCODILES

Castro Casal, Antonio, Merchán, Manuel, Cárdenas-Torres, Miguel, Torres, Cárdenas, Velasco, Fernando, and Garcés-Restrepo, Mario. "Uso histórico y actual del caimán llanero (*Crocodylus intermedius*) en la Orinoquia (Colombia-Venezuela)." *Biota Colombiana* 2013, 0124-5376. 14. 65–82.

Edralin, Francesca. "From New Guinea to Florida, one of these crocs is not like the others." *Mongabay*, https://news.mongabay.com/2020/07/from-new-guinea-to-florida-one-of-these-crocs-is-not-like-the-others/.

Fermín Gómez, Mercedes. "Orinoco River." *Encyclopedia Britannica*, https://www.britannica.com/place/Orinoco-River.

IUCN Crocodile Specialist Group. "Crocodilian Attacks", http://www.iucncsg.org/pages/Crocodilian-Attacks.html.

IUCN Redlist. "Nile Crocodile", https://www.iucnredlist.org/species/45433088/3010181.

Moreno Arias, Rafael, and Ardila Robayo, María Cristina. "Journeying to freedom: the spatial ecology of a reintroduced population of Orinoco crocodiles (*Crocodylus intermedius*) in Colombia." *Animal Biotelemetry*, 2020: 8:15, https://link.springer.com/content/pdf/10.1186/s40317-020-00202-2.pdf.

Museum and Art Gallery of the Northern Territory. "Sweetheart, a large male Saltwater (Estuarine) Crocodile, is a legendary part of recent Northern Territory history." https://www.magnt.net.au/sweet heart-crocodile.

Sacred Natural Sites. "The Philippine crocodile in the Northern Sierra Madre, Philippines." https://sacrednaturalsites. org/items/the-philippine\-crocodile-in-the-northern-sierra-madre-philip-pines/.

Schaffer, Grayson. "Consumed." *Outside Online: The Horror Vault,* Feb. 7, 2011, https://www.outsideonline.com/1825851/consumed#close.

SDM Adventures. "Crocodile diving Banco Chinchorro, Mexico." https://sdmdiving.com/crocodile-diving.

Seijas, Andrés E., Antelo, Rafael, Thorbjarnarson, John B., and Ardila Robayo, María Cristina. *IUCN Report*: Orinoco crocodile *Crocodylus intermedius*, https://www.iucncsg.org/365_docs/attachments/protarea/11_C-ba6d215f.pdf.

Van Asch B., Versfeld, W. F., Hull, K. L., Leslie, A. J., Matheus, T. I., Beytell, P. C., et al. "Phylogeography, genetic diversity, and population structure of Nile crocodile populations at the fringes of the southern African distribution." *PLoS ONE*, 2019, 14(12): e0226505. https://doi.org/10.1371/journal.pone.0226505.

Velasco, Alvaro, Hernandez, Omar, Babarro, Ricardo, Sola, R. "Status of the Orinoco Crocodile (*Crocodylus intermedius*) in Venezuela /Estatus del caiman del Orinoco (*Crocodylus intermedius*) en Venezuela," *Revista de la Real Academia de Ciencias Exactas*, 2020, Fisicas y Naturales—Serie A: Matematicas. LXXX. 1–17.

World Wildlife Fund. "An Epic Journey." https://wwf.panda.org/discover/knowledge_hub/where_we_work/orinoco_river_basin/?.

CHAPTER 9. GHARIALS

Government of Nepal, Ministry of Energy, Water Resources and Irrigation, Department of Water Resources and Irrigation, Behri Babai Diversion Multipurpose Project, http://bbdmp.gov.np/pages/about-project.

Kumar, P., Barma, S., and Subba, B. "A checklist of fishes of eastern Terai of Nepal." *Nepalese Journal of Biosciences*, 1, 2013, 63–65, https://doi.org/10.3126/njbs.v1i0.7473.

Premathilake, R. "Human used upper montane ecosystem in the Horton Plains, central Sri Lanka—a link to Late glacial and early Holocene climate and environmental changes." *Quaternary Science Reviews*, 50, 2012, 23–42, https://doi.org/10.1016/j.quascirev.2012.07.002.

Terrenato, L., et al. "Decreased malaria morbidity in the Tharu people compared to sympatric populations in Nepal," in *Annals of Trop-*

ical Medical Parasitology, 1988 Feb. 82(1):1-11, https://www. ncbi.nlm.nih.gov/pubmed/3041928.

World Wildlife Fund. "Nepal set to become first country to double wild tiger population," Sept. 23, 2018, Press Release, https://www. worldwildlife.org/press-releases/nepal-set-to-become-first-country-to-double-wild-tiger-population.

Ziegler, Thomas, and Olbort, Sven. "Genital structures and sex identification in crocodiles." IUCN Crocodile Specialist Group, https://www.iucncsg.org/365_docs/attachments/protarea/Geni-4343c282.pdf.

CHAPTER 10. THE SERPENT IN THE GARDEN

Abanda Expedition. "The Orange Cave-Dwelling Crocodiles": http://www.abanda-expedition.org/orange-cave-dwelling-crocodile-012.html.

Cambridge, Ellie. "Jaws of death: Animal expert survives being attacked by an 18 ft crocodile by allowing colleagues to rip off his leg while it was in the beast's mouth." *Sun*, March 7, 2017, https://www. thesun.co.uk/news/3035289/animal-expert-attacked-by-crocodile-rip-off-leg-malaysia/.

Darwin, Charles. *The Expression of the Emotions in Man and Animals*. London: John Murray, 1872.

Dillon, Nancy. "Man says he survived alligator attack at Disney resort when he was 8, refutes officials who claimed tragedy was the first." *New York Daily News*, June 16, 2016, https://www.nydailynews.com/news/national/man-attacked-alligator-1986-disney-tragedy-not-article-1.2676459.

Evans, Luke J., Davies, Andrew B., Goossens, Benoit, and Asner, Gregory P. "Riparian vegetation structure and the hunting behavior of adult estuarine crocodiles." *PLos ONE*, 12(10) October 11, 2017, http:// DOI.org/10.1371/journal.pone.0184804.

Galdikas, B. M. F. "Crocodile predation on a proboscis monkey in Borneo." *Primates*, 26, 1985, 495–496, https://doi.org/10.1007/BF0238 2464.

Galdikas, B. M. F. and Yeager, C. P. Brief report: "Crocodile predation on a crab eating macaque in Borneo." *American Journal of Primatology*, 6, 1984, 49–51, https://doi.org/10.1002/ajp.1350060106.

Hance, Jeremy. "Orange cave crocodiles may be "mutating" into new species." *Guardian*, Jan. 29, 2019, https://www.theguardian. com/environment/radical-conservation/2018/jan/29/orange-cave-crocodiles-gabon-bushmeat-africa.

Hart, Donna, and Sussman, Robert W. *Man the Hunted: Primates, Predators and Human Evolution*. Basic Books, 2005.

Monbiot, George. *Feral: Rewildling the Land, the Sea and Human Life*, Penguin Books, 2013.

Njau, Jackson K. "Reading Pliocene bones," *Science*, 336, 2012, 46, https://DOI.org/10.1126/science.1216221.

Njau, Jackson K., and Blumenschine, Robert J. "A diagnosis of crocodile feeding traces on larger mammal bone, with fossil examples from the Plio-Pleistocene Olduvai Basin, Tanzania." *Journal of Human Evolution*, 50, 2006, 142e162.

———. "Crocodylian and mammalian carnivore feeding traces on hominid fossils from FLK 22 and FLK NN 3, Plio-Pleistocene, Olduvai Gorge, Tanzania, 2012." *Journal of Human Evolution*, 63, 408–417.

Plumwood, Val. "Being Prey," in O'Reilly, James, *The Ultimate Journey: Inspiring Stories of Living and Dying*, Travelers' Tales, 2000.

Ron, Santiago R., Vallejo, Andres, and Asanza, Eduardo. "Human Influence on the Wariness of Melanosuchus niger and Caiman crocodilus in Cuyabeno, Ecuador," 1998. *Journal of Herpetology*, 32(3), 320-324, https://Doi.org/10.2307/1565444.

Zamudio, F., Bello-Baltazar, E., and Estrada-Lugo, E. I. "Learning to hunt Crocodiles: social organization in the process of knowledge generation and the emergence of management practices among Mayan of Mexico." *Journal of Ethnobiology and Ethnomedicine*, 9, 35, 2013, https://doi.org/10.1186/1746-4269-9-35.

CHAPTER 11. GODS AND DEVILS

Allen, Benedict. *Into the Crocodile Nest*. Macmillan, 1987.

BBC Earth. "Villagers worship crocodiles in Madagascar!, Zoo Quest to Madagascar, August 6, 2014," YouTube, https://youtu.be/whU_cwRWIAo.

BBC News. "Why Some Men in Papua New Guinea Cut Their Skins to Resemble Crocodiles." August 26, 2018, *BBC Stories*, https://www.bbc.com/news/stories-45297699.

Campbell, G. Eating the dead in Madagascar. *South Africa Medical Journal*, 103, 2013 (12 Suppl 1):1032–1034, https://doi.org/10.71 96/SAMJ.7076.

Center for the Tebtunis Papyri. "About the Tebtunis Papyri," University of California, Berkeley (Web Page), http://www.lib.berkeley.edu/libraries/bancroft-library/tebtunis-papyri/about-tebtunis-collection.

Clark, Laura. "Papyrus found in a mummy mask may be the oldest known copy of a gospel." Jan. 21, 2015, https://www.smithsonianmag.com/smart-news/papyrus-found-mummy-mask-may-be-oldest-known-copy-gospel-180953962/.

CrocBITE. Worldwide Crocodilian Attack Database, "Frequently Asked Questions," http://www.crocodile-attack.info/node/4299.

Farrell, John. "Fragments of Mark's gospel may date to first century." Feb. 27, 2012, *Forbes*: https://www.forbes.com/sites/johnfarrell/2012/02/27/fragments-of-marks-gospel-may-date-to-1st-century/.

Graham, Alistair, and Beard, Peter. *Eyelids of the Morning*. Chronicle Books, 1990.

Hassan, Sayed Raza. "Pakistani pilgrims flock to crocodile shrines as Taliban threat recedes." Reuters, Oct. 15, 2015, https://www.reuters.com/article/us-pakistan-security-crocodiles/pakistani-pilgrims-flock-to-crocodile-shrine-as-taliban-threat-recedes-idUSKCN0S90JI20151015.

Ikram, Salima. "Crocodiles: guardians of the gateways." In *Thebes and Beyond: Studies in Honour of Kent R. Weeks*, ed. Zawi Hawass and Salima Ikram. American University in Cairo Press, 2010.

Molcho, Michal. "Crocodile breeding in the crocodile cults of the Graeco-Roman Fayum." *Journal of Egyptian Archaeology*, 100, 2014, 181–193, www.jstor.org/stable/24644969.

Pooley, Simon. "A cultural herpetology of Nile crocodiles in Africa." *Conservation and Society*, 14(4) 2016, 391-405.

Rathbone, Dominic. "A town full of gods: reimagining religious experience in Roman Tebtunis (Egypt)." April 2003, *The Center for the Tebtunis Papyri, University of California, Berkeley*, http://www.lib.berkeley.edu/sites/default/files/files/ATownFullofGods_Imagining ReligiousExperienceinRomanTebtunis.pdf.

Silverman, E. K. "The gender of the cosmos: totemism, society and embodiment in the Sepik River." *Oceania*, 67, 1996: 30-49, https://doi.org/10.1002/j.1834-4461.1996.tb02570.x.

Sipa, Masika. "The crocodiles' lake." *Mada Magazine*, http://www.madamagazine.com/en/der-see-der-krokodile/.

Vaillant, John. *The Tiger: A True Story of Vengeance and Survival*. Vintage, 2011.

Wylie, Dan. *Crocodile*. Reaktion Books, 2013.

CHAPTER 12. THE (ALMOST) LOST WORLD OF THE CROCODILIANS

Azevedo, Fernando, and Verdade, Luciano. "Predator-prey interactions: Jaguar predation on caiman in a floodplain forest." *Journal of Zoology*, 286, 2012, 200–207, https://doi.org/10.1111/j.1469-7998.2011.00867.x.

Beal, E. R., Rosenblatt, A. E. "Alligators in the big city: spatial ecology of American alligators (*Alligator mississippiensis*) at multiple scales across an urban landscape." *Science Report* 10, 2020, 16575, https://doi. org/10.1038/s41598-020-73685-x.

Brito, José C., Martínez-Freiría, Fernando, Sierra, Pablo, Sillero, Neftalí, and Tarroso, Pedro. "Crocodiles in the Sahara Desert: An update of distribution, habitats and population status for conservation planning in Mauritania." Feb. 25, 2011. *Plos ONE*, https://doi.org/10.1371/journal.pone.0014734.

Dunnell, Tony. "Guelta d'Archei, Chad: Camels and Crocodiles share the Black Waters of this Stunning Saharan Oasis." *Atlas Obscura*, https://www.atlasobscura.com/places/guelta-darchei.

Hansen, Thor Arthur, Koch, Carl Fred, et al. "Cretaceous paleoclimate." *Encyclopedia Britannica*, https://www.britannica.com/science/Cretaceous-Period/Paleoclimate.

Hurd, Barbara. *Stirring the Mud: On Swamps, Bogs, and Human Imagination*. University of Georgia Press, 2008.

Piana, Mark E. "Crocodilian fossils." Harvard University (website), https://www.seas.harvard.edu/climate/eli/research/equable/evidence_alligator.html.

Struebig, Matthew, and Banks-Leite, Cristina, eds. "Tropical biodiversity." *Journal of Applied Ecology*: June 13, 2018, https://besjournals.onlinelibrary.wiley.com/doi/toc/10.1111/(ISSN)1365-2664.TropicalDiversity.

U.S. Fish and Wildlife Service. *Okefenokee National Wildlife Refuge, The Swamp Walk Trail Guide.* March 2000, https://www.fws.gov/southeast/pdf/brochure/okefenokee-national-wildlife-refuge-swamp-walk-trail-guide.pdf.

Williams, Joy. *Ill Nature.* Reprint edition, Lyons Press, 2015.

CHAPTER 13. A FUTURE FOR CROCODILIANS?

Baynes-Rock, Marcus. *Crocodile Undone: The Domestication of Australia's Fauna.* Animalibus: Of Animals and Cultures Book 15. Penn State Press, 2020.

Bull, Bartle. "Hunter-conservationist or . . . Jekyll and Hyde?" *Time* July 31, 2015 (web page), https://time.com/3979165/hunting-conservation-teddy-roosevelt/.

Edwards, Phil. "All 512 animals Teddy Roosevelt and his son killed on safari." Vox (web page): Updated Feb. 3, 2016, https://www.vox.com/2015/7/29/9067587/theodore-roosevelt-safari.

IUCN Crocodile Specialist Group. "Farming and the Crocodile Industry." *International Union for Conservation of Nature* (web page), http://www.iucncsg.org/pages/Farming-and-the-Crocodile-Industry.html.

Medley, Cynthia. "One way to halt poaching—gator farming." *New York Times*, Jan. 18, 1970, https://www.nytimes.com/1970/01/18/archives/one-way-to-halt-poachinggator-farming.html?sq=%2522alligator%2520farm%2522&scp=2&st=cse.

Milián-García, Y., Ramos-Targarona, R., Pérez-Fleitas, E. et al. "Genetic evidence of hybridization between the critically endangered Cuban crocodile and the American crocodile: implications for population history and in situ/ex situ conservation." *Heredity* 114, 2015, 272–280, https://doi.org/10.1038/hdy.2014.96.

National Park Service. "The Story of the Teddy Bear." https://www.nps.gov/thrb/learn/historyculture/storyofteddybear.htm.

Ramp, D., and Bekoff, M. "Compassion as a practical and evolved ethic for conservation," in Bovenkerk, B., Keulartz, J., eds., *Animal Ethics in the Age of Humans*, International Library of Environmental, Agricultural and Food Ethics, 23, 2016. Springer, https://doi.org/10.1007/978-3-319-44206-8_23.

Thorbjarnarson, John. "Crocodile tears and skins: international trade, economic constraints, and limits to the sustainable use of crocodilians."

Conservation Biology; Issues in International Conservation, 13, no. 3, June 1999, 465-470, https://www.rhinoalive.com/wp-content/uploads/2016/06/Crocodile-tears-and-skins-International-trade.pdf.

U.S. Department of the Interior. "New 5-year Report Shows 101.6 Million Americans Participated in Hunting, Fishing and Wildlife Activities." Sept. 7, 2017. U.S. Department of the Interior, https://www.doi.gov/pressreleases/new-5-year-report-shows-1016-million-americans-participated-hunting-fishing-wildlife.

Wallach, Adrian D., Bekoff, Marc, Batavia, Chelsea, Nelson, Michael Paul, and Ramp, Daniel. "Summoning compassion to address the challenges of conservation." *Conservation Biology*, 32, no. 6, 2018, 1255–1265.

ACKNOWLEDGMENTS

THERE ARE MANY PEOPLE TO THANK for various help, insight, or time they gave me that allowed the completion of this book. First and foremost I would like to thank my wife Erin Moody, who supported my decisions to pursue this book even when it meant spending money and time apart. Erin also read, commented on, and made suggestions for most of what you'll find in this book.

I am also exceptionally grateful to Bruce H. Franklin of Westholme Publishing, who was kind enough to support an unknown writer with a publishing contract, advance, and encouragement when it was needed most. My copyeditor Noreen O'Connor-Abel, cartographer Paul Rossmann, and everyone else at Westholme also deserve my gratitude.

I am deeply indebted to the numerous scientists, other professionals, and writers (too many to mention here) whose publications I've referenced.

Below are listed other people I especially owe thanks to—in alphabetical order by last name because it would be impossible to quantify the help each of them gave me. I apologize if I missed anyone.

Acknowledgments

Ashish Bashyal, biologist of Biodiversity Conservancy of Nepal, made the entire chapter on gharials possible with travel advice, help, and detailed information on gharials and his research. Santosh Bhattarai, conservation officer with the National Trust for Nature Conservation, Nepal, was kind enough to invite me into his office to discuss gharial conservation, Chitwan National Park, and his organization's work. Dr. Adam Britton, biologist, answered questions about crocodiles and his work through email. Dr. Adam P. Cossette, paleontologist, answered questions about crocodiles, paleontology, and his own field work. Dr. Carlos de la Rosa, ecologist, answered my questions about caimans, tropical conservation, and his own work. Joshua Fitzner, my brother, read many chapters and gave me encouragement and constructive criticism on my writing. Robert Gaston, natural history artist, museum exhibit creator, and commercial paleontologist, gave me my first job in paleontology, introduced me to *Deinosuchus sp.*, and offered advice and encouragement after reading some of these chapters. Tika Ram Giri, former guide and managing director of the Chitwan Gaida Lodge, shared his insightful views on conservation and tourism in Nepal. Dr. Scott Hatch, Dr. Kyle Elliot, and Timothy van Nus, hired, mentored, and supervised me, respectively, on sea bird research; I drew on these experiences in this book. Dr. Shaya Honarvar hired me as a volunteer sea turtle technician, and some of that experience is also in this book. Dr. Jackson Njau answered questions about the intersection of anthropology and crocodilians and shared important scientific papers with me. Dr. Chitra Khadka, veterinarian, was kind enough to talk to me about gharials, his own work, and veterinarian medicine in Bardia National Park, Nepal. Doctoral candidate Anje Kidd-Weaver was generous enough to let me volunteer on her alligator urban ecology project and answer many of my questions about alligators, urban ecology, and golf etiquette. Michael Lee, natural history sculptor, read early sections of this book and encouraged as well as made recommendations; he also lent me two helpful books. Tom Lindgren, commercial paleontologist, was generous with enthusiastic encouragement and set me the task of preparing a fantastic Eocene crocodile specimen.

He also got me involved in helping prepare a *Goniopholis sp.* and gifted me historical slides of crocodilian photos. Dr. Michal Molcho, historian, answered many questions I had about the role of crocodiles in ancient Egyptian worship and supplied me with a copy of her own thesis on the topic. Rafael Moreno-Arias, biologist, answered my questions about Orinoco crocodiles, conservation, and field work in the llanos of Colombia. Zach Piotrowski, conservationist and volunteer coordinator for Aransas National Wildlife Refuge, hired me as a volunteer, was happy to share alligator stories, and give me advice on traveling the Everglades. Balbahadur Ranamagar, "Mr. B," guide and owner of Mr. B's Place, his family, and his wonderful staff provided me excellent lodging and service in guiding me through the jungles of Bardia National Park on my search for gharials. Dr. Hector Rivera, paleontologist, answered questions about crocodile paleontology in Mexico. Alex Ruger, paleontologist and graduate student, patiently passed on articles and information about crocodilians and gave some advice on my rough drafts. Dr. David Schwimmer, paleontologist, answered my questions about *Deinosuchus* and his work through email. Matt Seney, former zookeeper and current fossil preparator, answered questions and joined me on adventures in Nepal. Dr. Matthew Shirley took time out for a long and informative conversation with me about crocodilian conservation and biology. Merlijn van Weerd, ecologist and crocodile conservationist, answered my questions about Philippine crocodiles, his own work, and crocodile conservation. Dr. Alvaro Velasco, biologist and conservationist, answered my questions about Orinoco crocodile conservation in Venezuela. Dr. Thomas Walla, professor and biologist, introduced me to tropical field biology and caimans along with Dr. Aparna Palmer, Dr. Harold Greenie, and Fernando Vaca. Dr. Clifford Warwick, veterinary researcher and animal welfare expert, answered my questions about his own work as well as crocodilian welfare and conservation in general. Dr. Graham Webb, biologist and wildlife manager, answered many questions about crocodile farms, conservation, and his own career in science. Jay Young, zoo owner and keeper, told me about crocodilian behavior and intelligence he observed. Thanks finally to People for the Ethical Treatment of Animals for allowing me to ask questions of an anonymous animal welfare investigator.

INDEX

Index

Index